A HOUSE OF
PRAYER
FOR ALL PEOPLE

A History of
Washington National Cathedral

Frederick Quinn

Morehouse Publishing
NEW YORK

Morehouse Publishing, 4785 Linglestown Road, Suite 101, Harrisburg, PA 17112
Morehouse Publishing, 19 East 34th Street, New York, NY 10016
Morehouse Publishing is an imprint of Church Publishing Incorporated.

www.churchpublishing.org

Cover photo by Donovan Marks
Cover design by Laurie Klein Westhafer
Typeset by Denise Hoff

Library of Congress Cataloging-in-Publication Data

Quinn, Frederick.
    A house of prayer for all people : a history of Washington National
Cathedral / Frederick Quinn.
        pages cm
    Includes bibliographical references and index.
    ISBN 978-0-8192-2924-3 (pbk.)—ISBN 978-0-8192-2925-0 (ebook)
1. Washington National Cathedral (Washington, D.C.)—History.
2. Washington (D.C.)—Church history—19th century. 3. Washington (D.C.)—
Church history—20th century. I. Title.
    BX5980.W3C356 2014
    283'.753—dc23
                                                                    2014005188

Printed in the United States of America

Contents

Introduction: Origins of this Book

In the summer of 2011, I returned to Washington after completing the book I was working on and renewed my ties at Washington National Cathedral as a chaplain and participant in some weekday and Sunday services. I had visited the cathedral first in the spring of 1958, when I hitchhiked to Washington for a Foreign Service interview with my modest possessions packed in a brown plastic Samsonite suitcase. One Sunday afternoon I walked up the hill from downtown Washington to Mount Saint Alban for a sung evensong. The musicians were members of a visiting Welsh singing society. They filled the half-completed building with four-part harmonies on hymns like "All Hail the Power of Jesus' Name" and "Crown Him with Many Crowns." The descant—"Crown Him! Crown Him!"—rolled like late afternoon thunder through the vast, resonant space. Later I attended many other services and concerts at the cathedral before I left for assignment in Morocco in the summer of 1958, but they were always intermixed with the memory of that initial experience.

Although I came to know various cathedral and diocesan clergy as well as laity in the years ahead, I had never thought of writing about them. Until recently, I was unaware that an extensive, well-catalogued archive was housed on the fourth floor of the cathedral office building. Richard G. Hewlett, a professional historian, had carefully assembled it since 1980 after his retirement from the federal government. Both Hewlett and the cathedral's provost, Charles A. Perry, had worked at the Atomic Energy Commission, Perry in its public information office, Hewlett as its historian. But Perry had left to study for the ministry and Hewlett continued to compile his award-winning histories of the AEC over several decades.

I eventually decided that I wanted to explore some aspect of cathedral history but I did not want to write a traditional institutional history, one governed by observations like "When Window One was completed, they began Window Two." Nor did I want to write an extended guide to the cathedral's stained glass, sculpture, and gargoyles. Instead, I wanted to look over the shoulders of the dead and bring a few of them briefly back to life in the three-dimensional settings in which they lived and worked. I also discovered that figures like Henry Yates Satterlee were more complex than usually portrayed. Their formidable faces were frozen in black-and-white photographs of the time, bishops dressed in billowing white surplices and surrounded by symbols of office, including large carved wooden chairs and heavy leather-covered Bibles. They often appeared to distance themselves from their contemporaries, or they were skillfully distanced by photographers and portrait painters. Yet such portrayals of the WASP clergy of an earlier era often falls short of really disclosing who they were.

My writing task also largely depended on what the archives contained. Hewlett had written a probing study of Washington's first bishop, the patrician Henry Yates Satterlee, but there were still more than twenty stuffed archival boxes that remained from Satterlee's time, allowing a more extended picture of him, especially as he struggled with what was then called "the colored problem" and with construction of the cathedral.

There were only a few books about the early history of the Episcopal Church in Washington, including a volume on Satterlee by Bishop Charles H. Brent, a friend of his, who twice declined election as bishop of Washington, and the reminiscences of Bishops William Paret of Maryland and Alexander Mackay-Smith of Pennsylvania. The latter was rector of the important Washington parish of St. John's, Lafayette Square, and had nominated Satterlee as a compromise candidate when the original election for first bishop of Washington was hopelessly deadlocked.

Something else occurred to me as I was writing. Transparency and openness are not words that describe the operations of large religious institutions. A bishop or dean may write extensively about the meaning of Christmas or Easter, but there are few records about who was being considered as candidates for major positions or how and why a particular person was selected. Additionally, deans and bishops held their cards closely, volunteering little personal information about themselves beyond standard alumni magazine biographical fare.

A continuing challenge has been to portray accurately the participants in the historical setting in which they lived and not as twenty-first-century personalities. Satterlee did the best he could to advance the place of African Americans, but this did not include integrating Washington parishes of the 1890s. He never considered that possibility. A later generation might be initially impatient with the measured, clearly consistent but nonthreatening position taken by Cynthia Wedel in the sixties on the place of women in priesthood, but Wedel laid a solid foundation that made the work of the next generation of women's leadership easier.

The relationship is a disjunctive one between the history of National Cathedral and mainline Protestantism, and between the cathedral and the city of which it was a part. Many major movements in American Protestantism came and went with only a minimal response from the cathedral. Some included Prohibition, the Social Gospel, womens' suffrage, immigration, and (until after World War II) civil rights. Likewise, the deep racial, social, political, and economic disparities that were such a part of the District of Columbia did not become regular subjects for cathedral interest until the second half of the twentieth century.

There are three reasons for this. First, for years the cathedral's first priority was to complete the building, not to be a voice for causes. Second, it had no regular parish constituency, and those attending on any particular Sunday might reflect a variety of positions on any given issue, making it difficult for the cathedral's leadership to take public stands on controversial questions of the day and be sure of their support. Third, throughout its history the cathedral was consciously seeking to stabilize and expand its donor base. Thus most clergy, including Dean Francis B. Sayre, who was outspoken on many political issues, carefully shaped their remarks for a Washington audience. Put starkly, if a strong anti-establishment sermon came with any regularity from the cathedral pulpit, it might be difficult to recruit local bankers and lawyers as fundraisers or as members of the Cathedral Chapter. Strategically, it would be better to oppose sin than to spotlight individual sinners. Thus, the cathedral, like almost any large religious institution, faced the dilemma of balancing the gospel mandate to be prophetic and the corporate challenge of self-preservation. More often than not, its leadership chose a place in the (cautious, prudent, hesitant) middle.

The biographies of church figures often make for uneasy reading, sometimes resembling heavily sugared holiday fruitcake. I have tried to paint accurate portraits of the characters in this study, chronicling their achievements, yet showing them in their humanity, as in the generational and attitudinal differences between Bishop John T. Walker and Dean Francis B. Sayre over the roles of bishops and deans in cathedral leadership.

What follows is a series of episodes and sketches of different times and personalities, connected in that they were all part of the evolution of the cathedral and the Diocese of Washington. The city changed greatly in the century it took to build the cathedral, and a new cast of characters appeared periodically in church and state, bringing with them new priorities. This story begins in the time of Bishop Satterlee in the 1890s, when the cathedral plans were first developed, and it ends with the death of dean and bishop John T. Walker in 1989, when the building was nearly finished and its public mission clearly articulated.

Throughout its history, the cathedral has demonstrated several purposes, but they have not always been united seamlessly. It was always "a House of Prayer for All People," but over the decades the meaning of "all people" shifted. Likewise, it was always a national church, a place where presidential inaugurations were celebrated and a president is buried, where national calamities were wept over and triumphs were proclaimed. Art, music, and architectural splendor helped make it a numinous place of worship, a sacred space where individual and collective pilgrimages encounter the *mysterium tremendum,* the divine mystery. It is far easier for the historian to discuss the progress of a building than to chronicle examples of sacred encounters where the human quest and divine reality might meet, where, as Bishop Satterlee's hope early on, "the Word became flesh and lived among us" (John 1:14).

My own academic training is as a historian, which suggests some specific ways of writing about a subject. This should include a scaffolding of chronology and an explanation of why particular dates or subjects are chosen. It should also emphasize the context and the times in which a particular event took place, the personalities involved, and their response to the issues that they faced. The historian cannot expect the characters of another time and place to behave like contemporary parishioners.

The most interesting work of a historian is that of weighing evidence and evaluating how specific people responded to situations they faced: rendering such judgments is part of the historian's craft. The amassing of such information will invariably lead to the revision of opinions, or at least to their nuanced qualification. This is another way of saying that all history writing, even the most seemingly conclusive, is transitory, awaiting the findings of new generations. "Show me an eternal verity and I will tell you its date of origin," an experienced colleague once remarked. I looked carefully, but I found neither tyrants nor scandal, and only one murder.

Why did I only deal with a select number of bishops and deans, and not others? After all, several deserving personalities await their biographers, like the second Mrs. Bratenahl, the cathedral's master gardener, and Bishop William F. Creighton, who brought women clergy into the church in a carefully planned manner. My selection was determined by the obvious contributions of some key persons and the availability of archival sources. Material about Bishop Satterlee was readily available on everything from cathedral building to the issue of race. His successor appeared to be a kindly disposed, hard working, but far less interesting individual. Additionally, many able canons came and went, but few approached Anson Phelps Stokes or Michael P. Hamilton in achievement or range of interests.

It is useful to bear in mind the basic issues of architecture and construction of the cathedral across the years, because the larger life of the institution revolved around them. 1906 was a decisive year in cathedral planning. On May 21, the chapter voiced its preference for a Gothic design and on October 8 employed George F. Bodley and Henry Vaughan, two leading exponents of fourteenth-century English Gothic architecture, as cathedral architects. They produced a master plan by June 10, 1907. The cathedral foundation stone was laid on September 29 of that year, with addresses by President Theodore Roosevelt and the Bishop of London. Bodley died in Oxford that October. Vaughan, who lived in Boston, was his successor until his death in 1917.

Subsequent construction moved by fits and starts, governed by the availability of funds. Bethlehem Chapel was built between 1907 and 1912 as a memorial to Bishop Satterlee, who died in 1908. The apse and walls surrounding the high altar were completed between 1915 and 1919. Vaughan died on June 30, 1917, and in 1921 the

Boston firm of Frohman, Robb, and Little succeeded him, with Phillip H. Frohman as lead cathedral architect for the next several decades. The third phase was the early 1920s, when work on the Great Choir proceeded. By December 1924 nearly fifteen thousand persons had contributed four million dollars, allowing for the purchase of all property on the close, the start of an endowment, and a modest increase in construction. The cathedral library was built, the College of Preachers completed, as was construction on side and crypt chapels. The Great Choir roof was put in place and the first stones were laid for the transepts that would provide space for increased congregations. The remains of President Woodrow Wilson were entombed in the cathedral on February 6, 1924. The Bishop's Garden opened in 1926.

On May 1, 1934, as the Great Depression was ending, a contract was let for placement of a sculpted reredos behind the high altar, construction was relaunched on the north and south transepts, and the Great Organ was dedicated on November 10, 1938. In May 1937, Dean G.C.F. Bratenahl was succeeded by Noble Powell, who was later elected bishop of Maryland in 1941. A popular Washington cleric, ZeBarney Phillips, rector of Epiphany Church, succeeded Powell in November 1942, but died five months later. The first concert of the newly formed 150-voice Cathedral Choral Society under Paul Callaway, which featured Verdi's *Requiem*, became a memorial to Phillips.

Construction was curtailed during the war. After Bishop Freeman's death in 1943, he was succeeded by Angus Dun, who was consecrated as fourth bishop of Washington on April 19, 1944, with John W. Suter following as fourth cathedral dean on November 1, 1944.

As the war was coming to an end, a five million dollar fundraising effort was launched, work on the south transept was resumed in 1948, and in 1954 expansion of the nave began. The cathedral library was expanded, additions to the cathedral schools were added, and on October 20, 1957 the War Memorial Chapel was dedicated in the cathedral in the presence of President and Mrs. Eisenhower, Queen Elizabeth, and Prince Phillip. Between 1960 to 1964 contracts were signed for the building of an administrative building, the north cloister, and the Gloria in Excelsis Tower, which was completed on October 16, 1963 and dedicated on May 7, 1964. Our narrative concludes in 1990, with the building's last pinnacle in place and the retirement of Provost Charles A. Perry, although there was always additional construction or repairs to attend to and staff to be hired or let go as funding possibilities increased or diminished. Continuity and change were features of its life. (Although a major program expansion effort was announced for 2012 to 2014, on August 23, 2013, at 1:53 pm, a 5.8 magnitude earthquake knocked off tower pinnacles, sent gargoyles flying, and loosened roof and wall masonry, doing over twenty million dollars worth of damage to the cathedral. The building and its ministry remain a work in progress.)

The building's legal name is "the Cathedral of Saints Peter and Paul in the Diocese of Washington," but it is usually known as Washington National Cathedral, or National Cathedral, terms I employ in this book. Footnotes refer to archival holdings as NCA (National Cathedral Archives), followed by three numbers designating the record group, file box, and folder, such as NCA (8.10.1). The archives are ample, and many of the participants of an earlier generation are still alive. I have assembled the story that emerged from the documents as I read them; others will understandably have a different picture to present. It is a history that changes somewhat with each telling.

This book is organized as follows: an opening section discusses the life and times of Henry Yates Satterlee, Washington's first bishop, an advocate of the English Gothic ideal who acquired the land and the plans for Washington National Cathedral. Subsequent chapters deal with the leadership of Bishops Alfred Harding and George E. Freeman and the cathedral's first full-time dean, G.C.F. Bratenahl. Then Angus Dun, bishop of Washington from 1944 to 1962, and Anson Phelps Stokes, a remarkable figure who served as canon from 1924 to 1939, but who was also deeply interested in Africa, racial integration, and American constitutional history. There follows a unit on Theodore and Cynthia Wedel, major figures in cathedral, diocese, and wider church life in the 1940s through the 1960s. Two additional chapters discuss the tenures of Francis B. Sayre as cathedral dean from 1951 to 1978 and John T. Walker as bishop and dean from 1977 to 1989. A final section presents a survey of issues of the 1970s and 1980s, and discusses the emergence of women clergy at the cathedral in the post-1977 period, when the ordination of women became an official reality in the Episcopal Church. It is an account of continuity and change, of which the final chapter is yet to be written.

Richard G. Hewlett's careful organization of the Washington National Cathedral Archives, and his balanced writing about Bishop Henry Yates Satterlee, made my own work possible. Hewlett, well known as a professional historian, spent over twenty years as cathedral historiographer and archivist, bringing the cathedral archives into modern times. Diane Nye, his successor as manager of the archives, and Susan Stonesifer, historiographer of the Episcopal Diocese of Washington, were equally helpful. Diane Nye disappeared down darkened corridors and emerged with books and documents that would have remained on shelves, but were just what was needed at particular moments of research. A number of skilled archive volunteers were generous in their assistance as well. Detailed conversations with Deans John T. Walker and Samuel T. Lloyd, III and Provosts Sanford Gardner and Charles A. Perry were valuable, even before I thought of writing about the cathedral. Frank Wade, rector of St. Alban's Parish and acting dean of the cathedral, was helpful in his recollections of time spent at both institutions: David Booth Beers, longtime lay leader and former chancellor to the diocese, shared his insights based on nearly four decades of work as an attorney and policy consultant to parishes, deans, and bishops. The late Bishops Ronald H. Haines and Jane H. Dixon helped complete the picture. Deans Nathan D. Baxter and Gary R. Hall were unfailingly helpful as well. The editorial skills and scholarly insights of Frederick W. Schmidt, former canon educator at National Cathedral, made valuable contributions to improving the manuscript. I am grateful to Bishop Mariann Edgar Budde and her husband Paul, and to Bishop Carolyn Tanner Irish, my wife, and to David Dixon, Martha and Don Horne, Gina Campbell, Jan Naylor Cope, Samuel Van Cullen Jr., Duke DuTeil, and Kevin Thomas for their support. Ryan Masteller, production manager, Church Publishing, saw the book through to completion with high professionalism. The Library of Congress, American University Library, and the Bishop Payne Library at Virginia Theological Seminary were valuable resources as well.

The photographs used in this book come from the collection of Washington National Cathedral and are used with permission.

This book is dedicated in grateful thanksgiving for the ministry of Katharine Jefferts Schori, twenty-sixth presiding bishop of the Episcopal Church. Her leadership, preaching, and pastoral empathy for all sorts and conditions of people have been exemplary since her election at the church's General Convention on June 18, 2006. The former bishop of Nevada was invested at National Cathedral on November 4 that year and seated the following day in the presiding bishop's stall. As primate of the American church, she has been a regular presence at National Cathedral, representing a denomination with over two million members in 110 dioceses and sixteen countries of the wider Anglican Communion.

Frederick Quinn
Washington, DC

CHAPTER ONE

Henry Yates Satterlee:
The Bishop as Builder (1896–1908)

Henry Yates Satterlee was a figure of contrasts, a patrician New Yorker who moved to the growing southern city of Washington in 1896. A descendent of an old English family, he was deeply committed to work among the poor and "colored people." He also maintained strong international interests, undertook a mission to the tsar of Russia to plead about the plight of Armenian Christians, and served as provisional Episcopal bishop of Mexico. Satterlee (1843–1908), first bishop of the newly established Episcopal Diocese of Washington (1895), was also the person who moved the vague hope for a Washington National Cathedral to a reality.

His own beliefs were an amalgam. He was deeply committed to moral and social betterment, but he steered clear of the Social Gospel and the Oxford Movement, both prevalent in his era. Satterlee held to a carefully crafted vision of the "primitive church" and the historic episcopate, as he understood them, but rejected later additions like ritualism and "Romanist" practices among clergy. He was a

1

vocal advocate of church union, especially of splintered Protestant groups, and hoped for their coming together, but only if they did so by accepting Anglican formularies.

Yet, while his personal and working life was spent with prominent civic and church leaders, he is rarely mentioned among their numbers in later accounts, in part because in almost four decades of active ministry Satterlee avoided the limelight, while consciously steering others in directions of his clear choosing. Additionally, he is not well known because not much has been written about him and the early history of the Diocese of Washington. The standard work is Charles H. Brent's *A Master Builder, Being the Life and Letters of Henry Yates Satterlee, First Bishop of Washington*.[1] Satterlee's widow provided a fourteen-page outline, documents, and suggested references to the author, Bishop Brent (1867–1929), who twice declined election as Satterlee's successor in Washington. Parts of this lengthy work are traditional Episcopal hagiography, resembling one of the large oil paintings of Episcopal bishops commissioned for diocesan conference rooms in the days when the church had easy access to money for such purposes. Richard G. Hewlett has published an extensive appraisal of Satterlee's work in launching the cathedral, but little has been written in more recent times about the bishop's equally active role in creating a new diocese and his views on church issues of his day.

Much other writing about the cathedral resembles stone and stained glass history that links a person with the building, but, as noted earlier, often cathedral personalities and their times were more complex than might initially appear. This was also true of Satterlee, the active diocesan bishop and writer on church issues, who determinedly obtained the land and the plans for the cathedral, but for later audiences he remained in the shadow of his greatest achievement.[2] Since this book focuses on that institution and the personalities that contributed to its evolution, a discussion of Satterlee's role as cathedral planner is an appropriate point of departure for this narrative.

---

1 Charles H. Brent, *A Master Builder: Being the Life and Letters of Henry Yates Satterlee* (New York: Longmans, Green, 1916).

2 The author acknowledges the valued assistance of Richard Hewlett, archivist and historian, Diane Ney, manager of Archives and Records at Washington National Cathedral, and Susan Stonesifer, Washington diocesan historiographer.

The Quest for a National Cathedral

The quest for a National Cathedral, the best-known endeavor of Satterlee's episcopate, had deep roots in American national life. Major Pierre L'Enfant envisioned "a great church for national purposes" in his original plans for the city of Washington, but nothing came of the idea. After several meetings of leading Washington figures, including planning sessions in the home of Charles C. Glover, president of the Riggs Bank, the Protestant Episcopal Church Foundation was created on January 6, 1893, by Act of Congress and signed by President Benjamin Harrison. The foundation stone, imported from a field near Bethlehem, was laid on September 29, 1907, and in 1912, four years after Satterlee's death, the Bethlehem Chapel was completed and open for worship.

Two leading Washington clergy of the late nineteenth century were instrumental in moving the cathedral idea forward. They were George William Douglas (1850–1926), rector of St. John's, Lafayette Square from 1889 to 1892, and Randolph Harrison McKim (1842–1921), rector of another major downtown parish, Church of the Epiphany, from 1888 to 1920. Douglas was independently wealthy and married to a Newport heiress, and had served at Satterlee's old parish, Calvary Church, and Trinity Parish, Wall Street, before coming to Washington. When he left in 1892 because of his wife's ill health, he was succeeded by Alexander Mackay-Smith, also well known to Satterlee from his New York days. It was Douglas and McKim who conducted the negotiations with Bishop William Paret of Maryland that led to formation of the Washington diocese, and the duo also worked for incorporation of an independent Cathedral Foundation by Congress, and later served as its trustees.

Paret, for eight years rector of the Church of the Epiphany in Washington, had been a hesitant supporter of the independent diocese. He took credit for its emergence in his autobiography, but for over a decade the prospect had been a start and stop exercise.[3] Paret recognized the inevitability of the new diocese being split off from Maryland, but had no personal inclination to move from Baltimore back to Washington, and regretted the potential loss of several parishes in the nation's capital that were a part of his diocese. Still,

---

3 William Paret, *Reminiscences* (Philadelphia: George W. Jacobs, 1911): 151–163, 204–205.

in his address to the diocese in 1894 he introduced the division as "absolutely necessary before long," with the proviso that there should be a fair division of the territory and work, as well as adequate salaries for two bishops.[4]

The Search for a Site

Finding an appropriate site was a major issue facing the early cathedral planners. The closer to the White House the better, but land north of 1700 Pennsylvania Avenue was becoming both more expensive and scarce. The gift of eight valuable city lots for a cathedral by Mary Elizabeth Mann of St. John's Church was welcome, but the $80,000 property was encumbered with taxes and debts, and the offer was soon withdrawn. Meanwhile, a land developer, Francis G. Newlands, also a member of Congress from Nevada, offered 14.5 acres in the distant streetcar suburb of Chevy Chase. There were strong disadvantages to accepting the offer, the principal one being its considerable distance from the city center. Rock Creek was a winding stream and difficult to cross, without an accessible bridge or adequate road; and Connecticut Avenue North remained a dirt or muddy trail, almost inaccessible until a trolley line was built. The land north and west of Rock Creek remained thick woods or open country for several years. Who would want to build a cathedral so far away?[5]

Meanwhile, Douglas, who had made several visits to England, pushed through the Cathedral Foundation's draft constitution, even though after 1892 he was rarely in Washington. Following a traditional English model, he proposed an organization with roles for bishop, dean, chapter, and canons, but questions remained. Would it be under diocesan governance or stand alone? Would it be primarily a diocesan church or a national institution? Would Baltimore and Washington parishes have seats on its governing board, or would bishops from other dioceses be included as well?

A national university and theological school were both proposed for the cathedral close, as were boys' and girls' schools, housing for

---

4 Richard Greening Hewlett, *The Foundation Stone, Henry Yates Satterlee and the Creation of Washington National Cathedral* (Rockville, MD: Montrose Press, 2007): 54. As historiographer of the Diocese of Washington, Hewlett spent almost twenty years overseeing the cataloguing of early records that include twenty-one boxes of Satterlee material.

5 *Ibid.*, 49–50, 64.

over ten clergy, and a hostel for returning missionaries. The draft of the constitution written in 1894 established a complex structure with two governing boards and chapters with separate membership and authority. The cathedral would be both a national *and* a diocesan institution. Douglas also picked its formal name, "The Cathedral of St. Peter and St. Paul." This was intentional. If it was St. Paul's alone, that would be in the great English tradition, but by adding St. Peter, he said, "I want to proclaim to the Romanists that we allow them no monopoly of St. Peter."[6] A grateful Satterlee named Douglas as first dean of the cathedral, but Douglas never took up the appointment.

Opposing Views on a National Cathedral

Satterlee continually sought support for the creation of a national cathedral. Washington Episcopalians had already met to consider the concept before Satterlee had been elected bishop, so the ground was already laid for him to move ahead when he arrived in Washington. Still, Satterlee was not the only one hoping for a large new cathedral in Washington. In November of 1901 an Episcopal clergy member of the Washington diocese announced plans for a massive non-denominational cathedral, a world temple to be built in Washington, not far from the White House. Richard Lewis Howell, former rector of St. Margaret's Episcopal Church, envisioned "a Mecca for all men, open day and night," housing "the greatest system of organs ever built." Construction costs would be paid by the popular subscriptions of eighty million people who would contribute a penny each over several years.[7]

Nothing came of the wildly unrealistic plan, but Howell's letter to Satterlee asking for support triggered the bishop's pointed response voicing his complete misgivings. Religious unity for Anglicans could only come about through the Chicago-Lambeth Quadrilateral, he told Howell, and "in the intensity of your generous desire for a religious unity, you must have temporarily lost sight of those fundamental principles . . . I cannot but deeply deplore, as your personal friend and your bishop, the step you have taken: for it is one all past

---

6 *Ibid.*, 53.
7 Richard Lewis Howell to Henry Yates Satterlee, undated, NCA (2.12.19).
  "Church for All Men," *The Washington Post,* November 2, 1901.

experience proves leads not to unity but to disunion."[8] For good measure, Satterlee asked Howell's printer, who was also the diocesan printer, to stop producing Howell's leaflets, which the printer did. Nothing more was ever heard of the Howell plan.

Land for the Cathedral on Mount Saint Alban

After a long search, an attractive site for the future cathedral finally became available in 1898—a fifty-seven-acre parcel of land on Mount Saint Alban, overlooking the city. Bishop Satterlee believed the two tides of Washington's expanding population would converge there. Massachusetts Avenue was "destined to be the street whereon the residences of the wealthy, are and will be erected," and Wisconsin Avenue was "already being built up with houses which, until it comes to the neighborhood of the cathedral and Cleveland Park, are of a humbler class" but will be transformed by the revolutionary newly invented form of public transportation, electric tram-cars.[9]

Unfortunately, Amzi L. Barber owned the desired land. A former college professor who became a business entrepreneur, Barber was known as "The Asphalt King," and for several years held a near monopoly on its production. Barber was also a flint-edged tough negotiator. He knew Satterlee wanted the land on Mount Saint Alban and was unyielding in his exchanges with the bishop. Barber held the upper hand, offered no concessions, upped the price after negotiations were under way, and threatened to withhold the final piece of property. He would build his own large residence there, he told Satterlee, and could sell it later for a sizable profit. They finally agreed on a price of $245,000 and Satterlee personally guaranteed a $145,000 partial mortgage on the property.[10]

In 1898, three years after he had been installed as bishop, Satterlee made an expansive bid to gain national support for the cathedral. The Episcopal Church's General Convention brought its bishops, clergy, and lay leaders to Washington, and Satterlee planned to unveil a Peace Cross on October 23 to commemorate the end of the Spanish-American War. This would establish the cathedral as a

---

8 Henry Y. Satterlee to Richard Lewis Howell, November 15, 1901, NCA
    (2.12.18).
9 Hewlett, 73.
10 *Ibid.*, 65.

national institution, attract President William McKinley and other national leaders, and call attention to the Mount Saint Alban site. It would also be an opportunity to honor Admiral George Dewey, a recent war hero, who was a cathedral trustee from 1899 to 1917.

Friends of the bishop donated the stone cross, and it was shipped quickly from an Indiana quarry in time for the dedication. The Marine Band played, President McKinley spoke briefly, and the presence of the bishop of London gave the gathering an international flavor. The Washington bishop asked a prominent Virginia writer, Thomas Nelson Page, author of several period novels on the antebellum South, like *Befo' de War* and *Two Little Confederates,* to compile a Peace Cross book. Satterlee sent it to all American bishops with an article from the *New York Sun* describing Roman Catholic plans to establish a national university in Washington. The Methodists were building American University, the Baptists were building George Washington University—would Episcopalians be left behind?

In spite of the favorable publicity, funds remained difficult to come by. The parishes in Washington did not contribute much, nor did dioceses in other parts of the nation. A printing of handsome founders' certificates, to be sold nationally at a dollar each, did not cover the cost of printing. Satterlee held a round of "parlor meetings" in Baltimore, Philadelphia, New York, and Boston that led to the formation of local chapters of a National Cathedral Association. He estimated that while in Philadelphia he called on fifty-one persons.[11] When the land purchase debt was finally paid off in 1905, Satterlee wrote in his *Private Record,* "No one can ever appreciate what it is to be delivered from this burden. I feel like one released from prison, after having been in confinement seven years from 1898 to 1905."[12]

Satterlee left no detail of the cathedral's planning to chance, from picking the colors of its stones to meeting with potential donors. He obtained stones for the bishop's cathedra, or ceremonial seat, from Glastonbury Abbey in England. Large stones from the Holy Land went into the Jerusalem high altar, and those for the pulpit came from Canterbury. He also designed a total immersion baptismal font, to be initially installed outside the cathedral in a small building that later became the Herb Cottage.

---

11 *Ibid.,* 68–70.
12 *Ibid.,* 70.

Satterlee reasoned that, if the Episcopal Church was to be an agent for Christian unity, and other Protestant denominations practiced total immersion baptism, it should also engage in this practice when required. That was as close as he ever came to an ecumenical plan. The baptistery was rarely used after Satterlee's death. It became part of the Herb Cottage after World War II, and the baptistery was finally dismantled.[13]

Renaissance vs. Gothic? Architectural Choices for the New Cathedral

The most divisive issue facing the cathedral was the selection of the building's architectural style. Two main architectural types predominated in the new Washington, Federalist and Greco-Roman governmental, but neither was suggested in plans for National Cathedral, where the battle was over "Renaissance" versus "Gothic."

The differences were stark, represented in the work of two major American architects, the flamboyant Ernest Flagg (1857–1947) of New York and the solitary Henry Vaughan (1845–1917) of Boston, who had grown up in England as a follower and later a colleague of the celebrated George F. Bodley (1827–1907), champion of the English Gothic style. Initially, Flagg had the edge with his Paris-inspired Beaux-Arts plan.[14] He had successfully designed Washington's Corcoran Gallery of Art in the updated Renaissance style, and Charles C. Glover, a leading banker and promoter of both the art gallery and cathedral, asked him to draw up plans for the cathedral as well. This took place before Satterlee had been elected bishop of the new diocese in 1895. Flagg had the additional advantage of already being the architect-designate of the new girls' school on the cathedral grounds. Its donor, Phoebe Hearst, favored the Renaissance style, as did Douglas, who wrote the original bylaws. Everything looked set for the cathedral's future. Satterlee's opinion was the remaining question.

The cathedral board had also been weighing the Gothic versus Renaissance question and asked Flagg to draw up arguments for and against both traditions to share with the new bishop. Flagg, whose

---

13 *Ibid.*, 71.
14 Mardges Bacon, *Ernest Flagg, Beaux-Arts Architect and Urban Reformer* (Cambridge: The MIT Press, 1986).

commissions included the Scribner Building in New York and buildings for the U.S. Naval Academy in Annapolis, Maryland, argued that the Gothic ideal was now obsolete, a product of an earlier age with its limited construction techniques. It would mean a smaller, longer church, supported by flying buttresses, and it would require extended heights for roofs and towers. Flagg's comments on Gothic architecture were a setup, after which he carefully laid out his own position. "At the time of the Renaissance," he began, "men cast off Gothic art just as they cast off Gothic superstition. The Renaissance style is emblematic of modern times and liberal ideas, just as Gothic art is emblematic of medieval thought and superstition. . . . The grandeur of the interior of a church no longer depended upon extreme length and a great disproportion of the height to the width but all three proportions might be used simultaneously."[15]

Finally, he unveiled a breathtaking design for the cathedral and close in his own modern adaptation of a French Renaissance design. It centered on a huge single-domed structure that could only be called Vatican II, and colonnades that filled the grounds with boys' and girls' schools, and a university that was never built. The cathedral board accepted the plan and named Flagg its architect in January 1896. Articles appeared in architectural publications and his plans for the massive project were prominently displayed at the Pennsylvania Academy of Fine Arts and the National Academy of Design in New York.[16] The design question was settled, or so the board believed.

Notwithstanding the plans made by the board, those inveterate church politicians, McKim of Epiphany and Mackay-Smith of St. John's, still favored the Gothic design, and Mackay-Smith tried to convince the strong-willed Flagg to abandon the Renaissance design. Meanwhile, Flagg faltered badly and lost both the already launched cathedral and girls' school projects. He had accumulated high-cost overruns on the Corcoran Gallery, quarreled with its builders, and alienated major donors like Glover, a key figure on both architectural commissions. Flagg's strongly held views and inflexible manner did not leave a way for negotiation. When his plans for the $315,000 Hearst school came in far above the $175,000 the trustees had budgeted, they believed it was time to reconsider both architect and plans.[17]

---

15 Hewlett, 57.
16 Bacon, 69, 108.
17 Hewlett, 58.

Where did Satterlee stand? His preferences were always clear. He had called Gothic "God's style," and in parishes where he had spent almost three decades he had undertaken Gothic-inspired renovations. At his parish in Wappingers Falls, New York, he had taught a weekly adult course on church architecture for over four years, and on European tours had systematically studied the great cathedrals of Germany, Italy, France, Spain, and England.

His conclusions were succinctly expressed in a letter to a member of the cathedral's advisory committee, "First, last, and always, the Cathedral is 'A House of Prayer for All People' that was Our Lord's own description of the Church. . . . And experience has plainly shown that the Gothic is distinctively religious and a Christian style of Architecture which excels all others in inspiring prayer and devotional feeling among all sorts and conditions of men." A Gothic cathedral would provide a positive contrast "between it and the magnificent classic buildings in Washington."[18] At the same time, he declared his strong preference for a Gothic structure. "I am sure," he declared, "from many indications in past years that the Gothic style of architecture appeals most strongly to the people at large for a Church building."[19] There he left the matter, without further elaboration, but he also left no doubt as to his choice.

Hewlett, who closely followed the bishop's life, noted Satterlee's preference to work behind the scenes on controversial issues. He did not publicly enter into the Renaissance versus Gothic debate, at least not until the land was debt-free in 1905.[20] After Flagg's plans were rejected, Satterlee proposed an open competition, with finalists displaying their work at the Library of Congress or Corcoran Gallery. (He later withdrew the proposal). He also appointed a five-member advisory board that included Charles F. Moore, a Harvard University expert on Gothic architecture; Casper Purdon Clark, director of the Metropolitan Museum of Art in New York; Daniel H. Burnham, chief architect of the White City built at the Columbian Exposition of 1893 in Chicago; Charles F. McKim, a well-known New York architect; and Bernard S. Green, a civil engineer who had supervised construction of the Washington Monument.

---

18 *Ibid.,* 78.
19 *Ibid.,* 74.
20 *Ibid.,* 70–71.

On May 5, 1906, four members of the committee toured the proposed cathedral site with Satterlee. They approved the new location atop Mount Saint Alban, rejected the idea of an open competition for an architect, and split evenly on the issue of Gothic versus Renaissance styles—clear hesitancy about the position Satterlee thought he had secured. The determined bishop worked for passage of a trustees' resolution on May 21 that stated, "while fully recognizing the beauties of the classic style, [it] sees no reason why it should change its views as originally enunciated, and therefore adheres to its decision that the Gothic style shall be adopted."[21] "The one sentence in the official minutes of the meeting and Satterlee's two sentences in the *Private Record* represent the sum total of all that he reveals to the reader about the decision on style," Hewlett observed.[22]

George Frederick Bodley and Henry Vaughan, Master English Gothic Architects

Now that he had free reign to propose an architect, Satterlee moved quickly. From his visits to England and careful study of English cathedrals, he was familiar with the work of George Frederick Bodley, a leading architect of English Gothic churches. But an American presence was needed as well, and Satterlee was drawn to a former student and head draftsman of Bodley's, the Boston-based Henry Vaughan. The two architects had mentioned each other as possible collaborators. Both were Anglo-Catholics whose respect for the English Gothic ideal was unqualified; both sought as well to avoid any statements of personal style, and this was attractive to Satterlee. They were accepted as architects at the trustee's meeting of October 8, 1906.

Vaughan was a reclusive figure who spent his days alternating between a Beacon Hill rooming house, early mass at the chapel of the Society of St. John the Evangelist, and his solitary office, which lacked a secretary, typewriter, or telephone. Born in England, he had clerked with Bodley, and his goal was to design churches in the English Gothic tradition. Vaughan's best-known works include the chapels for Groton and St. Paul's schools, and three chapels in the Cathedral of St. John the Divine in New York City. "His

---

21 *Ibid.,* 76.
22 *Ibid.,* 76.

English stylistic repertory was never significantly modified during his thirty-six years in America," the architectural historian William Morgan wrote. "In fact, there is no reason to suppose that he would not have produced virtually the same type of designs had he stayed in England."[23]

Both Bodley and Vaughan visited Washington and met with Satterlee, and sought an extended statement of his views about the cathedral. Satterlee's response was not so much about the design, but about the building's intended use. He saw it as "the representative Cathedral of our own church in the Capital of the country" and of "the Anglican Communion in America."[24] It would also be a welcoming home to those Protestant denominations that had broken away from the Church of England during the Reformation. Statues and stained glass could reflect both aspects of American history and Protestant religious figures like John Bunyan, George Fox, and John Wesley. The crypt chapel would be the Chapel of the Nativity or Bethlehem Chapel, the great central tower would be the Gloria in Excelsis Tower, recalling the song the angels sang at Christ's birth. The whole building "would breathe the atmosphere of the triumph of the Christian faith."[25] Satterlee was deeply attracted to the concept of the Incarnation, God entering history through the person of Jesus at Christmas, a theme he explored in various writings. On the cathedral's foundation stone the incarnational idea was echoed in a quotation he selected from the King James Bible's version of the Gospel of John: "The word became flesh and dwelt among us" (1:14).[26]

On June 5, 1907, Bodley's first drawings arrived in New York. Satterlee had arranged for the custom house there to expedite their onward passage to Washington by night train. Two hours after their arrival in Washington on June 7, they were spread out for the trustees to view. Satterlee described a setting "of the subdued serene pleasure with which all the members of the chapter contemplated the

---

23 William Morgan, *The Almighty Wall, The Architecture of Henry Vaughan* (Cambridge: The MIT Press, 1983): 8.

24 Hewlett, 79.

25 *Ibid.*, 80.

26 After the Bethlehem Chapel was completed, Satterlee's sarcophagus, containing a recumbent effigy of the bishop by W.D. Caroe, resident architect of Canterbury Cathedral, was placed behind the altar. It was set above the foundation stone and under the cathedral's main Jerusalem altar. Four surrounding pillars represented the Chicago-Lambeth Quadrilateral, written by Satterlee's friend, William Reed Huntington. (Hewlett, 82).

two perspective drawings." Vaughan explained the features of the fourteenth-century English Gothic style building.[27] Inspirational as the plans might be, Satterlee had numerous corrections to make: the nave required expansion to hold a congregation of three thousand persons, the West End towers were too low, the choir needed to be raised, and the red stone suggested for the building was far too dark. Also, Satterlee wanted a more easily accessible approach to the building's main entrance.[28]

The building that emerged, long after Satterlee's time, would have a central tower of 676 feet above sea level, making it the highest point in the District of Columbia. It would be the sixth largest cathedral in the world, and second largest in the United States, the largest being St. John the Divine in New York. Its West End Rose Window would be 26 feet in diameter and contain 1,500 pieces of colored glass, many of them an inch thick. Some 288 carved angels would adorn the two west towers, and inside an organ with 10,650 pipes would play for services and concerts.

Satterlee's extended correspondence with Vaughan was filled with practical construction and design suggestions. Satterlee's primary achievements regarding the cathedral are that he obtained the plans for an English Gothic building, purchased the land, and launched the National Cathedral Association that would be a future source of funding and support for the project. Although his name is the first one listed in any history of that building, in fact he spent even more time launching the new Washington diocese during his twelve-year episcopate than he did on the cathedral. Satterlee was an intensely hard-working church leader.

Satterlee's Early Years: "A Happy, Healthy Boy" in Albany and New York City

Any understanding of the Satterlee who came to Washington in 1896 must begin with an examination of his New York origins and long

---

27 *Ibid.*
28 Bodley died in 1907, Satterlee in 1908. Vaughan continued as architect until his death in 1917 after which the long tenure of Philip Hubert Frohman as chief architect began. "Washington Cathedral would be mostly his monument," Morgan wrote of Frohman, representing "more of an academic exercise in Gothic than that envisioned by Bodley and Vaughan. And it lacks the freshness and originality of the Englishmen's design." *Ibid.*, 81–82.

and active ministry there, as he was a fully formed person by the time he was elected bishop. Both old English and Dutch roots were parts of Henry Yates Satterlee's ancestry, and in New York society of the mid-nineteenth century he was either related to or knew most of the main players, connections he drew on constantly during his nearly twelve years in Washington.[29] The family name was traceable to the English Middle Ages and the county of Suffolk, where Edward IV had seized the family manor house and lands after the War of the Roses.[30] Henry's paternal grandfather was a wealthy merchant in Albany, New York, and president of the Albany Gallery of Fine Arts. Henry's father, Edward, was born in 1815, and lived off family money while trying his hand as an artist and cultivated gentlemen of leisure.

Handsome and well educated, Edward married Jane Anna Yates, whose ancestry included a colonel in the American Revolution, and a governor of New York. Jane spoke fluent French and Dutch. Her family, like her husband's, was descended from New York's original Knickerbocker aristocracy. The couple married in Schenectady, New York, in 1838 and, after their first daughter was born in 1840, moved briefly to New York City, where their son, Henry, was born on January 11, 1843 at the family home at 112 Greenwich Street, near the Battery.

At least six Satterlee families were living in lower Manhattan in the affluent district just north of the island's tip.[31] In 1845 Edward returned to Albany, joined the family business, and moved into the spacious Yates family mansion, set on several acres, where he and Jane raised six children. Henry's older sister remembered her younger brother as "a healthy, happy boy, fond of reading, especially of making all sorts of collections of insects, minerals, etc."[32] Like many affluent families of the time, Henry was schooled at home by a private tutor, then attended the Albany Academy. He grew up speaking both English and "New York Dutch."

After nearly a decade of idyllic life in busy, hospitable Albany, his father again returned to New York City in 1854, this time to a town

---

29 *Ibid.*, 54.
30 "People of Sotterley, Herbert L. Satterlee, Retaining a Piece of Colonial America (1863–1947)," http://www.sotterley.org/satterlee.htm7/27/2009.
31 Hewlett, 1.
32 *Ibid.*, 3.

house on Twenty-Third Street, a block east of Broadway. New York was changing. Waves of European immigrants had pushed into lower Manhattan in recent years, and New York society was migrating up town. Henry resumed schooling at the Columbia Grammar School, and in 1858 was accepted into Columbia College. His was the sort of family Edith Wharton wrote about and Henry James might have described.

The Grand Tour—England, Europe, Egypt, and the Holy Land

Fifteen-year-old Henry delayed his entrance into college for a nine-month-long family trip to Europe and the Middle East that began in September 1858. From his artistically inclined father he gained a lasting interest in European art, architecture, and sculpture, especially English works. The family visited England—Henry returned there frequently during summers and made a lifelong study of its cathedral architecture and governance. The initial trip also included Paris, Vienna, and Rome, with additional time in Egypt and the Holy Land. It gave the observant youth an awareness of international issues, European culture, and the religious setting of the early Christian church, topics he would often return to in later life.

After returning to New York in 1859, Henry lived at home but attended Columbia College, where he wrote essays, fiction, and youthful poetry. He also had a deep interest in moral questions. In a student essay on "The Power of the Will," he argued that mind could subdue matter, both among persons and nations, and could cause individual and societal progress. Themes of the struggle of will with good and evil became foundational to his writing. The Creator gave powers of self-improvement to people to both rule themselves and others; he wrote, "Man is endowed by the Creator with certain powers of mind that if rightly exercised or wrongly, will produce good or evil alone depending wholly upon the intellectual zeal or moral power he possesses."[33]

Henry also became president of the college debating society, which is important because his essential writing style was that of a polished debater. His arguments were always well marshaled, clearly

---

33 *Ibid.*, 7.

aware of the point of view of the audience he was addressing, usually ending on an upbeat, positive note after having refuted the other
person's position. He was neither an original stylist nor especially
imaginative in discourse. Had he chosen a different career, he could
have joined his relatives in a major law firm.

Satterlee graduated from college in 1863, at the height of the
Civil War. He sought an appointment to the U.S. Military Academy
at West Point, and collected letters of recommendation from several
New York members of Congress, but there were no vacancies at the
officer candidate's school. He retained a lifelong admiration for the
military. As bishop, Satterlee instituted a longstanding relationship
with the military, which included friendships with leading officers
and frequent appearances of military musicians, including the Marine
Band at major services. One of his heroes was Admiral George
Dewey, victor of the Battle of Manila Bay.

Alfred Cleveland Coxe and General Theological Seminary, 1863–1865

A number of vocational options were available to the nineteen-year-old
Columbia graduate. He would have been a welcome addition in several major banks, businesses, and law firms, and his father had encouraged a gentleman's tastes in the fine arts and literature. But Satterlee
was always interested in the moral and ethical dimensions of life, and
he was drawn to a career in ministry.

This was no sudden decision, but a gradual unfolding of his life's
interests. His ancestors had been active in both the Dutch Reformed
and Episcopal churches, and Henry was probably baptized in the
Dutch Reformed Church, although he would be rebaptized in the
Episcopal Church on Easter eve 1864 by Arthur Cleveland Coxe,
rector of Calvary Church, and confirmed on Easter Day by Bishop
Horatio Potter at Trinity Church, Wall Street.[34] The influence of his
mother may have been at work here. She regularly attended Sunday
afternoon services at St. Paul's, Albany, and often took young Henry
with her. Such letters of hers as remain "reveal her to be a prayer-
centered person with a simple but intensely real faith."[35]

---

34 *Ibid.*, 6–7.
35 *Ibid.*, 6.

As he weighed denominational options, Satterlee drew on his extensive family contacts. A Columbia professor, Milo Mahan, an uncle of the famous naval strategist Alfred Thayer Mahan, suggested Satterlee contact Alfred Cleveland Coxe at Calvary Church, four blocks from the Satterlee home on affluent Twenty-Third Street. Calvary was an anchor parish and Coxe a major figure in the Episcopal Church of his time. The Roosevelt family lived nearby and attended Calvary, where the Astors and Vanderbilts were also members. Since the 1840s Calvary had attracted moneyed New Yorkers, whose places were secured by renting pews clearly marked with their names and reserved for exclusive family use. There were no free seats. Visitors did not sit in pews for which they had not paid. This prevented Calvary and other Episcopal parishes from attracting a wider, more diverse congregation. Calvary's response to its changing neighborhood was to build a chapel a few blocks away, and even Satterlee, years later when he became rector of Calvary, could not break the hold of the pew rent system.

Coxe was rector at Calvary from 1853 to 1865 and combined the various strains of mid-nineteenth-century Anglicanism that Satterlee reflected as well. Conventional wisdom paints a high church versus low church rivalry in the Episcopal Church at this time, but a considerable number of mix-and-match clerics occupied space somewhere in the middle. Satterlee's beliefs focused on both an attraction to the historic episcopate and the early church, which moved him somewhat toward the high church column, but he was equally a product of his time and class, with its call for moral uplift and social betterment of the less fortunate, a position often associated with the Social Gospel. Like many contemporaries, he saw no need to tidy up loose ends and could live comfortably with what might appear as inconsistencies in churchmanship. That was true of his mentor as well.

Son of a Presbyterian pastor, Coxe called himself an Old Catholic but was a sharp critic of Pius IX whose first Vatican Council (1869–1870) proclaimed the doctrine of papal infallibility. Coxe was opposed to revised translations of the English Bible, but also to newly promulgated Roman Catholic doctrines like the Immaculate Conception and the virgin birth of Mary. Coxe, like many clerics of his time, expressed his religious sentiments in poetry. He had a fascination for the early church and its liturgies, which he popularized in a series of sausage-like poems called *Christian Ballads*.[36] One of Coxe's most popular poems reflected sentiments that Satterlee repeatedly employed in various writings and sermons:

> O where are kings and empires now
> Of old, that went and came?
> But Lord, thy Church is praying yet,
> A thousand years the same.
> We mark her goodly battlements
> And her foundations strong;
> We hear, within, the solemn voice
> Of her unending song.[37]

Suspect About the Social Gospel, Selective About the Oxford Movement

Satterlee was suspect of the newly emerging science of "sociology" and its claims that solutions to the grim conditions of working class families could be resolved by society itself. Instead, he believed that problems of political failure, economic inequities, and loose morals could only find solution through accepting the religious principles of a loving God represented by Jesus. During a trip to England he visited Toynbee Hall, a settlement house in urban London that provided a setting for meetings, exhibitions, concerts, and lectures. He also visited Oxford House, in London's East End, a religiously based institution that, in Satterlee's observation, "puts first things first, it takes men as they are and tries to develop their characters in the state of life in which God has placed them."[38] Hewlett concluded, "His work contributed to the Social Gospel movement, but he would not be part of it."[39]

Satterlee's position on the Social Gospel, a phrase he never used in his own writings, was, "It is one thing to welcome and assimilate

---

36 Peter-Ben Smit, "An Old Catholic Anglican: Bishop Arthur Cleveland Coxe's Positioning as an Old Catholic in Episcopal-Roman Catholic Polemic," *Anglican and Episcopal History*, Vol. 80, No. 2 (June 2011): 174–192.

37 The work was contained in several hymnals, including *Hymns Ancient and Modern, Standard* (Norwich, UK: Canterbury Press, 1922): No. 165.

38 Hewlett, 33.

39 *Ibid.*, 37.

the truths that science has discovered in the natural world; it is another thing to adopt and push the scientific method of research into the spiritual world. The danger of error comes not from the science itself, but from a Christianity which would form a partnership with science."[40]

Marriage to Jane Lawrence Churchill, June 30, 1866

In September 1863 Saterlee moved further down Twenty-Third Street to attend the General Theological Seminary, a domain of high church ritualists under its Anglo-Catholic dean, George Franklin Seymour. Satterlee deftly avoided aligning himself with any church party. He worked periodically at the "colored" Church of the Messiah on the Lower East Side, and graduated from General on June 28, 1866. Two days later he married a wealthy New York merchant's daughter, Jane Lawrence Churchill, his intellectual and social equal. Henry and Jane (Jennie) had met at West Point during the summer of 1863, where the two young people and Henry's mother ran a church school for children.

Like so many comparable women of her time, his future wife consciously kept herself in the background, assuming a role as a church group leader, choir director, and as Satterlee's personal secretary after the couple moved to Washington. She also taught Sunday school and provided a constantly welcoming table at the rectory. Her father, Timothy Gridley Churchill, was descended from old English families and was a prominent New Yorker of the Civil War period. Her mother, Patience Riker Lawrence, came from a family of wealthy landowners in eastern Long Island. "Like most upper-class Victorian matrons, Jennie lived in the shadow of her husband," Hewlett wrote. "We know virtually nothing about her background, education, or interests except what can be gleaned from the dozens of letters that she wrote to her husband, children, and family."[41] The letters were plainspoken, solicitous, and caring, voicing her concern for her family, her constant faith, but little about her other interests.

---

40 *Ibid.*, 37.
41 *Ibid.*, 14.

Wappingers Falls in the Hudson Valley, 1865–1882

Satterlee followed the path of several leading young clerics of the Diocese of New York and began his full-time ministry in a lower Hudson Valley parish, in his case, Wappingers Falls, a rural textile town seventy miles north of New York City. The rector of Zion Church there was old and ill, but had no pension or retirement possibilities, so he held on while the parish sought an energetic young assistant. Ordained to the diaconate on November 21, 1865, during his third and final year of seminary, Satterlee stayed in Wappingers Falls until February 1882 and his return to Calvary Church. His activities there set the pattern he followed later at Calvary and as first bishop of Washington. He plunged into multiple projects, encouraged the proliferation of church groups for women and men, became a civic presence, and supported libraries and social work among mill workers and the poor.

The Satterlees arrived in Wappingers Falls in the summer of 1865, with no housing and a salary of $750 a year. Fortunately, on a country walk the newly arrived cleric encountered Irving Grinnell, who came from a social background similar to his own, and who offered the young couple lodging in a house on his nearby 2,500-acre estate. Grinnell, like Satterlee, was a graduate of Columbia College and the son of a wealthy New York shipbuilding family, and he attended a Unitarian church a block away from Calvary Church. Grinnell was captivated by Satterlee's enthusiasm. He and his wife, Joanna, soon became close friends with the Satterlees. The two couples taught two evenings a week at a parish night school, and Grinnell donated a community library and held the post of senior warden of Zion Church for thirty years.

Zion Church, "A Warm Spiritual Home"

Satterlee paid equal attention to the landed gentry and the working class members of the community. He supervised the Sunday school, and in typical, methodical fashion, wrote a comprehensive manual for teachers that contained both questions and answers for classes. He was a busy parish minister as well, calling regularly on church members and civic leaders. That led to his campaigning for improved sanitary conditions for workers' homes, a workingman's club, debating society, and reading room. The flour mills of Wappingers Falls had been destroyed in a flash flood in 1834 and replaced with a calico mill that employed over a thousand workers, many of them from England. By 1880 Zion Church's membership included over three hundred families. More than a thousand persons participated in its various activities.

Satterlee wanted to make the church "a warm spiritual home." He hoped to dissolve class prejudices through personal contact in parish social gatherings, and by "cooperation in all forms of church work from the election of the Vestry down to the choice of officers in a workingmen's club."[42] His intent was "to give everyone something to do and something for everyone to do." This included both helping each individual find his or her own personal mission in life while "never doing himself what he could get others to do."[43] It was a formula he used in both New York City and Washington.

Meanwhile, the local church gained members, and a new building in the Gothic style was constructed. When the longtime rector, George B. Andrews, who had hired Satterlee in 1865, died in 1875 at age ninety, Satterlee formally took over the expanding church and recruited his own assistant. The Satterlees also raised two children, Churchill (b. 1867), who became an Episcopal clergyman, and Constance (b. 1874). But his seemingly endless activity gradually took its toll on Satterlee's health; in his late thirties the future bishop put on weight, complained of weariness, and looked forward to taking the cure during summers at a European spa. Although he noted an interval of nine years without a proper vacation, month-long stays in Europe or at a family estate near West Point became part of the pattern of his life. Henry once wrote a family friend, J. P. Morgan, "You were crossing the Atlantic in one direction while I was crossing it in the other." The trips allowed him to deepen his appreciation of European art and continue a study of the English Church, its architecture, ethos, and governance. He was a staunch Anglophile.

In 1880 Henry and Jennie boarded a ship for Europe and a fourteen-month vacation, duplicating part of the grand tour the Satterlee family had taken in 1858. While the Satterlees were in

---

42 *Ibid.*, 15–16.
43 Itemized List of Articles Sent to Bishop Brent, NCA (2.12.10): 13–14.

Europe, church members built a new parish hall, but could not raise all the needed funds. Satterlee paid the remainder from his own money several years later.

His successful work in Wappingers Falls brought Satterlee to the attention of other parishes and bishops. Although, he declined offers of posts in New York City, New Haven, and St. Louis, he retained his strong New York City ties and was invited to join the Clerical Club, a gathering of leading New York Episcopal clergy, who read papers and held discussions on religious topics. When his sponsor, Edward A. Washburn, rector of Calvary Church, died in 1881, Satterlee was his expected successor, a call that he accepted in February 1882 and where he stayed for the next thirteen years.

Return to New York City: Rebuilding Calvary Church, 1882–1895

> The day was fresh, with a lively spring wind full of dust. All the old ladies in both families had got out their faded sables and yellowing ermines, and the smell of camphor from the front pews almost smothered the faint spring scent of the lilies banking the altar. Newland Archer, at a signal from the sexton, had come out of the vestry and placed himself with his best man on the chancel step of Grace Church. The signal meant that the brougham bearing the bride and her father was in sight, but there was sure to be a considerable interval of adjustment and consultation in the lobby, where the bridesmaids were hovering like a cluster of Easter blossoms.[44]

The Grace Church portrayed in Edith Wharton's *The Age of Innocence* was the Calvary Church to which Satterlee returned as rector from 1882 to 1895.[45] Wharton was a member of Calvary Church and lived nearby. She chronicled the dress, speech, and manners of the patrician class of this leading lower Manhattan religious institution. Wharton's description of Newland Archer could have

---

44 Edith Wharton, *The Age of Innocence* (New York: Modern Library, 1990): 133.
45 www.calvarystgeorges.org/pages/history

fit many members of Calvary Church, and several members of the Satterlee family or their friends and relatives:

> He had been, in short, what people were beginning to call "a good citizen." In New York, for many years past, every new movement, philanthropic, municipal, or artistic, had taken account of his opinion and wanted his name. People said, "Ask Archer," when there was a question of starting the first school for crippled children, reorganizing the Museum of Art, founding the Grolier Club, inaugurating the new Library, or getting up a new society of chamber music. His days were full and they were filled decently. He supposed it was all a man ought to ask.[46]

Archer was the sort of person Satterlee knew well, and would go to time and again at Calvary Church, and later as bishop of Washington, for leadership and financial support.

The Calvary Church that the thirty-nine-year-old returned to was not the same place he had left. It had lost many of its core members as New York's social and financial elite had moved their homes further uptown. Some vestry members proposed the venerable institution near Gramercy Park, now heavily in debt, be sold for $250,000. Seventy pews remained unrented, depriving the church of a major source of revenue.[47] Although Satterlee opposed the pew rent scheme because it denied outsiders a place to worship, the vestry was unyielding, and the system prevailed of each family renting its own pew, like a box at the opera.

The new rector also undertook a major interior refurbishment of the building designed by James Renwick, Jr., architect of St. Patrick's Cathedral and the Smithsonian Institution. Seeking to rearrange the "big parlor" chancel he inherited, Satterlee brought the organ down from the west balcony, installed a vested choir, moved the altar to the east end, installed a communion rail to clearly separate the congregation from the sanctuary, and instituted frequent communion services on Sundays and saints' days.[48] At Calvary he founded the Olive Tree Inn and the Galilee Chapel, the former as a workingmen's lodging

---

46 Wharton, 258.
47 Hewlett, 23.
48 *Ibid.*, 24.

house that charged fifteen cents a night for a clean room, the latter as a free chapel refurbished from a decrepit storefront. Calvary started a Chinese Sunday school, an industrial school where young women learned to sew, a kitchen garden, and a program to provide home visits and counseling to those seeking employment.[49] The rector was a strong supporter of temperance programs, including a church temperance legion for boys under fourteen. Legionnaires wore uniforms, joined in military drills, and swore to abstain from drinking liquor until they were twenty-one. Female members of Calvary regularly visited prisoners at the Tombs, the homeless on Blackwell's Island, and the sick in three hospitals, where the parish regularly provided fifteen woman visitors.[50]

Soon Calvary's staff grew to five clergy members, with four choirs and over seven hundred students and a hundred teachers in its large Sunday school. "In one sense he had no organization plans at all," Hewlett observed. Satterlee simply tried to match needs with possible responders.[51] A lay member of Calvary said, "I do not know of any church in the City of New York which has a larger, more substantial body of young men workers, between the ages of twenty and forty, and these are ready to stand in the breach and shoulder very real burdens."[52]

Time and again Satterlee sought the people he knew he could count on for financial support, like Frederick W. Rhinelander, who came from a family of highly successful sugar merchants and investors and who married Satterlee's daughter, Constance, in 1910; Rhinelander's younger brother, Philip, who grew up in the parish and later became bishop of Pennsylvania and a cathedral trustee; and Alexander M. Hadden, who served as Satterlee's personal secretary without pay in New York and Washington. Hadden, like a character in a Wharton novel, described himself as "a man not over occupied in business, going about in society, and somewhat of a clubman." Satterlee tasked Hadden, who "rather unwillingly" ran two large parish organizations at Calvary. Another close collaborator was Dr. William C. Rives, III, from an old Virginia family, who had studied medicine at Harvard, Oxford, and in Vienna, and could

---

49 Ibid., 27–30.
50 Ibid., 35.
51 Ibid., 30.
52 Ibid., 31.

always be counted on for a discreet donation. It was Rives who anonymously provided the Washington Peace Cross in 1898.

Attractive offers came to Satterlee while at Calvary: he declined elections to the episcopate in Ohio (1887) and Michigan (1889). Probably other possibilities would have come his way if he had shown an interest, but he concentrated on the busy parish and the expanding mission work generated through its programs. For decades, he was a director of the Episcopal Church's Domestic and Foreign Missionary Society, whose headquarters were within easy walking distance of Calvary Church. He also paid for a missionary to Mexico from his own funds.

Changes at Calvary

The thirteen years Satterlee spent at Calvary Church resembled the seventeen years he had spent at Zion Church. If the 1880 record of Zion Church showed twenty-eight groups started or sustained in Wappingers Falls, the 1895 yearbook for Calvary Church recorded sixty-one groups and over two hundred pages worth of activities. Worship was central to the rector's life, and he maintained a steady round of services, but he was also active in Sunday school promotion and the betterment of living conditions for slum dwellers, including colored people. Convinced that overheating was a major contributor to the spread of disease, one of his pleas was to place a thermometer in each home in the slums.

Satterlee's "New Testament" Churchmanship

A wide circle of church, family, social acquaintances, and supporters awaited Satterlee's return to New York City. His old sponsor, Bishop Horatio Potter, had retired and the bishop's nephew, Henry Codman Potter, was his successor. The younger Potter and Satterlee had grown up together in intersecting social circles. When Potter moved to Church House, he was replaced at Grace Church, a major parish in lower Broadway, by William Reed Huntington, a leading voice in the Episcopal Church of his time.

Like Satterlee, he was a member of the Clerical Club. Huntington was an often cited influence in Satterlee's writings, particularly for the important Chicago-Lambeth Quadrilateral of 1886 and 1888 that he authored. It provided a defining statement about Anglican beliefs, that the Holy Scriptures contained "all things necessary to salvation," and the Apostles' and Nicene creeds represented sufficient statements of the Christian faith. Its final two provisions were that the two main sacraments instituted by Christ were baptism and the Supper of the Lord, and that structurally the church was based on the historic episcopate locally adapted to the varying needs of the nations and peoples.[53] Huntington was also a leader in the movement to update the church's Book of Common Prayer, including the once controversial step of adding prayers for industrial workers. Figures like Huntington and Coxe influenced Satterlee's intellectual and spiritual development. Educated Americans, with a knowledge of the Church of England, yet holders of distinctive viewpoints, they drew on a range of English sources. Satterlee likewise steered his own course, calling his distinctly articulated beliefs "New Testament Christianity." In his valedictory statement to the people of Calvary Church, he summed up his views:

> Now, I believe the Anglican Church comes nearest to this ideal of any Church in Christendom. I believe not only that one hundred years from this time the Anglican Church will be larger and more important than the Church of Rome, but that the more one understands the "genius" of the Anglican Church, the better he will understand the New Testament itself.[54]

The Rector as Author, Carving Out a Distinct Position on Theological Issues

Satterlee was more a parish minister and organizer than a theologian. Still, he wrote several substantive books while maintaining an active parish and civic presence. These works represent clear statements of Christian belief with titles like *Christ and His Church* (1878), *Life Lessons of the Prayer Book* (1890), and *The Calling of the Christian* (1902). Mostly they were manuals for Sunday school teachers or for

---

53 *Prayer Book and Hymnal, Containing The Book of Common Prayer and The Hymnal 1982, According to the use of The Episcopal Church* (New York: Church Publishing Incorporated, 1986): 876–878.

54 Hewlett, 40.

those joining the church. His prose style was plain, unencumbered by illustrative examples or overly original commentary. He would recycle much of this material in sermons and addresses when he became bishop of Washington.

Theodore Roosevelt, whom he had known in New York and Washington, caught the essence of Saterlee in action when he wrote Satterlee's daughter Constance years later: "I had long known your father; I was brought into intimate contact with him first when I was Police Commissioner. . . . I soon discovered that he was one of the clergymen who was a genuine force for civic righteousness and that his deeds made good his words. He was a practical idealist."[55]

A Creedless Gospel and the Gospel Creed

A summation of Satterlee's central beliefs is contained in a book he completed at Calvary, *A Creedless Gospel and the Gospel Creed*.[56] He systematically rejected the advances of science, art, literature, economics, law, politics, and the insights of other religions if they claimed to have any lasting worth independent of Christianity. Other religions fell short of providing a true reflection of God's revelation in history. "The radical distinction between all these man-made religions, on the one side, and Christianity on the other, is that the first are human philosophy, or a meditation upon God, while the second is a divine life, wherein Jesus Christ gives to those who believe on His name power to become sons of God."[57]

Satterlee's presentation of contemporary scientific, philosophical, and social thought was incomplete, and his comments on other religions were roundly dismissive of their falseness. When he surveyed the sweep of Western history from the early church to modern times, he did so with bold but erratic leaps. He concluded:

> Christ's disciples have not, as yet, felt called upon to draw together and present a united front in the way of this so-called progress of civilization, or to oppose as wrong what civilization encourages as right; but if that day ever comes,

---

55 *Ibid.*, 34
56 Henry Y. Satterlee, *A Creedless Gospel and The Gospel Creed* (New York: Charles Scribner's Sons, 1895).
57 *Ibid.*, 7.

it will witness as autocratic and relentless, though of course not as cruel and bloody, a proscription of Christ's followers as that decreed by the imperious Roman Empire in the days of yore.[58]

Incarnation, Ministry, and the Anglican Future

Three concepts were distinctive in Satterlee's religious writings: his understanding of the Incarnation, "the invisible Vicar of Christ," and the "representational" as distinct from "mediatorial" priesthood—essentially placing the priest among the people rather than above or away from them. Collectively, he presented a distinctive, carefully thought-through understanding of Christian ministry, one that Roman Catholics and some Anglicans would find objectionable, and one many Protestants would find novel as well.

In the Incarnation, Satterlee saw a close unity between the Divine and human life, where "we behold the ethical and divine lineaments of our manhood perfected" in Jesus who "was on the natural, as well as the spiritual side, the Ideal Man."[59] But then Satterlee left the human aspect of Jesus unexplored: "It was a human nature without a human selfhood, without the separations that human individuality necessitates."[60] In such a view, Jesus was "not a man," but the Son of Man, Universal Man, or Elder Brother of the whole human race. The Incarnation for Satterlee remained an important, but incompletely developed concept.

The image of the Vicar of Christ on earth received an entire chapter in *New Testament Churchmanship,* but the vicar was *not* a human being, not a pope, a prelate, or a representative of the institutional church. The actual presence of Christ was replaced by the ongoing reality of the spirit: "The world cannot receive Him because He is unseen, and because He is beyond the world's power of perception."[61]

Next came priesthood, not the "false" *mediatorial* priesthood of the Roman Catholic or high church Anglican tradition, but a

---

58 *Ibid.,* 192.
59 Henry Y. Satterlee, *New Testament Churchmanship, and the Principles Upon Which it was Founded* (New York: Longmans, Green and Co., 1899): 37.
60 *Ibid.,* 42–43.
61 *Ibid.,* 139.

representative priesthood. Satterlee made a clear distinction between the two possibilities and clearly rejected the former: "If the priesthood were vicarious the priest would be a personal mediator between Christ and the people and offer up a kind of sacrifice which the people cannot offer; in the representative priesthood he is simply the minister of Christ's priesthood to the people, and the minister of the people's priesthood to God."[62]

What emerged for Satterlee was a particular set of working theological concepts: an idea of the Incarnation, another of the Vicar of Christ, and a clearly Protestant understanding of the representational priesthood. If his ideas were incomplete for the professional theologian, few parish priests or bishops of his time wrote so comprehensively at the practical level. A lawyer teaching a Sunday school class at Calvary could read an hour's worth of Satterlee on Saturday night and feel confident in dealing with the subject matter the next day.

The church he envisioned was the embodiment of New Testament ideals, as represented in the "primitive church" (a key concept for Satterlee) before it came under centralized Roman Catholic control. Both centrifugal and centripetal tendencies opposed one another, as socialism and individualism contested one another in society, or individual religiosity confronted the church as a collective body. To this list of tensions, he added those generated by the historical collision of the Protestant Reformation with the expanding Roman Catholic Church. His conclusion was "in the Anglican Communion itself, we behold perhaps the closest approximation to the description of the Church, by St. Paul, that we have witnessed since the Apostolic Age."[63]

There he stopped. He made no effort to engage with other Protestant groups. Relations with Roman Catholics were distant and the content of other world religions remained within the banished realm of paganism. The Anglican way was the preferred way: it represented the "sense of justice . . . inbred in the Anglo-Saxon mind" that grounded Christian believers. If they could avoid "any semblance of injustice . . . any lack of charity, honesty, or courage" somehow a day of reunion would be forthcoming.[64] The implication was that

---

62 *Ibid.*, 211.
63 *Churchman's League Lectures, The Fundamental Principles of Christian Unity* (Washington: The Church Militant, 1902): 11.
64 *Ibid.*, 13.

others would look seriously at the New Testament and Western history and accept an Anglican approach, but Satterlee, reflecting the era in which he lived and wrote, never became more specific.

Saterlee, now in his early fifties, was fully formed in his vocational and spiritual interests, and ready to move on, although he was perfectly content with his setting. He had turned down two elections as bishop, and others would have come his way, if he had shown an interest. The person who would become the first elected bishop of Washington was an immensely active person, the busy and successful leader of a major New York parish. Born into and well connected with the world of civic and business leaders, he knew the key players of the national and New York Episcopal Church, and was the friend or colleague of most of them. His brand of churchmanship was in the moderate middle, his theological views safely within the orthodox camp. He could safely be trusted to head a diocese.

One of the glaring needs in Washington was for a cathedral, a challenge for which Satterlee was well prepared. A staunch Anglophile, he knew the history and forms of governance of the Church of England and unabashedly favored English Gothic architecture. His contacts with Roman Catholicism were limited and would stay that way. Other Protestant bodies were welcome, the implication being that somehow, someday they would be part of a larger church modeled on Anglicanism. Equally important for Satterlee and his vision of a future cathedral is that it would be American, a place to honor the nation's history and heroic moments.

As people came from all over the expanding country, the growing capital needed a national church to stand along with its other institutions. The 1890s would represent a fortuitous moment: Washington was by now a city ripe for the leadership Satterlee would provide in finding land and funding for a cathedral. Satterlee was also ready for Washington and especially to give shape and definition to a new diocese and a hoped-for cathedral.

CHAPTER TWO

A New Diocese, Bishop, and Cathedral (1895–1908)

In 1895 the Episcopal Diocese of Washington was formed. It included the growing national capital of Washington, DC and four additional counties originally part of the Diocese of Maryland, which had been incorporated in 1781. The national capital was expanding in size and importance, the proposal for a national cathedral had been raised earlier, and the movement for a new diocese finally coalesced. On May 29, 1895 the convention of the Diocese of Maryland, with the support of its bishop, voted for the independent diocese, and on October 8, the Episcopal Church's General Convention, meeting in Minneapolis, confirmed the move. The Diocese of Washington became a reality.

A diocesan convention gathered in Washington on December 4, 1895 to elect Washington's first bishop. Several prominent East Coast clergy were candidates. Satterlee was not among them. But after five ballots no candidate received the required two-thirds clerical vote and the convention was deadlocked. On its second day it cast a wider net. The prominent rector of St. John's, Lafayette Square, Alexander Mackay-Smith, nominated Satterlee as a candidate he hoped would be acceptable to all factions. Mackay-Smith (1850–1911), an unsuccessful candidate himself, had known the nominee when Satterlee was at Calvary Church and Mackay-Smith had been an assistant at St. Thomas' Church and archdeacon of New York.

As other names fell off the list, the number of votes for Satterlee rose and he was elected on the eleventh ballot with forty-five votes, two more than required. Reached at home in New York by a reporter that Saturday evening, the bishop-elect expressed surprise at news of the election and voiced his initial reluctance to accept the new position. This came not from coyness or false modesty, his full commitment until now was to his work in New York. As he did with any major decision, Satterlee made a list of reasons pro and con, nine reasons for staying at Calvary and eighteen against. He found thirty-seven reasons in favor of accepting the Washington election, eight against it. Meanwhile, letters flowed in from the clergy in Washington, urging him to accept.

A huge congregation spilled out onto Fourth Avenue at the new bishop's consecration at Calvary Church on March 25, 1896. The procession consisted of nearly five hundred people and included Satterlee's former mentor from Calvary Church, Bishop Arthur Cleveland Coxe, representing the presiding bishop, who was old and ill. Ten other bishops were present, including co-consecrators Henry C. Potter of New York and William Paret of Maryland. Fellow Clerical Club member and now bishop Frederick D. Huntington of Central New York preached on "The Power of the Church in National Life." The Washington clergy came up *en masse*, and there were delegations from General Theological Seminary, the Board of Missions, and Colored Missions. His son, Churchill, ordained three years earlier, was Satterlee's chaplain.[1]

Methodically, the bishop-elect presented his vision of a new ministry. He spoke about Washington's expanding "colored" population, the city's growing parishes, and the less active ones in southern Maryland. The rich and poor of North and South would be welcome in the diocese. Satterlee would continue his national and international interests, including working on the troubled Mexican mission, and advancing the

---

1 Hewlett, 72.

cause of church unity. He would also work actively for building a national cathedral and in the words of the King James Bible, a "house of prayer for all people" (Isaiah 56:7). He wrote to the people of Washington:

> The first words which, as your Bishop, I write unto you
> are words of deep gratitude for the unity of spirit which
> so manifestly pervades the diocese. . . . May this unity of
> the spirit in the bond of peace become the ruling influ-
> ence in the Diocese of Washington. Through all coming
> days and years let us guard and treasure it, and then hand
> it on to our successors as a pearl of great price; for upon us
> is resting the God-given responsibility of forming now, in
> the beginning of our history, the tradition of the future.[2]

Bishop Satterlee Comes to Washington

Meanwhile, there was the business of moving to Washington. The Satterlees found a comfortable residence on Thomas Circle and a nearby diocesan office on Rhode Island Avenue, later moved to 1407 Massachusetts Avenue. St. Mark's on Capitol Hill became the diocesan pro-cathedral. Later it was moved to the Church of the Ascension, at Twelfth Street and Massachusetts Avenue, two blocks from the bishop's residence. The bishop's annual salary was set at $5,000, plus housing. He hired as his secretary Lucy Vaughan Mackrille, who was also a skilled seamstress, founder of the cathe-dral Altar Guild, and later author of an illustrated book on church embroidery and vestments.[3]

After almost thirty years of intensely active ministry, Satterlee prepared for the challenges that would consume his remaining twelve years of life—a new diocese in the burgeoning national capital of the 1890s. It was a quickly growing city, whose character was in for-mation, a Southern city with a growing population of Northerners. Satterlee recognized that Washington had a large floating population, mostly of people coming to work for the government or the mili-tary or as tourists, students, or temporary residents. Unlike London or Paris, "It was not a city to which the government came, but one

---

2 *Ibid.*, 44–45.
3 Lucy Vaughan Mackrille, *Church Embroidery and Church Vestments* (Chevy Chase, MD: Cathedral Studios, c. 1939).

which the Government itself created." Its "homespun provincialism" was fast giving way to a new cosmopolitanism, bringing affluence to the city, but without the new residents displaying any matching civic, moral, or religious fervor, he believed.[4]

It was also a city whose population was at least one-third African American and had a large number of low-income residents. Satterlee eagerly began his work there, time and again calling on the New York social and financial elite he knew well for support. William C. Rives moved to Washington and stayed close to Satterlee. Philip M. Rhinelander, a clergy protégé of Satterlee's at Calvary Church, came to St. Alban's Church on the cathedral grounds.[5] The bishop also engaged Washington leaders, like Charles C. Glover, philanthropist and bank president, and Admiral George Dewey. There were also numerous "holy women," as Satterlee called them, generally wives of leading men, widows, or inheritors of family money.

Time and again they came through with the funds he needed to advance a project. Their biographies remain unrecorded and their views on most matters are unknown. Some of the names include Mary Elizabeth Mann, who originally offered downtown Washington land for a cathedral; Phoebe A. Hearst of California, who made a large gift to the cathedral and $200,000 for a girls' school; Mrs. Percy R. Pyne, wife of a financier/philanthropist at Calvary Church, and an early cathedral benefactor; and Maria Massey, a major donor. Others included Mabel Thorp Broadman, founder of the American Red Cross, whose remains were interred in the cathedral; Beatrix Farrand of the Rhinelander family and a noted landscape designer, who laid out initial plans for the cathedral gardens; Mary Frick Garret, wife of the president of the Baltimore & Ohio Railroad, who chaired the cathedral's Baltimore Committee; Huybertine Lansing Hall, a prominent Boston attorney's wife and member of the cathedral's Boston committee; Harriet Lane Johnson, niece and official hostess for President James Buchanan, widow of a Baltimore banker and railroad builder, who gave the original $300,000 for the boys' school that became St. Albans; Hope B. Russell, a Providence, Rhode Island member of the cathedral committee; Emily Borie Ryerson, a leader of the cathedral committee in Chicago; and Bessie Kibbey,

---

4 *Journal of the Diocese of Washington, 1904–1905,* 38–39.
5 Hewlett, 63.

who donated the cathedral carillon. Margaret F. Buckingham, Isabel Freemen, and Mary M. Barringer were all major donors. Cassie M. Julian-James donated the last $50,000 to pay off the debt on the cathedral property in October 1905.[6] The list is long—what is most memorable about it is how willingly and generously women gave to build the cathedral and its schools, and volunteered as altar and flower guild members and docents.

One of Satterlee's most elaborate statements of his financial and emotional plight was contained in a letter to Matilda W. Bruce, an early donor. The bishop wanted to build "a Protestant school for girls that will hold its own against those Romanist convent schools to which the daughters of senators, congressmen, and prominent officials are being sent." He needed an additional $20,000 to hire a principal for the girls' school, but the money was not forthcoming.

> The wealthy winter residents with one exception, have refused to give a single cent for any object that I have ever appealed for, and dear Miss Bruce I am in despair— I came here to do God's work, and it is nothing but begging for money morning, noon, and night—I am losing all my spirituality and serving tables. You can't imagine the cross it is for me to come to you again—I went to others first for the past two days I have done nothing but pay calls to raise funds. I can expect no help from the Cathedral board for they say that we have all we can do to pay the $104,000 mortgage without this additional burden of a $20,000 guarantee fund for the girls' school . . . I have opened my heart to you.[7]

Satterlee was fifty-three when elected, six feet two inches tall, and of impressive military bearing. "There was about him an air of determination, serious intent, and moral rectitude that made him the epitome of a Victorian cleric," Hewlett observed.[8] He was also self-contained, guarded, and stubborn. His lengthy *Private Record* provides few clues about his frank attitudes toward issues and other people.

---

6 *Ibid.*, 53, 55–56, 70, 183–191.
7 Henry Yates Satterlee to Matilda Bruce, ND, NCA (1.8.1).
8 Hewlett, 61.

When they appear, it is in the same carefully guarded language he used in official documents. His letters to family and colleagues were similar in their cordial but cautious tone. Satterlee made no claims to being a colorful preacher, nor would he stand out as the obvious leader of a peer group. He was less a visionary and more a capable implementer. Satterlee was also strong-willed, often arbitrary in his decisions, and, at heart, a list maker who carefully weighed the pros and cons of each question he faced. Once he made the decision, he stuck to it. Self-doubt and hesitancy were not part of his makeup, neither was closeness with those with whom he worked. Photographs of him in various ministerial poses show a formal person, somewhat distant from others, looking beyond or away from them, elbows or arms out a few inches to guard the space around him. He was polite with all, intimate with few. The gift of easy approachability was not his, and he cultivated a certain distancing from others.

He felt passionately about slum dwellers and minorities in general, but he claimed few persons beyond his own circle as more than passing acquaintances. "He was a master at achieving his goals without alienating those who disagreed with him," Hewlett wrote, "He was willing to take risks for a good cause, and he knew how to raise money and recruit talented men and women to help him."[9]

Virtually all doors were open to him, from the White House and halls of Congress, to those of the city's leadership. The easy nature of his relationship with President Theodore Roosevelt is reflected in this 1907 letter about the appointment of Episcopal clergy as Army and Navy chaplains, a responsibility that fell to Satterlee as bishop of Washington. "Secretary Taft tells me that although the Episcopalians have considerable more than their quota, yet you give such admirable men that he will appoint one other chaplain for you. Will you communicate directly with him? I am extremely glad to be able to write you this."[10] On February 17, 1906, Satterlee performed the wedding of Roosevelt's daughter, Alice, in the East Room of the White House. It was Washington society's glittering event of the year, although one guest commented that Satterlee "had the voice of an auctioneer."

After coming to Washington, he joined the Cosmos Club, a group of leading men in the sciences, arts, and civic leadership.

9 *Ibid.,* 63.
10 Theodore Roosevelt to Henry Yates Satterlee, May 26, 1907, NCA (2.12.18).

Although Satterlee was a strong advocate of the temperance movement, like men of his class, he enjoyed a good cigar. He sent his son
a supply of "Plantations" and kept a choice box of Henry Clay's to
share with special guests.[11] Almost Puritanical in personal bearing,
he had little interest in New York or Washington society, unless it
was to relieve members of their money or engage their support for
one of his projects.

Satterlee was intensely hard working as bishop, and although
later accounts focus on him as a cathedral builder, he actually put
more energy into the daily round of building a new diocese. In 1902
and 1903 he celebrated 97 communions, participated in 503 other
services, confirmed 1095 persons, preached 130 sermons, gave 289
addresses, and sat through 227 meetings. The summary list of his
official acts covered twenty pages of the diocesan annual report, with
entries like: "May 2. Went to the Cathedral School and gave the
usual weekly lecture. May 3. Conference with Mr. Pellew regarding
King Hall. Took midnight train to New York. Returned at night.
Called on President Roosevelt regarding Navy chaplains. Made two
sick calls. Spent rest of the day at the Retreat for Clergy." He also
looked forward to summer vacation time, although he stayed in frequent communication by mail with the diocese from a family vacation site in rural New York state.[12]

The "Silent Congregations" of Southern Maryland

An enduring problem the new bishop faced was bridging the differences between growing city and struggling small country parishes,
especially those in the four counties that had been hived off from
the Diocese of Maryland to create the Diocese of Washington. In his
take-charge manner, Satterlee assumed direct responsibility for the
small Maryland mission congregations, many of them lacking funds,
numbers, and leadership. It was to be a consuming problem without
a solution, for him and for his successors a century later.

In a pastoral letter dated 1904 entitled "The Distress in Southern
Maryland," the bishop spoke of "the silent churches of Southern
Maryland" and asked all diocesan churches to withhold sending any

---

11 Hamilton Schuyler, *A Fisher of Men; Churchill Satterlee, Priest and Missionary—An
   Interpretation of His Life and Labors* (New York: E.S. Gorham, 1905): 55.
12 *Journal of the Diocese of Washington, 1902–1903*, 65.

contributions to the national church or special missions outside the diocese until the full sum designated for diocesan missions had been paid. The problem was longstanding. Fifteen years earlier Bishop Paret had launched an appeal to reopen several parishes that had been closed for many years, noting that in recent years "seven of these old historic parishes, dating back to the days of William and Mary, Queen Anne and the Georges," had become silent churches without rectors. The heart of the matter was their inability to come up with a thousand dollars a year for a rector's salary and attract capable clergy. "We can secure exactly the kind of clergymen we need for a salary of $1,000 a year, but not for $650 or $700 a year." Satterlee asked, "Do you think that you could support a family, keep a horse and wagon, send your children to school, maintain your position with fitting dignity as a prominent member of the community, all for six hundred and fifty dollars a year?" To reinforce the point he added, "How much do we pay our coachman, our gardener? What wages do we give in our kitchen and household?"[13] Clergy salaries in southern Maryland did not compare favorably with those of stone-cutters, carpenters, and masons.

Satterlee as Sabbatarian

Satterlee was always clear about the moral stands he took on issues. He was a strict Sabbatarian and frequently laid down rules for conduct in the church schools. For example, in response to a query as to whether or not girls from National Cathedral School should be allowed to attend the opera during Lent, he wrote:

> The opera managers make a special point of coming at a sacred season when there are no festivities, in order that they may increase their own receipts. . . . I cannot believe any blessing will come upon any of us, who support such sordidness. The musical advantages the girls will gain will be at the cost of a great spiritual disadvantage in the sight of God. I comprehend perfectly that there are parents and scholars, to whom all this is mere words, and therefore

---

13 "The Distress in Southern Maryland, A Pastoral Letter from the Bishop of Washington," December 9, 1904, NCA (2.12.3).

I am willing that every girl should decide that the case of conscience should be put distinctly and clearly before each one, so that she may realize her own personal responsibility in making the decision.[14]

On Divorce, Marriages with Catholics

He had little sympathy for divorce and wrote a woman seeking his advice, "The growing prevalence of divorce is blasting family life in America. . . . The marriage bond must be kept as a sacred vow, first, because the integrity of family life depends upon it, second, because the family, not the individual is the unit of civilization, and third, because the loose ideas of the marriage bond brings inevitable future degradation upon womanhood, for in the end, womankind always suffers most intensely from a cause like this." He elaborated, "One's sympathies go out to those who after having made an unhappy marriage are thus precluded from marrying again, while the other party lives, but this is only one instance out of a hundred of the different ways in which individuals have to be martyrs for the sake of society, but the blessing of God always comes in largest measure upon the innocent, who thus voluntarily suffer."[15]

The difficulties of an Episcopalian marrying a Roman Catholic were also real. Satterlee wrote a young woman he knew, "I am sorry my dear child to hear that you are to marry a Roman Catholic, and not one of our church, because although you and your father have always belonged to the Catholic church, the Roman Catholics deny the fact, and indeed to speak frankly, treat us as though we were heathen."[16]

He also took sharp public issue with the Roman Catholic Church. In a pastoral letter about marriage issued in 1902 he disputed the "Romanist" position that no marriage could be considered an authentic Christian marriage unless it was solemnized in the Roman Catholic Church. Satterlee quoted from its *Manual of Prayers for the Catholic Laity,* which explicitly forbid any church celebration

---

14 Henry Yates Satterlee to Lois A. Bangs, February 25, 1904, NCA (2.12.10).
15 Henry Yates Satterlee to Charlotte Watson, New York City, March 16, 1905, NCA. (2.8.4).
16 Henry Yates Satterlee to Katharine Crane, California, Maryland, ND. NCA (2.8.4).

of "mixed marriages." Such marriage ceremonies could not be held in a church, nor could the witnessing priest wear vestments, say any prayers, or give a blessing. Satterlee told the Washington Diocese this "treats our own devout churchmen or churchwomen as though they were infidels or heathen people who have no bond or union with Christ and His Church and no right to expect any blessing from God Himself upon their marriage."[17]

An article in a church magazine also observed that "Bishop Satterlee had taken vigorous ground against the dissipations and frivolities of what is known as high society, and had preached in advocacy of higher ideals among the 'smart set.' He had bitterly denounced the divorce evil and had expressed the belief that the modern apartment building is a large factor in the lack of harmony in modern homes."[18]

Overseas Interests: "God Is Behind America"

Throughout his episcopate, the bishop continued to speak out in sermons and pastoral letters on moral issues, especially those affecting families, such as those detailed above. He was no less interested in international questions, and spent several years as a member of the Episcopal Church's missionary board, where he spoke out on behalf of persecuted Armenians. He was, at the same time, highly suspect of any efforts at interfaith dialogue, and positively linked American expansionism of the Spanish-American War era to his country's civilizing mission. On international issues, he basically echoed the Manifest Destiny political rhetoric of his time in religious language.

During the nineteenth century many believed that it was America's destiny to expand across the North American continent and beyond; and conflicts with countries like Cuba and the Philippines would understandably be settled through armed conflict and conquest. From that point of view, America was not one nation among many, but the world's leader, the biblical "city on a hill" expected by God to expand Christian civilization globally.

At the Episcopal Church's General Convention in Minneapolis in October 1895, Satterlee was principal drafter of a resolution

---

17 "To the Clergy and Laity of the Diocese of Washington," Pastoral Letter, October 1, 1902 (VTS. PAM 1902.1).
18 "Death of Bishop Satterlee," *The Living Church* (February 29, 1908).

condemning Turkish persecution of Armenian Christians. It noted the Turkish army's "wholesale slaughter of men and the violation of women" and called for sending funds to a relief committee in Constantinople. In July 1896, a few months after his consecration as bishop, he went to St. Petersburg on behalf of the American and British churches to meet with Tsar Nicholas II of Russia. Satterlee was kept waiting three weeks for an audience with the tsar and tsarina, and delivered an unanswered petition that asked the Russian leader to exert his influence "to secure, in combination with other Christian powers, safety of property, life, and honor to those [Armenians] who still survive."[19] There is no indication the Russians ever acted on the petition.

The Parliament of World Religions, Satterlee's Dissenting Voice

Although he dealt with a constant flow of international mission questions as part of the Episcopal Church's missionary body, Satterlee was sometimes faced with questions of interfaith relations as well. One such issue was how to respond to the World Parliament of Religions, part of the Columbian Exhibition in Chicago in September 1893, which met two years before the Diocese of Washington was formed. The World's Fair also included representatives of Eastern and Western religions. The archbishop of Canterbury and several leading theologians and civic and cultural figures endorsed the event, but not Satterlee. "The inevitable impression will be conveyed, not only to Brahmans and Buddhists, but to the outside world, that Christianity is only a man made religion like all the rest, and that it has as much to learn from them as to impart to them," Satterlee wrote of the Congresses' deliberations . . . "Already there are thousands who see no other difference between the Light of the World and 'The Light of Asia' than a difference in the degree of inspiration."[20]

There was no place for dialogue and toleration in such a viewpoint. All contact among members of various religions, Satterlee believed, must be viewed from the cross of Calvary, and from the

---

19 Hewlett, 41–42.
20 Henry Y. Satterlee, "The Parliament of Religions, An Inquiry," *The Churchman* (May 20, 1893): 681–682.

unique claims of Jesus to be the Light of the World. This results in an absolute judgment of other religions. "The world is to be led, not by the spirit of the age, but by the Spirit of Truth . . . not by bringing to remembrance what Buddha, or Confucius or Mahomet has said, but by what Christ has said."[21]

The Progress of Civilizations: "Never Take Sides Against the United States"

Satterlee's views of other religions were congruent with his position about the leading place of America among world civilizations, a theme he elaborated on in a 1900 talk at Princeton University.[22] Here he enthusiastically endorsed the progress of civilizations idea widely accepted in nationalistic political and religious thought of the time. His premise was that Greece and Rome had fallen, and stagnant European monarchies had given way to American constitutionalism with its twin emphases on individual liberty and national responsibility. Still, the American experience was not flawless. While national politics were comparatively pure and uncorrupt, he believed, unscrupulous local politicians at times corrupted the activities of government.

America in the late nineteenth century was now the major world civilization, called to a higher moral responsibility among the nations, he argued. Satterlee spoke in the aftermath of the Spanish-American War of 1898, which he read as a God-given vindication of the United States, a country driven by a law of brotherhood that united all nations of the world.[23]

During his long membership on the Board of Foreign and Domestic Missions of the Protestant Episcopal Church, Satterlee's main interest was in supporting a missionary presence in America's overseas possessions and in Mexico. His May 5, 1898 diocesan address came in the midst of the Spanish-American War, and with a flourish he predicted the conflict's outcome would "elevate the position of America among the nations . . . marking an epoch in

---

21 *Ibid.*
22 Henry Yates Satterlee, "The Ethics of American Civilization," *The Princeton Alumni Weekly*, 1, No. 15 (1900): 4–12.
23 *Ibid.*, 11.

civilization itself." What Europe refused to do in Armenia, he concluded, America would do for the people of Cuba.[24]

America had seized Spain's former possessions, Puerto Rico,
Guam, and the Philippines, but Satterlee detected no trace of imperialism in such conquests. "I see no spirit of imperialism in all
American history," he confidently wrote, and the acquisition of
"certain islands" has made them de facto American territory. There
was no turning back; America was challenged "to keep pace with
the growing civilization of the world" and avoid the danger of dis-
engagement and arrested development. The choices for American
civilization were either growth or decay, in his view. He ended by
repeating the advice of a leading statesman of an earlier generation
to "never take sides against the United States . . . because—God is
behind America."[25]

Satterlee on Race: "Concentrate the Whole Energy of the Church Upon the Evangelization of the Negro Race"

> There is no longer Jew or Greek, there is no longer slave
> or free, there is no longer male and female; for all of you
> are one in Christ Jesus. (Galatians 3:28)

In addition to launching the new diocese and building Washington
National Cathedral, another major Satterlee focus in Washington was
on "the race problem." But if his efforts to build a cathedral produced land, a supportive community, and a set of building plans,
he fared less well on issues of race. And, although the cathedral was
to be "a House of Prayer for All People," there was no mention of
including black clergy or laity in its numbers. "Next to the Cathedral
of Washington, the welfare of King Hall has been the greatest burden
that I have had to bear, and its welfare the greatest cause for concern
and anxiety," the bishop wrote.[26] King Hall, a struggling seminary

---

24 *Journal of the Diocese of Washington, 1897–1898*, 26.
25 "The Ethics of American Civilization," 12.
26 Henry Yates Satterlee, "The time has now come when I as Bishop of
   Washington and President of the Board of Trustees of King Hall . . . " nd,
   (probably February 1905), 5–6, NCA (2.8.6).

built on the Howard University grounds, never attracted support from southern bishops, who believed its students were unlikely to eventually leave Washington and return to isolated rural parishes. It closed in 1906, lacking both students and funds.

The 1907 Diocesan Convention Address

Satterlee's most extensive public treatment of racial issues came in his May 15, 1907 diocesan address. Negroes should have opportunity for education, self-help, and development comparable to those available to whites, he stated. The question was a national, not a local one. Out of a population of ninety million Americans, ten million were part of the "weaker race" whose numbers would increase to fifty million by century's end. Out of a Washington population of three hundred thousand, some one hundred thousand were African American. He cautioned:

> No stream can rise higher than its fountainhead; and the history of the Negro race in the past forty years is a great historic lesson. Though for more than a generation the Negroes have been made the political equals of the whites by universal suffrage, the result has only brought out more plainly than ever before, the fact that they are morally and intellectually a weaker race, and that, even if they should become great land owners, men of wealth and men of education, race antagonism would only become stronger and more sharply defined.[27]

He cautioned against political activism by Christians, repeatedly urging that worship and voting were separate categories that should not be mixed. His skewed reading of church history was that "the Primitive Church refused to become entangled with any political questions whatever" and church members must "work for the establishment on this earth of the Kingdom of Heaven, and ignore all political questions whatsoever."[28] Specifically on "the Negro problem,"

---

27 "Address by the Rt. Rev. Henry Y. Satterlee. D.D., LL.D., Bishop of Washington," St. Alban's Episcopal Church, Washington, DC, May 15 and 16, 1907. *Journal Diocese of Washington,* Twelfth Annual Convention, 38.

28 *Ibid.,* 35.

Satterlee believed that "those burning differences of opinion which divide Northern Churchmen and Southern Churchmen enable both to unite with one heart and mind . . . and thus concentrate the whole energy of the Church upon the evangelization of the Negro race."[29]

Satterlee should be looked at through the prism of his times, not that of a later century. His views on race, like those on other issues, were not much different from other church leaders of his era, and among peers he would be in the more forward-looking camp. He did not resist change, nor was he an agent of change. He was a hard-working, centrist figure, trying to weigh the merit of both Northern and Southern positions, while maintaining an appeal for the greater unity of the church.

Later Years and the Loss of His Son

Despite his joy at securing and paying for land for the cathedral and working on plans for the building, the later years of Satterlee's episcopate weighed heavily on the bishop. The loss of his son Churchill to a heart attack at thirty-six in 1904 deeply affected Satterlee.

Churchill, like his father, had attended both Columbia College and General Theological Seminary, and he held a small parish in Morgantown, North Carolina, from 1895 to 1901, and a somewhat larger one in Columbia, South Carolina, from 1901 to 1904. Afflicted by intermittent bouts of ill health, Churchill wrote constantly to his parents. He served as his father's chaplain at the bishop's consecration and in conveying President William McKinley by carriage from the White House to Saint Alban's Hill for the dedication of the Peace Cross in 1898. Satterlee loomed large in his son's life. When Churchill was considering the call to Morgantown, unbeknownst to him, his father took a train to the mountainous town, and interviewed the vestry members and outgoing rector before advising his son to accept the offer.[30]

Death and Burial

Satterlee died at home at 7:30 am on Saturday, February 22, 1908. A severe cold he had contracted a week earlier in New York had

---

29 *Ibid.*, 36.
30 Schuyler, *Fisher of Men*, 3–4.

turned into pneumonia, but he continued with parish visits and con-
firmations until bedridden. He asked for Holy Communion to be
celebrated, and after he was told his end was near, he tried to join
in singing the Gloria in Excelsis, and continued to murmur "Holy,
Holy, Holy" from the Sanctus as he died.

The reading of the burial office was held at the Pro-Cathedral
of the Ascension on the afternoon of February 25, with President
Theodore Roosevelt among the mourners. A solemn procession
wound its way up Massachusetts Avenue to Mount Saint Alban,
where a committal service was held in the Little Sanctuary, a temporary church used until construction started on the cathedral with
the building of the Bethlehem Chapel, which would be Satterlee's
memorial.

Its cornerstone was laid on All Saints' Day, 1910. The chapel cost
about $200,000, a hefty sum for the time, and additional gifts from
the bishop's family and friends of $35,000 provided five stained glass
windows, seating, altar furnishings, and a small organ. By 1911 the
chapel, the work of the master architect Henry Vaughan, was complete. Services were held regularly in it and work was started on the
cathedral sanctuary, the worship space above it, which would take
nearly another two decades to complete.

A Summing Up

The hard-working Satterlee accomplished much in his forty-three
years of active ministry. He was more a doer than a theorist, a tireless
fundraiser and launcher of projects. A list-maker on all major decisions, he was decisive and stubborn in temperament. Generally, this
produced favorable results.

On racial issues, on linking foreign missions with American
political and military interests, and on arguing there were weaker and
stronger races, his views were conventional in their time, somewhere
in the broad middle of the Episcopal Church in that era. Satterlee's
work was steady, and the new diocese was solidly launched thanks to
his efforts. He worked carefully on the detailed plans for the cathedral, yet he knew it would never be built during his lifetime. Still,
he bought the land and articulated a vision of what the cathedral
might become.

CHAPTER THREE

Years of Gradual Growth
(1909–1939)

The three decades after Satterlee's death were a time of gradual, steady growth for National Cathedral. The sanctuary was built and a start was made on the nave. Several stained glass windows were designed and placed, a music program was established, and office space built. All this took place during World War I and the Great Depression, when funds were hard to find. A visitor arriving at Mount Saint Alban in 1909 would have only the construction site and school-related buildings to visit, but by the eve of World War II a partially completed cathedral would be in place, with daily and Sunday worship services and a small but active staff.

Alfred Harding, Satterlee's successor, was bishop of Washington from 1909 to 1923, and de facto dean of the cathedral from 1909 until 1916. His goal was to build the cathedral in five years, which became his successor's hope as well, although neither came close to realizing their aspirations.

Harding was born in Northern Ireland on August 15, 1852, and came to the United States as a teenager in 1867 when his parents settled in Brooklyn, where he found a job in a manufacturing concern. Next he graduated from Trinity College, Hartford, Connecticut in 1879, and distinguishing himself as class valedictorian and a member of Phi Beta Kappa. He attended the Berkeley Divinity School in Middleton. Harding became a deacon in 1882 and a priest in 1883. After time spent in Geneva, New York, and Baltimore, he began a long tenure as rector of St. Paul's, Washington, DC, from 1886 to 1909. He had strong pastoral skills and was popular among diocesan clergy and laity. Harding became first secretary of the diocesan standing committee, a position he held until he was elected bishop. He also became a canon of the cathedral and was part of the national church's effort to compile a mission hymnal. In Washington he became secretary to the board of governors of the Columbia Hospital for Women and president of the Episcopal Eye, Ear, and Throat Hospital. Bishop Satterlee called Harding "my right hand man" in building the cathedral and highly endorsed him when Harding was being considered as candidate for bishop in another diocese. Satterlee wrote that Harding always received by far the highest number of votes as a member of the standing committee, as a delegate for the General Convention, and for every other position to which he had been elected.[1]

Harding's most memorable cathedral activity was building the Bethlehem Chapel as a memorial to Bishop Satterlee. Additionally, foundations of the entire building were laid and the sanctuary and part of the choir were erected as well. World War I occurred during his tenure, however, severely limiting fundraising possibilities, and Harding also lacked the extensive affluent East Coast contacts that Satterlee long cultivated.

Shortly after his consecration as bishop in 1909 he announced that contracts had been let for the Satterlee Chapel and laying the foundation walls for the cathedral. Differences over building with red brick or Indiana limestone were settled in favor of the latter, and Harding estimated that the total cost of the Bethlehem Chapel would be about $200,000, exclusive of interior furnishings. By 1911 the chapel was completed and the cathedral had a resident staff of three clergy, Archdeacon Richard P. Williams, Canon William L.

---

1 Satterlee to Hodges, January 4, 1908, NCA (2.4.12).

De Vries, and Canon G. C. F. Bratenahl, who would became dean in 1916.

Harding was often on the road to Baltimore, Philadelphia, New York, Boston, Cleveland, Chicago, and elsewhere, accepting a string of donations from $1,000 to $25,000 from local committees and individuals. By 1917 the cathedral could boast that its assets had grown from almost nothing at all in 1898 to over $2.4 million, of which $1.5 million had been raised in Harding's time. Although money was raised for the Bethlehem Chapel, larger sums were not forthcoming for additional major construction.

World War I had impacted life in Washington and the work of the cathedral. "Our formerly serene and quiet Washington has become a city over-run with a vast influx of people, some on business with the Government, but the larger number workers for the Government," the bishop observed in 1918, adding, "The housing problem has become acute. Traffic in our streets has become congested. . . . New conditions confront us, which demand new methods and new agencies to meet them." A negative sign of the times was "the growing disregard for the Lord's Day in Washington," with cinemas open all day every day, and theaters now opening on Sundays as well. A Sunday Law was needed for Washington, Harding believed, to provide reasonable restrictions on amusements and Sunday commerce.[2]

As for the war, Harding called it "a veritable Crusade" to halt German worldwide domination and asked parishes to support the Allied cause. "We are at war with a powerful and relentless foe," he said. "We can hardly overestimate the gravity of the situation. . . . We have an absolutely righteous cause and every true American is thrilled with pride and with mingled emotions of relief and joy." The war "is a war against autocracy as interpreted in the cruel oppression manifested in the deeds and purposes of those now governing the German people."[3]

---

2 "The Bishop's Address," *Journal of the Twenty-Third Annual Convention of the Protestant Episcopal Church of the Diocese of Washington,* Chapel of the Good Shepherd, Washington, DC, May 16 and 17, 1918, 45, 47, 55.

3 "The Church in the Nation's Crisis," *Journal of the Twenty-Second Annual Convention of the Protestant Episcopal Church of the Diocese of Washington,* St. Andrew's Church, Washington, DC, May 23 and 24, 1917, 68.

Cathedral Music: Edgar Priest, First Organist and Choirmaster (1910–1935)

One of Harding's goals for the cathedral was to build a music program appropriate for such an institution. An English organist and
choirmaster, Edgar Priest, became the cathedral's first full-time
music director, hired by Harding, who had known his work from
St. Paul's, Washington, where Harding had been rector. Priest was
born in West Riding, Yorkshire, on February 26, 1878 and attended
a school run by his father. A child prodigy as a pianist and organist,
he had a fine tenor voice and was a graduate of the Royal College
of Music, and an assistant organist at Manchester Cathedral, until he
moved to the United States in 1901. There he worked as organist at
churches in Kingston, New York; New Haven; and Saratoga Springs
before moving to Washington in 1907 as music director at St. Paul's.
Harding took Priest with him to what would become National
Cathedral, whose services were held initially in nearby St. Alban's
parish on Sunday afternoons until construction on the Bethlehem
Chapel was completed on May 6, 1912.[4]

Priest's original assignment with the cathedral was to direct a
choir for the laying of the foundation stone on September 29, 1907.
When Harding became bishop on June 19, 1909, he arranged dual
appointments for Priest, part-time at St. Paul's and part-time at
the cathedral, which benefitted from a choir school that eventually
became St. Alban's School.

"Daddy" Priest enjoyed a reputation as a skilled builder of choirs,
and from 1912 to 1922 the Washington Cathedral boys' choir schedule
included two hours of daily rehearsal time, Monday through Friday,
plus participation in several weekday and three Sunday services. By
1932 the cathedral's main altar and choir stalls were in place and the
choir contained twenty boys and twelve men, whose performance
was broadcast nationally each Sunday afternoon. Priest insisted that
choir members keep their eyes on him at all times during a service.
He and his wife frequently invited choir members for dinner, kept in

---

4 Kitty Yang, "A Musical History of the Washington National Cathedral,
 1893–1997, A Dissertation Submitted to the Graduate Committee in Candidacy
 for the Degree of Doctor of Musical Arts," Peabody Conservatory of Music
 (Baltimore, MD: May 1998): 11–25.

touch with them after they left school, and built a growing informal association of choir alumni.

Priest helped found the Washington chapter of the American Guild of Organists, gave organ recitals, and taught music at St. Alban's School from 1910 to 1918. He engaged the well-known American organ builder Ernest M. Skinner to construct an organ for Bethlehem Chapel and a larger instrument for the cathedral proper. An outdoors enthusiast, Priest also raised prize-winning hunting dogs. A composer of Edwardian-era choral music, some of Priest's hymn tunes, anthems, and service settings still exist in manuscript form in the cathedral archives, but would attract little interest from future generations of church musicians because they represented byproducts of the English choral music of their era. He died suddenly on March 30, 1935.

Harding's successes were real but not dramatic during his fourteen year episcopate. He was responsible for successfully building the Bethlehem Chapel, which opened for daily worship in 1912, and for construction of part of the choir and sanctuary, and laying the foundations that allowed for the building's eventual expansion. A skilled administrator and caring pastor, his attentions were increasingly focused in his later years on the steadily expanding Diocese of Washington and his work with the national church.

Harding's final years were busy ones, and his work for the diocese and cathedral covered over his personal grief. A son, Nathan, died at age five, and his wife, Justine, died on February 9, 1909, less than a month after his consecration as bishop on January 25. Harding died on April 30, 1923. His wife and young son were buried with the bishop in his sarcophagus in the cathedral's Resurrection Chapel. A carved representation of his dog, Kiddo, was curled at his feet, as a symbol of fidelity.

Robert Barrow, Second Organist and Choirmaster (1935–1939)

Priest's unexpected death in 1935 left the cathedral music program without a leader. Robert Barrow, a graduate of St. Alban's School and former cathedral choirboy, was named Priest's successor in September 1935. He lasted four years.

Barrow, who held B.A. (1932) and B.S. (1933) degrees from Yale University, had won a number of recital prizes, and had spent a year in London studying composition with Ralph Vaughan Williams and others. He then held a two-year appointment at Trinity Church, New Haven, and when interviewed by the cathedral, replied that he probably knew "more of Mr. Priest's methods than any man alive" and was willing to return to Washington for a salary of $2,400 a year. Of the seventy applicants, Barrow was the leading candidate.

The Great Choir of National Cathedral had opened for worship in 1932, and funding for a large Skinner organ had been raised. Barrow was expected to train a choir of men and boys that would sing at two major services on Sundays and at five regular weekly choral services. Barrow would also be responsible for care and maintenance of the cathedral organs. He entered into his job with enthusiasm and soon asked for funds to add four additional choir members (at $25 a month) to increase antiphonal singing and help with the expanded choral repertoire he hoped to introduce. He also wanted to recruit an additional choir of male and female voices, which did not happen in his time.

Barrow disliked organ preludes in services because of the noise and distractions of congregations arriving, and suggested that a major organ solo follow the sermon, an idea that never took hold. He likewise opposed processional and recessional hymns, which he believed could not be adequately heard by the choir, and was opposed to chanted psalms, which he thought congregations could not adequately sing.

By November 1938, E. M. Skinner had completed the Great Organ, and Barrow played a dedicatory recital on November 10. By 1939 the demands as musician and administrator had taken their toll on him, and some of Barrow's impulsive decisions had not sat well with cathedral leadership. He was considered high-strung and opinionated, a skilled musician without matching administrative skills. There were also complaints about the uneven quality of cathedral music, and Barrow, without telling anyone, had contracted with a local firm to maintain the organ, which disturbed Skinner greatly.

During 1938, Barrow applied for a position with the Williams College music department, which he joined in May 1939. He and his wife stayed there for thirty-seven years until he retired in 1976. He died in 1987.[5]

---

5 *Ibid.,* 26–38.

Philip H. Frohman, Cathedral Architect for Over Forty Years

In addition to building a music program, construction of the actual cathedral building was a major concern during this time. George F. Bodley and Henry Vaughan, the original cathedral architects, both died before the structure was built. Beginning in 1921, Philip Hubert Frohman, an American architect, planned and supervised on-site construction for the next half century. The resultant building was largely his work—in the spirit of an English cathedral of the fourteenth century, as interpreted by Frohman in a Washington setting.

The architect's ancestors had been French architects and civil engineers, and Frohman had long been attracted to the cathedral. A graduate of the California Institute of Technology, in 1914 as a young architect he visited the Bethlehem Chapel and called it "a more beautiful crypt than any I have seen abroad" and "the most satisfying example of church architecture in America."

Frohman had looked in detail at the original cathedral designs and talked with Vaughan in Boston, and with Bishops Harding and Freeman and Dean Bratenahl in Washington while assigned to the U.S. Army near Washington during World War I.

Frohman took over as architect in 1921. This became his consuming task, and the resultant building was as much his as Bodley and Vaughan's, although the intensely modest Frohman would not claim such credit for himself. "I am proud I am an anachronism," Frohman said at his eightieth birthday on November 16, 1967. He constantly maintained the Gothic style remained both logical and functional. Although Bodley's original design was sometimes called an English Gothic cathedral, it combined pronounced French elements as well in the polygonal shape of the apse and the decorative addition of flying buttresses, in addition to its English square towers and long nave.

Frohman's most extensive statement of his plans was contained in a report to the Cathedral Chapter of October 21, 1921. In it Frohman repeated the comments others had made that the original plans were a fine expression of fourteenth-century English Gothic architecture, but lacked aisles and side chapels, and the west front was somewhat small and weak compared to the rest of the building. He would make the towers and front larger, and add a much larger rose window. The original design, he concluded, lacked the refinement and polish that would come from the expected dialogue between cathedral clergy and architects from which a completed design would emerge.

Frohman had definite ideas about how to improve the original design. He both extended the towers further westward and made them higher, and raised the central Gloria in Excelsis Tower to be much taller. Several nave windows were lengthened to allow for more light, and the rose window on the west façade became four times larger than in the original plan.

Frohman noted that the Bethlehem Chapel followed Bodley's original design, but by 1919 several revisions were undertaken to modify the other original building plans, adding crypt chapels of St. Joseph of Arimathea, the Resurrection Chapel, and the Children's Chapel where "we have endeavored to develop the original design into what we hope is resulting in an even more impressive and ideal cathedral." He added that, were the cathedral just being designed, he would make a case for a series of chapels to be built off the central apse instead of surrounding it with flying buttresses: otherwise he would stay with the basic Bodley-Vaughan concept.

A person of deep faith (he became a Roman Catholic in 1934), he supervised a small staff of drafting clerks and a secretary from an office on the top floor of National Cathedral School's Hearst Hall. If he was not in the office, poring over drawings, he was up on scaffolding with the masons or supervising construction in the building. Frohman wrote little and participated only minimally in the professional associations of architects, and although he designed more than fifty churches during his long career in Washington, the National Cathedral was his consuming interest.

As lead architect, Frohman was joined by E. Donald Robb, a Boston architect, who had done extensive work on St. Thomas' Church in New York. They added Harry B. Little, who had worked on the Cathedral of St. John the Divine in New York, to their small staff. Robb lived in Boston until his death in 1942. Little stayed there until he died in 1944. Frohman moved to Washington and in 1920 reassuringly wrote the dean: "We regard the Washington Cathedral as the most important structure being built in America, and possibly the entire world."[6]

---

6 Richard T. Feller and Marshall W. Fishwick, *For Thy Great Glory* (Culpeper, VA: Community Press, 1965): 21.

"There is a certain geometrical relation which should always determine the height and width of towers in relation to the height and width of the nave," Frohman wrote. "This is no matter of guess work or personal taste; it is just as much a matter of law as are the rules of harmony in music. The application of mathematics to architecture does not tend to lessen the spiritual and emotional value of a structure . . . a cathedral should express the fact that the Christian life is one of ordered freedom and that the whole universe exists in accordance with fixed laws."[7]

When he retired in 1971 after fifty years on the job, Frohman was succeeded by Richard T. Feller, clerk of the work. Frohman died on October 30, 1972. He had been hospitalized after being struck by a car in August while walking to the cathedral from his home on nearby Macomb Street.

A builder of major hotels, churches, and other buildings, the George A. Fuller Co. was awarded several contracts to build chapels: the apse, the eastern sanctuary, and the cathedral's altar, its center of worship. For much of the twentieth century, construction was by fits and starts. Capital campaigns were announced, suspended, and then completed. Wars and economic downturns occurred. Plans were announced for the central tower, windows, and aisles, then put on hold until money was found. Staff was hired and let go. Cathedral life was episodic yet ongoing.

It is difficult, as a result, to ascertain how much the cathedral cost. Feller and Fishwick, in their book *For Thy Great Glory*, estimate the actual construction contracts totaled $13 million between 1909 and 1964. This includes the initial $360,000 for the Bethlehem Chapel through the $1,575,000 for the central tower in 1962, but not money for operating expenses, furnishings, staff, and programs.[8]

Construction gains were modest at the cathedral during the 1920s and 1930s; it was the time of the Great Depression and World War II, but the stage was set for building and program expansion in the postwar era.

---

7 Philip Hubert Frohman, "Excerpts from Mr. Frohman's Report to the Cathedral Chapter, October 21, 1921," in Richard T. Feller and Marshall W. Fishwick, *For Thy Great Glory* (Culpeper, VA: Community Press, 1965): 87.

8 Feller and Fishwick, *For Thy Great Glory* (1965): 95. Feller was a lay canon and clerk of the works at the cathedral for many years. Fishwick was a historian of American popular culture.

Three strong, colorful personalities dominated cathedral life in the 1920s and 1930s after Harding's death. Washington's third bishop, James E. Freeman, a former New York railroad financial executive, was elected bishop in 1923. The cathedral's first full-time dean, the former rector of nearby St. Alban's Parish from 1915 to 1936, G.C.F. Bratenahl, had some success in fundraising, but as his health waned, his interest in Christian symbolism and the details of construction issues remained the focus of his daily activity. Anson Phelps Stokes, who spent many years in administrative posts at Yale University, emerged as a major cathedral voice, especially on racial issues, during his long incumbency, 1924 to 1939.

Freeman, Bratenahl, and Stokes, each a major figure in their settings, tended to relate to one another in concentric circles. The dean and bishop maintained polite, formal contact. The bishop's relations with the dean were productive but somewhat distant. With Stokes they were a bit closer, for the bishop sought the latter's help in fundraising. Stokes, however, had accepted the canon's position in 1924 with the understanding that he would only receive a half salary and could take time to pursue other interests, such as supervising a family foundation, writing several books, and traveling in Africa to promote closer African and American ties.

James E. Freeman, Washington's Third Bishop (1923–1943)

Washington's third bishop, James E. Freeman (1866–1943), like his predecessor, Alfred Harding, hoped to complete building National Cathedral in five years, and like Harding, he made some progress toward expanding the structure, but it would take almost a half century after his death for the building to be completed.

Born in New York City on July 24, 1866, Freeman attended public schools there and began work at an early age in the accounting department of the Long Island Railroad. After spending nearly fifteen years with the Long Island, Hudson River, and New York Central railroads, he switched careers and studied for the ministry with Bishop Horatio Potter of New York. Potter, who had been in business himself, sought Freeman out after hearing him speak at a political rally. The bishop urged Freeman to study for the ministry. Freeman resisted at first, saying "I am a railroad man," but eventually changed his mind. Potter arranged for him to study with three prominent New York clerics.

Ordained a deacon in 1894 and a priest in 1895, Freeman served two growing parishes in Yonkers, before moving to St. Mark's, Minneapolis, in 1910. He stayed there until 1921 when the Church of the Epiphany, a key parish in downtown Washington, DC, called him as rector. Meanwhile, he declined an election as bishop coadjutor of West Texas in 1911, lost an election to be bishop of Colorado by one vote, and declined the dean's position at the Cathedral of St. John the Divine, New York City, where a building program was in full swing.

Freeman was a civic presence wherever he went and was often invited to speak at Liberty Bond rallies, school dedications, and Community Chest events. In Washington he estimated that he spoke at thirty-five or forty banquets a year. Freeman was active in a campaign to suppress tuberculosis in Yonkers, was asked to be arbiter in a street railway strike there, and maintained a continuing interest in labor-management questions. Congregations grew under his tutelage, and church administrations ran more smoothly than before. He built new parish halls in several places and modernized church plants. "When the church took him, it deprived the New York Central Railroad of a future president," a senior railroad executive said of Freeman.

Freeman stayed as rector of Epiphany from 1921 until 1933 when he was elected third bishop of Washington on the seventeenth ballot. He was also a skilled user of print and broadcast media. A columnist and public speaker, as bishop he wrote several articles about introducing Christianity to the "man-on-the-street." *The Washington Star* carried his weekly column, and national radio networks broadcast his seasonal sermons. In an article called "Why a National Cathedral?" he wrote, "The sermons broadcast Sunday by Sunday from its pulpit have met with a response from people of every shade of religious belief, and at times I am compelled to employ two or more stenographers to answer the daily mail received from radio listeners. In this connection, I have come to believe that it may be that radio will do more to break down intolerance, bigotry and indifference than any agency hitherto employed."[9]

---

9 James E. Freeman, "Why a National Cathedral?" *The Washington Star* (October 2, 1926), NCA (4.3.3).

Freeman was a popular figure in Washington, a broad churchman who saw himself as someone who could also appeal as well to the Episcopal Church's high church faction when he ran for the post of presiding bishop in 1924. However, he received only a handful of votes and was greatly disappointed at the lack of support.

Two world wars and the Great Depression affected what Freeman could do at the cathedral. Funding possibilities were reduced, but he was resourceful and successfully sought donors in several cities for the cathedral. The College of Preachers was built with a $1.5 million gift from a former Yonkers parishioner and philanthropist, Alexander Smith Cochran, the carpet king, and Freeman completed construction of the cathedral's choir, the Children's Chapel, the St. Mary's, St. Joseph's, and Holy Spirit chapels, and a crypt chapel. Construction of South Transept advanced, new designs made the Central Tower and nave higher, and the position of the high altar was made more attractive and depth was added to the Sanctuary. Freeman also urged that brighter colors be used in stained glass windows and saw the Great Organ construction completed in the choir in 1938. Cathedral construction was incremental but real.

During his time as bishop, Freeman traveled about the country on numerous speaking engagements, meeting with potential donors, speaking to garden clubs and church groups. There is a photo of him sharply attired in an army major's uniform, a rank he was awarded in the Chaplain Corps for speaking in military camps and to Liberty Bond rallies. He travelled more than seventy thousand miles and spoke to more than four hundred and fifty thousand troops in army camps.[10]

"His frame was large and well-proportioned," a colleague wrote of Freeman. "The mouth suggested the orator; showed character, strong feeling and fine sentiment. Altogether, he presented a splendid appearance—stalwart, vigorous, distinguished, every inch a man." His sermons "were couched in a most forceful and distinctive diction, well phrased and flowing with unfailing smoothness. With their unfoldment, his delivery rose to a climax; his voice thundered; the gestures grew more vigorous," often moving listeners to tears.

---

10 Elisabeth Ellicott Poe, "Bishop Freeman, Twentieth Century Prophet of the Church," Reprinted from *The Washington Post* (June 10, 1923): 14, NCA (4.3.2).

"He had a way of pausing to remove his glasses; then grasped the edge of the pulpit and leaned forward to talk in a very personal and intimate manner."[11]

Woodrow Wilson Buried in Cathedral

Woodrow Wilson died late Sunday morning, February 3, 1924, at his home on S Street in the Kalorama District of Washington. A short service was held there the following Wednesday afternoon, February 6, led by two Presbyterian ministers and Bishop George E. Freeman, who had offered Edith Wilson burial space for her husband in the still incomplete Washington National Cathedral.[12]

Crowds lined both sides of Massachusetts Avenue, and were separated by lines of marines and army troops, and at least fifty thousand people gathered outside Bethlehem Chapel, which could only seat three hundred. Radio and loudspeakers broadcast the service to those outside. Bishop Freeman and two other cathedral clergy read the Office of the Burial of the Dead as the casket rested before the altar. As the congregation departed the organist played the Easter hymn "The Strife is O'er, the Battle Done," and Wilson's casket was lowered into a vault under the marble floor. A bugler sounded "Taps" outside the cathedral and another repeated the call across the Potomac.

In 1956 the president's remains were reinterred in the Woodrow Wilson Bay in the cathedral's nave in a service led by the president's grandson, Dean Francis B. Sayre. After Edith Wilson's death at age eighty-nine, her remains were placed by his side. The Woodrow Wilson Bay remains one of the cathedral's most visited sites.

Shortly after he was elected bishop, Freeman tried to recruit Anson Phelps Stokes, recently resigned as secretary of Yale University, as the cathedral's fundraiser for metropolitan New York. Stokes, from an affluent New York family, had raised six million dollars for Yale through individual pledges of $25,000 each. This was the sort of fundraising Freeman wanted to see at the cathedral, but Stokes preferred to leave fundraising behind and be a full-time minister and advocate

---

11 Van Rensselaer Gibson, "A Distinguished Bishop in the Making," *The Right Reverend James Edward Freeman, Bishop of Washington, 1866–1943* (Washington, DC: *The Cathedral Age*, Michaelmas, 1943).

12 A. Scott Berg, *Wilson* (New York: G.P. Putnam's Sons, 2013): 739–741.

of improved racial relations. The cathedral was urged to find him "a permanent and adequate position in the Cathedral itself, which would be dignified, and give him an opportunity for service."[13] What Stokes wanted was a cathedral position that would both allow him to preach and take services of a regular schedule, and to write and travel.

When Stokes moved to Washington, Freeman soon wrote to ask him "with [his] very large knowledge of prospective donors to the Cathedral" could he produce a list of "preferably elderly women of large means to whose doorsteps a path of approach might be made" for Freeman. The bishop suggested joint calls with Stokes and added that, with proper advance work, "we might accomplish large results."[14] Stokes's response is unknown, but he deflected the numerous requests of him to lead fundraising efforts.

In Stokes's *Reminiscences*, he listed Freeman's strengths as being "a deep interest in evangelical religion; great capacity as a preacher, especially to men, being unusually effective before Chamber of Commerce and similar organizations" plus a "deep interest in Christian unity, and friendliness to all religious bodies," and strong support for the cathedral. However, "he was not a very deep man and he was a somewhat vain man. He loved to talk about the 'big men' who were his friends, especially Andrew Mellon, whose name he always mentioned with great reverence."[15] Freeman wrote a lengthy memorandum of conversation of his hour-long meeting with Secretary of the Treasury Mellon on February 3, 1930, "the longest [meeting] I have had with him for some time." Freeman said Mellon had found the latest drawings for the south transept "very artistic." Freeman asked how future building of the cathedral might be financed. Mellon suggested that ten backers be found to underwrite a long-term loan for a million to a million and a half dollars, and that two or three Washington banks might make such loans, and if that didn't work, Freeman should return and Mellon would make other suggestions.[16]

---

13 "Memorandum in Regard to Strengthening the Administrative Force," (January 16, 1924), NCA (112.5.3).

14 James E. Freeman to Canon Stokes, June 24, 1933, NCA (112.8.3).

15 Anson Phelps Stokes, *Reminiscences of Anson Phelps Stokes, 1874–1954, for His Children and Grandchildren, With Family Traditions, and Stories and Some Comments and Reflections* (Lenox, MA: publisher unknown, 1956). Typescript in Washington National Cathedral Archives.

16 "Memorandum of Conversation with Secretary Mellon, By Bishop Freeman," February 3, 1930, NCA (4.8.1).

In some ways, Freeman was always the businessman–bishop. He kept careful records of cathedral and diocesan funds and his own expenditures. He delighted that the Pennsylvania Railroad gave him a complimentary pass to ride any train in its system. When he was on the road, he sought to make maximum use of his time by calling on potential donors or meeting with them over meals. A memo for a trip to New York contained capsule comments on nineteen persons to be possibly visited. As his briefing memorandum stated, they included potential donors, such as "Mr. and Mrs. Bernard Baruch— This devoted friend of President Wilson has an office in the neighborhood of our New York office. With his wife he gave $25,000 in 1925 to the W.H. Page School for International Relations at Johns Hopkins. Mr. Seymour ought to be able to advise you on the approach to Mr. Baruch." And "Adolph Ochs—Your friend on *The New York Times*, with whom you usually lunch when you are in New York, recently gave $5,000 to the Clarke School for the Deaf and helped Martha Berry raise $1,000,000 for her school in Georgia. Has not the time come for us to definitely ask Mr. Ochs to make a gift to Washington Cathedral and would it not be more appropriate in view of his race to request his gift for the Boys' School rather than for the Cathedral, itself?"[17]

Although clever and a facile writer, Freeman had neither a college nor a seminary education, and his writing lacked broad scope. His sermons were laced with quotes from English poetry and aphorisms from Greek and Roman writers. In a 1930 Thanksgiving Day cathedral sermon, he said of America, "She is a veritable El Dorado, whose hidden resources are as yet but dimly understood and appraised. Her pacific attitude towards the nations of the world, as well as her capacity for furnishing men and markets to meet universal needs, is generally and widely conceded." The National Cathedral represents "a glowing temple, rising in the Capital of the Nation, while it bears the name of one of the religious bodies of the country, it is too vast in its dimensions, too noble in its architecture, too utterly splendid in its design and purpose to be a house of prayer and worship for any exclusive group."[18]

---

17 Edwin N. Lewis to Bishop Freeman, "Bishop's Visit to New York, May 20th to 25th," May 18, 1929, NCA (4.8.8).

18 James Edward Freeman, "Drifts and Tendencies," Thanksgiving Day Sermon, November 27, 1930, NCA (4.3.2): 12–13.

Most of his clerical correspondence was to "Dear Bishop" or "Dear Dean," with first names rarely used. His extensive letters to G.C.F. Bratenahl were focused on fine points of cathedral construction, while prodding the dean to further action, without showing any irritation. At one point, when reminded that some designs were several years late in being produced, the dean offered Freeman the opportunity to name someone else to oversee cathedral iconography, but Freeman failed to act on the possibility.[19]

In a 1931 report to the Cathedral Chapter, Freeman said that salaries paid to cathedral clergy were smaller than those paid to assisting clergy in large parishes: $5,000 to the dean, and $4,000 to the warden of the College of Preachers and two of the canons, $3,500 to other clergy, and $3,000 to Canon Stokes, who had other sources of income. He recommended consolidating administration of the funds of the cathedral and its boys' and girls' schools in a single office, and increase the tuition at both schools, especially among affluent parents, to help cover increased operating costs.[20] As for the cathedral, it received $2,638,455 in 1930, $1 million of which came from the estate of Alexander Smith Cochran, and $250,000 from the estate of George F. Baker, a wealthy New York banker. Freeman expressed concern that several members of the Chapter never attended meetings, and that monthly gatherings did not allow time for detailed, reflective discussion of architectural, administrative, and artistic plans.

"The demands that are made upon me by the Diocese, to which I am primarily committed, as well as those laid upon me by the Cathedral, grow in volume with the passing of time," Freeman noted. "Were I freer to press the claims of the Cathedral and its several institutions, I am confident I could effect larger results. The problem as to how I shall be able to render a more efficient service to the Diocese and to the great work to which the Chapter is committed is yet to be solved," the bishop concluded. His successors would raise the same question in later decades.

After a decade as bishop, Freeman reflected on changes in the church and nation as he experienced them. The Diocese of Washington had grown to 26,545 members, 12,198 of whom he

---

19 G.C.F. Bratenahl to James E. Freeman, April 1, 1929, NCA (4.8.1).
20 James E. Freeman, To the Chapter of Washington Cathedral, Confidential Report, February 5, 1931, NCA (4.8.2,9).

had personally confirmed. After forty years of active ministry, he had "never known conditions more favorable to the Christian cause than I have witnessed in more recent years." He worried about the church's failure "to make its proper appeal to the so-called masses of our people. For reasons that are hardly justified, the great body of our working people, and they constitute a majority, have come to feel that . . . the Church as an institution is largely designed for the capitalistic class. To the wage-earner, religion seems a rather costly luxury to be enjoyed only by those who can afford to pay for it."[21] Freeman recalled his fifteen years spent in the accounting departments of major railroads, a period "that very largely shaped my course and colored my preaching," and his outlook on social and economic questions. He saw the Great Depression lifting and a new age on the horizon. Some seven million dollars had been raised to advance cathedral construction during the last decade, and "the commanding influence of the Cathedral as a spiritual power-house has outdistanced the material fabric," he believed.

From the death of Bishop Satterlee in 1908 to the death of Bishop Freeman in 1943, cathedral growth was sporadic but real, and its influence in Washington and beyond increased, due in part to the energetic and determined work of Bishops Harding and Freeman, and the efforts of clergy like Dean G.C.F. Bratenahl and Canon Anson Phelps Stokes, and a widening circle of lay supporters.

G.C.F. Bratenahl (1862–1939), First Resident Cathedral Dean (1915–1936)

From his arrival as deacon at St. Alban's parish in 1898 until his forced retirement as dean of the cathedral at age seventy-four in 1936, George Carl Finch Bratenahl (1862–1939) was an enduring presence on Mount Saint Alban for almost four decades. Carl, to the few who knew him on a first-name basis, served as rector of St. Alban's from 1898 to 1915, a cathedral canon beginning in 1903, then dean from 1915 to 1936.

A hard-working, details-oriented administrator, originally trained as an accountant in a business firm, Bratenahl helped build up the

---

21 "Interview on His 10th Anniversary, Dictated by Bishop Freeman, 9/14/33," NCA (4.8.4).

St. Alban's congregation. The congregation also founded missions in its rapidly expanding suburban neighborhood, including St. Columba's, St. David's, St. Partick's, All Saints', and St. George's, a colored mission in Tenleytown.

As dean of the cathedral, issues of war and peace, of the Great Depression and the racial demographics of Washington, were of secondary interest to Bratenahl, whose major concerns were iconography and details of the cathedral's building plans. He was both dean and, as chair of the building committee, de facto construction superintendent of the building. The cathedral archives contain several folders of his detailed letters about the color and type of stones, plumbing problems, the proposed location of access roads, the delivery of stained glass windows, and staff schedules. He also kept in touch with chapter members and donors.

His second wife, Florence, was a skilled, self-taught horticulturalist, who did much to landscape Mount Saint Alban's, founded the All Hallows Guild gardeners, changed an unused outside building into the Herb Cottage, and designed what would become the Bishop's · Garden. She was his confidant and partner in every sense.

Early Years: Cleveland and London

Carl was born on May 4, 1862 in Lake Shore, Ohio, where his German immigrant family had acquired sixty-five acres of uninhabited lakeshore property and developed a farm that sold vegetables to nearby Cleveland. (Bratenahl, a small, affluent community on the shore of Lake Erie, still exists, with its own postal address and zip code.)

After her husband Charles's death in 1870, Mrs. Bratenahl sold the property and moved to England with her two sons, and then to Massachusetts. Carl attended school in England, the Greylock Academy in South Williamstown, Massachusetts, and nearby Williams College, where he graduated in 1883. He obtained an accountant's position in New York City with the Ansonia Clock Company, a major manufacturer of clocks, and in 1889 was sent to England as their European representative with a comfortable salary of $5,000. He also married Louisa Oakey Hall, daughter of a former mayor of New York, in 1889.

His assignment was to reorganize Ansonia's London office, and Bratenahl dismissed its twenty-two employees and hired replacements.

He also devoted his spare time to settlement house work at Toynbee
Hall, a well-known church-sponsored center for London's poor and
struggling.

One evening, while walking home, he passed Westminster
Abbey where he heard choral music, which turned out to be a performance of Handel's *Messiah*. The young office manager was trans-
fixed and, by his later accounts, was determined to reorient his life.
Although raised a Presbyterian, he began studies for confirmation in
the Church of England. After five years with the clock company, he
returned to New York City and began to prepare for the ministry
with Henry Yates Satterlee, then rector of Calvary Church.

When Satterlee became first bishop of Washington, he brought
Bratenahl with him, where the latter became rector of St. Alban's.
The nearby cathedral was under construction, and as it grew, in 1902
Bratenahl took on additional duties as canon precentor in charge of
worship. He also returned to England when possible, to study the
organization of English cathedrals.

At St. Alban's, he was highly regarded for his administrative
skills, and for his equitable, steady temperament, and for his pastoral ability.[22] He was tall, with Teutonic facial features, a carefully
trimmed moustache, and a military bearing. As a youth, his vocational goal had been a military career, but a West Point appointment eluded him. There is almost no mention of him as a preacher,
although Anson Phelps Stokes, who must have heard him frequently
at the cathedral, called him a wretched preacher and one of the few
fundamentalists he had ever known.

To the Cathedral

In 1912 Bratenahl's wife, Louisa, died, and he moved from
St. Alban's to the cathedral, where he stayed for over two decades.
He also accepted responsibility for missions and outreach for the
Diocese of Washington, which included raising a million dollars for
missions and oversight of groups like the Girls' Friendly Society, the
House of Mercy, and the Home for the Incurables. Bishop Alfred
Harding named him head of the cathedral building committee, as

---

22 Ruth Harwood Cline, *Church at the Crossroads, A History of St. Alban's Parish,
Washington, DC, 1854–2004* (Chevy Chase, MD: Posterity Press, 2009): 49–50,
102–128, 130–131, 155–156.

well. Harding knew of Bratenahl's skills in business and his interest in Christian iconography. In addition to raising money for construction of the building, there were commemorative stones to be carved, stained glass windows to be ordered, wrought iron decorations to be made, wooden screens to be carved, a massive organ to be designed, a reredos—the stone screen behind the high altar—to be built, and donors to be found. It was a full-time job and then some.

On June 16, 1915, Bratenahl married his second wife, Florence Cornelia Brown Finn, a clergy widow from Cleveland, and on May 1, 1916 he was formally installed as first elected dean of the cathedral. The term "elected" can be misunderstood: there was no public contest for the position. Harding made the nomination and the Cathedral Chapter elected his choice.

In 1917 the Bratenahls began construction of a large dean's residence at 3525 Woodley Road, across the street from the cathedral. It was built from their own funds and was eventually known as Bratenahl House. The building was later sold by the Bratenahl family to the Pulitzer Prize-winning journalist Walter Lippmann, who lived there from 1945 to 1967, and wrote in one of his columns, "I can't think for those damned Cathedral bells," after which the cathedral covered part of the bell tower's north side with baffles to deflect the bells' sound. With Lippmann's departure for New York, the house was sold to the cathedral, and rented to Senator Eugene J. McCarthy from 1967 to 1973.[23]

Bratenahl summarized his vision of the cathedral as representing four "Ps": "It is PRIMITIVE, the oldest of all Christian organizations: it is PROGRESSIVE, though not necessarily from a political viewpoint. It is a POPULAR institution, able to bring all sorts and conditions of men together. It is the one organization that outlasts the rise and fall of governments—the most PERMANENT of all institutions."[24] While he demonstrated an interest in the early church, he never formally studied the subject, and his 1930 manuscript on Washington cathedral iconography failed to make any notice of the rapidly evolving fields of biblical studies and church art. His view of history, even for his time, was narrow, lauding, for example, the "courage, courtesy, loyalty (and) mercy" of the

---

23 Robert E. Kendig, *The Bratenahl Haus, An Interim Report* (Washington, DC: publisher unknown, 1993).
24 Quoted in Feller and Fishwick, 20.

Crusaders.[25] The military windows were "to include . . . Joan of Arc, General Gordon—the type of warrior who in taking the sword, always remembers he was a soldier of the Cross."[26] Virtually all present and most proposed windows were described in detail in the report, and represented the standard Christian triumphalist vision of the 1920s.

Although Bratenahl started his work as cathedral dean with enthusiasm, his energies waned after a decade as the result of a continuing heart condition, but his attention to detail never flagged. He was advised by the chapter to hire an energetic assistant to take over some of the day-to-day work, but that never happened. Bratenahl seemed serene in his personal relations, and was never known to voice irritation or anger with others, nor in his voluminous correspondence, much of it dealing with leaky roofs, missed deadlines, and other construction problems. His annual reports to the chapter were short and to the point, and he did not comment on wider moral or political and economic issues facing Washington and the country during the 1920s and 1930s. He was a member of several fraternal and patriotic societies: a photo of the dean in clerical garb, blessing the hounds at the Washington Riding and Hunt Club's first chase, appeared in a newspaper in October 1932.

An Unquiet Retirement

Due to his growing infirmity, Bratenahl's activity was limited by the late 1920s and focused largely on his study of iconography and work with the building committee. Chapter members, while maintaining personal affection for him, believed it was time for the dean to retire. He could spend only a few hours each week at work. Their plan was to have a chapter member gently talk with him, and suggest that he reapply for his position as usual, and when it was offered to him, decline it and announce his retirement plans. In turn, the chapter would name him dean emeritus, provide a full salary for life, and allow him to retain his post as chair of the building committee.

Negotiations dragged out over two years, and when the chapter thought they had the dean's agreement, they announced his pending

---

25 G.C.F. Bratenahl, *Washington Cathedral Iconography, Preliminary Report,*
    typescript, October 1930, NCA (129.11.3), 3.
26 *Ibid.*, 9.

retirement set for May 1, 1936. At this point an irate Bratenahl, age
seventy-four, said he was being forced out and declined the offer.
He published a lengthy letter to this effect in the fall 1936 issue of
Cathedral Age. Sides were chosen within the wider cathedral community and public, and lawyers were consulted. The dean vocally
defended his position, and the controversy bubbled along beneath
the surface.

Bratenahl finally left in late 1936. In retirement the couple moved
to the Weathered Oak Herb Farm in Bradley Hills, Maryland, which
Mrs. Bratenahl ran with Charles H. Merryman, a former cathedral
master gardener. It was a large farm devoted primarily to landscape
gardening and was later sold by the two Bratenahl sons after their
parents' death. Bratenahl died on February 29, 1939, his wife on
May 14, 1940.

Anson Phelps Stokes: Cathedral Canon, and Internationalist (1924–1939)

Any list of clergy who made lasting contributions in the life of the
cathedral should include the name of Anson Phelps Stokes, a major
although largely unrecognized figure. Stokes, who came close to
being president of Yale University, was an active cathedral canon,
especially in calling attention to the need for improved educational,
economic, and housing possibilities for minorities in Washington,
and for heightened American foreign policy interest in Africa. His
carefully reasoned disagreement with the Daughters of the American
Revolution over their refusal to allow a Marian Anderson concert
at the D.A.R.'s Constitution Hall in 1939 became the subject of
national media interest and brought the question of racial segregation
to wider church and public attention.

Stokes was as influential as any bishop or dean in advancing
Washington National Cathedral's aspirations during his fifteen years
as a canon of the cathedral, from 1924 to 1939. Tall and thin, with
craggy features and a carefully trimmed Van Dyke beard, he could
have stepped from an El Greco painting. Stokes (1874–1958) was
descended from a long line of English mercantile, social activist, and
philanthropic ancestors, and inherited considerable wealth from both
parents.

Stokes spent nearly three decades as a student and then a senior administrator at Yale University. As secretary, third-ranking official after the university's president and provost, he had been a major fundraiser at Yale, built up an alumni association, and helped the university acquire property in New Haven for expansion. Stokes attended General Theological Seminary after graduating from Yale, was ordained a deacon in the Episcopal Church, and was active at both St. Paul's, New Haven, and with the Yale University chaplaincy.

In 1924 he came to Washington with his wife, Carol, and three children, where he interacted with several presidents, leading diplomats, church and civic leaders, members of Congress, and justices of the Supreme Court.

Staten Island Childhood

A large family house set on seven acres in New Brighton, Staten Island, was the scene of Stokes's early childhood. Its influences were life-long and often referred to by Stokes in later life. The spacious house contained school rooms, quarters for eight indoor servants, and a large library where the family gathered for daily prayers and spent their evenings reading by gas lamps before a large open fireplace. A twenty-six volume illustrated Bible allowed the children to pore over original works by famous artists like Albrecht Dürer. Eventually electricity and a telephone were added to the house. It was an idyllic life for children, grounded in family attention, intellectual challenge, and strong social and philanthropic commitments.

Stokes's father, also Anson Phelps Stokes, was a banker in a highly successful family firm. Skilled at amassing wealth from banking and investments, the family supported groups like the American Bible Society and the Y.M.C.A. Stokes's mother, Helen Louisa Phelps Stokes, raised the large family, managed at least three households and over fifty servants, and organized a constant round of family activities in New York; at Shadow Brook, a huge family house in Lenox, Massachusetts; and during summers at a family camp in the Adirondacks. Shadow Brook, built in 1893 on a 727-acre property, was America's largest house at the time, with more than a hundred rooms and over three acres of floor space.

On Sundays the family divided into two teams to play a biblical guessing game. The Stokes children may not have been aware of it, but they were gaining a religious education at the same time they were learning to read, write, and perfect their skills in outdoor sports, and for Anson, biblical literacy was an ingrained part of his upbringing, inseparable from the rest of life's activities and central to his work as pastor and preacher.

Although the family was originally Presbyterian, by the late nineteenth century they had migrated toward the Episcopal Church. The whole family walked together each Sunday to church, followed by a noon dinner that ended with large blocks of vanilla and strawberry ice cream and long walks with their father. Innumerable small gestures affected their lives as well. By giving up ice cream during Lent, the family raised enough money to provide a scholarship for a female American Indian student at Tuskegee Institute.

In New York, the family built a mansion at the corner of 37th Street and Madison Avenue, where it was possible to see boats on the Hudson River from the front porch and on the East River from the back porch. From the roof, the tower of the family house at New Brighton was visible.[27]

While an undergraduate, Stokes honed his writing skills as chair of the *Yale News* and a member of the Harvard-Yale Debate team. He made Phi Beta Kappa and Skull and Bones, was awarded several prizes for public speaking, conducted Bible classes on the life of Christ and the life of St. Paul, and on Sunday evenings helped the Yale Hope Mission minister to New Haven's "down and outs."

At the same time, Stokes met many men who would become national religious leaders and lifelong friends, such as William Sloane, head of the Y.M.C.A. during World War I, and Henry Coffin, later president of Union Seminary. His writings are filled with encounters with the major figures of his time. "I was lunching with a friend at the New York Yacht Club when I saw Alex come into the room. I went over to greet him" could have been the opening lines of innumerable Stokes letters. But Stokes was not a namedropper. He generally let others lead in conversations. He was a patient listener, and although assured and self-confident, was not a self-promoter.[28]

---

27 Stokes, *Reminiscences*, 13.
28 Anson Phelps Stokes to George E. Freeman, Brook Farm, Lenox, MA, August 6, 1927, NCA.

A Call to Ministry

Although he had seriously considered the law as a profession, Stokes was also long-drawn to a career in ministry. He interviewed with a major New York law firm, and for good measure consulted a leading phrenologist, who confirmed the bumps on his head pointed toward either career choice. He wrote in *Reminiscences,* a memoir for family members, "I had been convinced by my experience, study, and thinking, especially at Yale, that the Christian Church represented in many ways the greatest opportunity for service for a person of my particular interests and characteristics."[29]

The Episcopal Theological School in Cambridge, Massachusetts, was his choice among seminaries, representing "the spirit of Phillips Brooks, and [standing] for a broad and spiritual interpretation of the Church's position."[30] "What Christ Thought of Himself," his graduation thesis, was later expanded into a book. It was a biblically based appraisal of the humanity and divinity of Christ, drawing in part on the methodology of German biblical criticism of its time. The book, which a modern reader would find conventional and uncontroversial in content, raised vocal opposition at its publication, and some critics said Stokes should be denied priestly ordination because of its modernist contents. Stokes wrote a minutely detailed six-page letter explaining his viewpoint to an inquiring bishop in 1924.[31]

Return to Yale, 1899–1924

Even before he finished Episcopal Theological School, the twenty-five-year-old Stokes was called back to Yale by its president, Arthur T. Hadley, and was offered the position of secretary to the university. This included planning for the Yale Bicentennial in 1901, building up the university's chaplaincy programs, beginning the Yale-in-China educational and missionary presence, and Yale University Press. His work included the acquisition of several choice New Haven locations that allowed the college to expand into a university, the organization of a systematic alumni contact program, and targeted efforts to acquire major gifts from wealthy donors.

---

29 Stokes, *Reminiscences,* 63.
30 *Ibid.,* 63.
31 Anson Phelps Stokes to Bishop Philip M. Rhinelander, December 23, 1924,
   Yale University Manuscripts and Archives, Stokes Collection (186.267).

Stokes was ordained a deacon in 1900 and in New Haven established a nearly twenty-year relationship with St. Paul's, a major downtown Episcopal church, where he generally preached at the Sunday evening service and sometimes gave Lenten courses on major figures in church history. He declined an opportunity to be chaplain at Yale as well, but participated actively in Sunday and daily services and in selecting speakers.

Stokes was much in demand as a guest preacher in East Coast universities and private schools. "In my college preaching I always tried to avoid both the popular or athletic sermon on the one hand, or the complicated or philosophical sermon on the other. I tried to present the foundations of Christian truth in a simple and effective way," he reflected, adding he hoped to present a religion "squarely based on past revelation and experience, but moving forward in relation to the problems of the time, and helping people to meet them."[32]

There was clarity to his style, and simplicity of presentation that remained unwavering through the years. Rhetorical flourishes and stridency were absent, elegant understatement was a hallmark of his use of language. The careful honing of his writing style from editorial writing days at the *Yale News* was evident in his later sermons and books. The extensive Stokes archives at Yale contain many notebooks filled with his sweeping handwriting, particularly outlining the meaning of key biblical words and concepts.

Marriage to Carol Mitchell, December 30, 1903

The pattern of Stokes's life changed with marriage in late 1903. A special car was attached to the train from New York and over a hundred people, mostly family members, gathered on December 30, 1903 at St. Bernard's Episcopal Church, Bernardsville, New Jersey, and then at "Pennbrook," the bride's family's newly built estate, for the wedding of Carol Mitchell and Anson Phelps Stokes. Although it was a small gathering, the couple had sent out five thousand announcements, mostly to Yale, New York, and New Haven connections. A two-week honeymoon in Camden, South Carolina, was later followed by a cruise.

The couple had met at their respective family camps in the Adirondacks, and during the autumn of 1903, before a large fireplace

---

32 Stokes, *Reminiscences,* 105.

in the main Mitchell cabin, Stokes asked "Miss Mitchell" to be his wife. When she consented, he switched to her first name, Carol. The Mitchells, from Charleston, South Carolina, were similar in civic and religious interests to the Stokes family, though without comparable great wealth. "Mother and I were a team," Stokes later wrote of Carol. "We worked together with unusual sympathy. We were equally interested not only in Christian ideals in the home, but in the advancement of the Negro, in missions, in cooperation between the churches, in American international responsibilities, and in many other matters. She proved an invaluable collaborator or helper in my four major jobs—Yale, the Cathedral, the Phelps Stokes Fund, and *Church and State*," the book Stokes completed after retirement. He added, "She felt that a married woman's first job was to provide a joyous, well-ordered and inspiring home for her husband and children, and in this she succeeded marvelously."[33]

The Phelps Stokes Fund

One of the pillars of Stokes's life was the Phelps Stokes Fund, founded in 1911 by his sister, Caroline, from her own inheritance. Stokes served as its president until he retired at age seventy-five. Its purpose was "the improvement of tenement house dwellings in the city of New York for the poor families of that city, [and] . . . the education of Negroes, both in Africa and the United States, North American Indians and needy and deserving white students."[34]

The family had long supported missionary educational institutions. "The first flag of the Republic of Liberia was made in my great grandfather Anson Phelps's home on the East River," Stokes remembered.[35] Stokes knew most of the leading black educators of the period, including J.K. Aggery, a Gold Coast scholar who took a medical degree at Columbia University and was a principal figure in interracial relations. Stokes often quoted a phrase of Aggery's as his own mantra, "You can play some sort of music if you play only the white keys, and some sort of music if you use only the black keys, but if you want real harmony, you must use both the white keys and the black keys."[36]

---

33 *Ibid.*, 79.
34 *Ibid.*, 110.
35 *Ibid.*, 111.
36 *Ibid.*, 112.

On racial issues, Stokes was a gradualist. He was opposed to the federal government trying to legislate integration, especially in the American South. The federal courts, shifting public opinion, and education would bring about the ultimate demise of school segregation, he believed, but racially segregated social patterns were strong in the South, with deep historical roots, and change should be gradual. He counted on enlightened Southerners of all races to provide on-the-ground leadership for integration. Meanwhile, his interests remained focused on minority education; the prevention of discrimination; opening employment, including federal government jobs, to Negroes; and bringing civil rights cases before the courts. Like others of his time, he saw his place in the pulpit and boardroom, and not on a picket line.

Washington National Cathedral, 1924–1939

Stokes was happy with his position as secretary to Yale University when its president, Arthur T. Hadley, retired in 1921. A strong movement among trustees and the Yale community supported Stokes as his successor, but equally strong voices were raised for a new president who was not a clergyman and who would bring a fresh perspective to the post. Stokes backed off gracefully, and looked at other possibilities. He declined the rectorship of St. Paul's School and several inquiries about university or foundation presidencies, and in 1923 began negotiations that led to a position as canon of Washington National Cathedral a year later.

Bishop George E. Freeman wanted Stokes to lead the cathedral's development efforts. Stokes was more interested in finding an opportunity to preach regularly and participate in worship services. He also wanted to write his never-completed book on the history of universities, engage in efforts to advance Negro education, and travel internationally, especially in Africa, where he could also promote educational advancement and improved race relations. This meant he would be part-time at the cathedral with long absences from Washington, for which he would accept a reduced salary of $3,000 a year.

An agreement was reached by the fall of 1924, and the family headed for Washington with their children, Anson, who years later would become bishop of Massachusetts; Isaac, who would become a New York attorney; and Olivia, who became Mrs. John D. Hatch of Norfolk, Virginia. However, Stokes had an initial obstacle to overcome in Washington. He had not been ordained as a presbyter or priest, although he had been a deacon for almost a quarter century. The Washington ordination process required him to take a set of examinations again, and in the oral interviews, he encountered opposition from a clergy and a lay member over his interpretation of the doctrine of the Trinity and the virgin birth—based on explanations he had given in his book, *What Jesus Thought of Himself.*

Stokes found eminent scholars who supported his position, plus written statements from the archbishops of Canterbury and York generally supportive of a position similar to his. The opposition was short-lived. Freeman had already decided to ordain him, as was the bishop's prerogative, and Stokes was ordained in the Bethlehem Chapel of National Cathedral on March 30, 1925.

His duties consisted of preaching usually twice a month, participating in other services, and sometimes conducting the cathedral's popular Sunday afternoon radio services. Actual cathedral work probably took up a quarter of his time. The rest was spent in many civic and philanthropic activities, especially those dealing with minority education and advancement. As a member of the Cathedral Chapter, or board of governors, he joined Bishop Freeman, who hoped—unsuccessfully—to add non-Episcopalians "possibly starting with Presbyterians" to the board.

This proved too radical a move in the 1920s, although a Methodist, Baptist, and Presbyterian were eventually added as cathedral canons. During the summer of 1933 he hoped to have Frances Perkins, secretary of labor and active church member, speak at the cathedral on Labor Day. "I know you are very conservative about women speakers at the Cathedral and I did not wish to approach her even indirectly without getting your approval in advance," he wrote Dean Bratenahl.[37] The dean was the central castings model of an Episcopal cleric of his time. Stokes wrote of him, Dean Bratenahl "deserves tremendous credit for doing more than any one else to work out the Cathedral plan and to develop the iconography. He was, however, one of the few Fundamentalists I have ever known intimately, and he was a wretched preacher."[38]

---

37 Anson Phelps Stokes to G.C.F. Bratenahl, Washington National Cathedral, July 3, 1933, NCA.
38 Stokes, *Reminiscences,* 174.

Stokes also made a strong effort to preach in parishes around the diocese, and gave more than a hundred lectures, illustrated with lanternslides, made from his trips to Africa and South America. He also spoke on the history of biblical translation, which he illustrated from his own sizable collection of historic manuscripts and Bibles printed in several languages.

Racial Issues in Washington

Washington was a deeply segregated city, and Stokes was quick to join with those who would frontally address race relations, especially in housing and education. When he asked his friend Chief Justice William Howard Taft to recommend other persons to join the effort, the latter replied, "Why, Anson, if you asked me in Cincinnati, or in New Haven, or even in New York, I could tell you who the best white people were" to join such an effort, but in Washington "I have no idea who they are here. Washington is all divided up into watertight compartments, no one being in close contact with the others. You have the Army, Navy, diplomatic group, the old Washingtonians, the business interests, etc."[39]

Largely through broadly constituted groups like the Community Chest, the Committee on Race Relations gathered a core group of black and white leaders who published a report on *Negro Housing in Washington* that attracted wide attention. Still, it was not easy going. "Town hall" meetings were a popular forum for discussing civic issues in Washington, but Stokes could not persuade local organizers to invite a black speaker or directly discuss race-related topics. Although the cathedral was open to all races as a place of worship, the College of Preachers would not welcome non-whites to its conferences, until by accident they invited a distinguished participant to speak based on his curriculum vitae, unaware he was a Negro, after which the color ban dissolved in that institution.

Carol worked with Mrs. Herbert Hoover on the Girl Scouts and succeeded her as district commissioner, helping establish "the Colored Girls . . . on a par with white Girl Scouts" and finding a prayer book for Girl Scouts that would be acceptable to Protestants, Catholics, and Jews. Stokes worked hard on public housing, especially on the

---

39 *Ibid.,* 173.

"alleys," the poorest black neighborhoods of Washington, some of them not far from the White House. Eleanor Roosevelt was a strong advocate of the project and her husband named Stokes to the Alley Dwelling Authority, where he served as its president.

The Alley Dwelling Authority was established by Congress in 1934 with the goal of ridding Washington of its over three hundred inhabited alleys within ten years. Such slum dwellings were an outgrowth of the original L'Enfant plan for the new federal city. L'Enfant's design contained many sizable, irregularly designed blocks, often with alleys that opened on the backyards and houses of the new city. As there was no provision for housing freed slaves and migrants to Washington, many ended up as squatters on unused public lands or built flimsy structures from discarded packing materials or scrap wood. They crowded into alleys, without electricity, water, gas, or toilets. By 1934 it was estimated that ten thousand blacks and five hundred whites lived in such conditions, a situation which slum landlords were quick to exploit.

The authority was crippled from the start by inadequate funding and hostility from the real estate community. The group tried to obtain support from real estate developers for housing for people who made less than $2,000 a year, but they failed to gain any such support.[40]

At the same time, Stokes maintained his strong interest in national political issues. He was asked by the Senate Judiciary Committee to testify against President Roosevelt's court-packing plan to add several justices to the Supreme Court. He opposed the plan and answered numerous questions from the panel, which sent out thousands of copies of his testimony to the press and the public. His civic interests were widespread. "The religious activity to which I devoted most attention outside of the Cathedral," he wrote, "was the 'Committee on Religious Life in the Nation's Capital,'" an ecumenical group that planned a welcoming process for the sizable number of new people who were pouring into Washington as the city and government agencies expanded in the 1920s and 1930s.

Stokes was quick to link race, religion, and employment as related issues. He was distressed to learn in 1937 that when the Board of Public Welfare decided to limit its grants to "unemployables," some

---

40 *Ibid.*, 182.

four thousand people had lost their welfare grant support, and only a thousand people had found jobs, leaving another three thousand without income. He called for a public rally to attract congressional attention to the problem and for a redoubled effort by local churches to engage in a ministry of feeding the hungry and finding jobs for the unemployed.[41]

The Marian Anderson Concert, April 9, 1939

The Washington activity for which Stokes is most remembered is probably his 1939 role in support of the Marian Anderson concert after the Daughters of the American Revolution (D.A.R.) refused to allow her to sing in four-thousand-seat Constitution Hall, at that time the most sought-after indoor concert venue in Washington. His pamphlet *Art and the Color Line* went through several printings and was widely circulated. It was largely a historical survey and a legal brief written for consideration of the executive committee of the D.A.R. who rejected it at the time.

Stokes's basic point was that it was poor public policy for an organization to discriminate against Negro artists because this opened the doors to further prejudice. "I felt up against a stone wall of prejudice," he said of the D.A.R., who several years later changed their policy. Stokes also worked closely with Eleanor Roosevelt, who resigned her membership in the D.A.R. over its failure to change its Constitution Hall policy.

The twenty-six-page document noted that Marian Anderson had appeared to interracial audiences previously in the District, and that singers such as Paul Robeson and Roland Hayes had appeared as well, and that at a recent confirmation service at the cathedral about a third of the participants were people of color. Stokes carefully pointed out that no local law or ordinance required segregation. He also quoted from a wide variety of American newspapers in urging the D.A.R. to lift its color ban, letters signed by the entire Philadelphia orchestra, and several national musical leaders.[42]

---

41 Extract from Minutes of "Committee on Religious Life in the Nation's Capital, March 8, 1937," Yale University Manuscripts and Archives, Stokes Collection (188.330).
42 Anson Phelps Stokes, *Art and the Color Line* (Washington, DC: October 1939): 16.

After a careful survey of legal and editorial comments on the matter, Stokes concluded: "We see no adequate reason why the color line should be drawn in the case of a really great singer such as Marian Anderson. We repeat this is a matter of art. We ask in this American democracy—especially at a critical time in our history when foreign social and political ideologies inconsistent with our national traditions are clamoring for acceptance, for fair play for American genius—for an opportunity for white and colored persons interested to hear world famous artists, when they come to Washington, in Constitution Hall—the only suitable hall in view of the regrettable absence of a municipal auditorium."[43]

Instead, the concert was held at the Lincoln Memorial where, on April 9, 1939, over seventy thousand people gathered to hear the American contralto sing a short program ranging from operatic arias to Negro spirituals. The music included the national anthem; "America;" Donizetti's "O mio Fernando;" Schubert's "Ave Maria;" two American Negro traditional works, "Gospel Train" and "My Soul is Anchored in the Lord;" followed by the encore, "Nobody Knows the Trouble I've Seen." The artist inscribed a copy of the program, "Gratefully to A.P.S by Marian Anderson."

Entertaining at 2408 Massachusetts Avenue

As important as anything in the Stokeses' efforts at racial integration was their extensive entertaining of black and white guests at a constant round of teas and dinners. One servant estimated that, during a twelve-month period in Washington and Lenox, over a thousand people had been entertained, most of them in Washington. A well-known local architect, Nathan N. Wyeth, designed their centrally located spacious house at 2408 Massachusetts Avenue in stately Beaux-Arts style. Stokes added to it, including a comfortable third floor study for himself, and a porch and other rooms overlooking Rock Creek Park.

It was, he noted in his memoirs, midway between the cathedral and the White House. "The house was a center for all sorts of meetings in the interest of interracial work," he noted, "social welfare, cathedral activities, interdenominational efforts, educational

---

43 *Ibid.,* 24.

interests . . . It was one of the of the few houses of white people in Washington at the time where people felt that they could come and feel reasonably at home."[44]

The Stokeses were friends of Chief Justice Taft, and also frequently saw or were at dinners with President and Mrs. Herbert Hoover. "Franklin Roosevelt I knew reasonably well, but not intimately," Stokes wrote. "F.D.R. always greeted me by my first name when we met at receptions or elsewhere, but this meant little, as he was probably the greatest artist in American history at calling people by their first names . . . in spite of his being much of a politician, in some respects he was magnificent in foreign affairs and did much for social welfare in the country." Of other presidents, he noted, "I did not know Mr. Truman. On the whole he did better than would be expected of a man of his background and experience. I felt that he deserved great credit for deciding that opposition to Communism made it necessary for us to enter the Korean War." As for General Eisenhower, "I had no acquaintance with him, having only met him casually."

African Trips and Interests

Africa was an enduring interest for Stokes, and improving education, especially in Liberia and South Africa, were perennial projects of his, largely realized through the Phelps Stokes Fund and through his trip reports. Stokes and his wife made a memorable five-month-long trip from Capetown to Cairo in 1932 to 1933 under Carnegie Corporation sponsorship. He lectured on "Race Relations in the U.S." at universities in the Union of South Africa, and gathered material for the widely circulated *Report of Rev. Anson Phelps Stokes on Education, Native Welfare and Race Relations in East and South Africa* (1934). The survey contents were moderate in tone. Its purpose was to call increasing Western attention to African problems that would require multi-governmental attention.

His personal observations of Africa included seeing "hundreds of native Africans who looked like American Negroes with one difference—they did not have the American Negro's smile and cheerfulness." This was due to Boer and conservative British oppression in South Africa, based on the belief that native Africans were inferior beings.[45]

---

44 Stokes, *Reminiscences,* 185.
45 *Ibid.,* 196.

Race Relations in Africa

In 1934 the Carnegie Corporation of New York published his *Report of Rev. Anson Phelps Stokes on Education, Native Welfare, and Race Relations in East and South Africa.* The document attracted attention in Washington and London for what would be considered progressive recommendations in that era. The lengthy Cape to Cairo trip included stops in South Africa, Southern and Northern Rhodesia, the Belgian Congo, Tanganyika, Zanzibar, Kenya, Uganda, Sudan, and Egypt.

Stokes and his wife were accompanied by their daughter, Olivia, who served as secretary, and Marvin Breckinridge, who became a well-known ethnographer and photographer. Stokes was welcomed both for his Carnegie connection and as president of the Phelps Stokes Fund, which would soon begin active African programming of its own. He kept an active schedule, preaching most Sundays in an Anglican cathedral or mission station, and speaking on race relations in America at many schools and universities wherever they visited.

Stokes was interested in promoting cooperation between the races, especially in the Union of South Africa. He commended the work of the Institute of Race Relations, headquartered in Johannesburg, for bringing representatives of different races together for thoughtful discussions. "The problem of adjustment between the white man and the black man is probably both the most difficult and the most important one which the African continent faces," he concluded."[46] He especially cited difficulties in South Africa, including the lack of educational and medical facilities for indigenous people, and the Pass system that kept people restricted to specific lands and dwellings. Despite such difficulties, Stokes provided several specific recommendations for scholarships and support of African institutions.

Retirement in Lenox, Final Reflections

By the summer of 1939 it was time to leave Washington, and *The Washington Post* greeted Stokses's departure with an editorial praising the canon's wide range of community endeavors, including his work of improving racial relations and public housing. His staff gave him a

---

46 *Ibid.,* 32.

fountain pen and a set of finger bowls made by one of the cathedral stained glass artists. Stokes kept only two of his multiple Washington memberships, with the National Cathedral Association and the Brookings Institution.

He planned to complete two books. One was a history of universities from their inception to the present, for which he had amassed a library of 2,500 volumes in several world languages. It would be a multi-volume work, but it was never finished. The second work was a history of church-state relations in the United States since the time of the Constitution contained in his three-volume *Church and State in the United States.*[47]

The Stokeses retired to Lenox, Massachusetts, in July 1939. He was sixty-five, with lingering health problems. He and his wife continued their multiple activities, though in a diminished manner. The weddings of their daughter, Olivia, and sons, Newton and Anson, were large family gatherings at Lenox. Shadow Brook, the huge family estate, had been sold to Andrew Carnegie. Eventually it became a Jesuit novitiate, before it was gutted by fire.

In his summary reflections in *Reminiscences,* Stokes wrote, "I have seen the rise of modern biblical scholarship, which has made the personality of Christ and the other great figures of the Old and New Testament, much more vital." He also witnessed:

> the application of Christianity to social problems, and an enormous growth in the Ecumenical Movement, due largely to persons in England and this country whom I have had the privilege of knowing well. People have also begun to realize the vital importance of religion to democracy. Without the Fatherhood of God and the Brotherhood of Man, as shown by Thomas Jefferson in the Declaration of Independence, our Government simply could not exist effectively.[48]

Stokes described his general point of view on questions of politics, religion, and education as those "of the old-fashioned liberal, as distinguished from that either of the extreme conservative or

---

47 Anson Phelps Stokes, *Church and State in the United States,* in three volumes.
   Introduction by Ralph Henry Gabriel (New York: Harper & Brothers, 1950).
48 Stokes, *Reminiscences,* 216.

radical." He concluded "the path of progress is through middle of the road liberalism. A person should have his feet on the ground but his eyes on the stars. We must live close to the past but we must not be satisfied, as Christians, with our present achievement in any field, and work toward better things."[49]

---

49 *Ibid.,* 219.

CHAPTER FOUR

A New Era Begins
(1943 through the 1960s)

The next three decades of cathedral history contained the same issues as before, but with a new cast of characters and a new emphasis. Construction issues remained a major concern, but the nave went up and the towers began to rise. Slowly but surely questions of racial integration were steadily introduced and reference was even made to the possibility of ordaining women to the priesthood.

The first Washington bishop to have been a seminary dean, Angus Dun, became fourth bishop of Washington in 1944. An articulate supporter of racial integration and the ecumenical future, Dun was supportive of the cathedral, but had little interest in its day-to-day operations, having a growing diocese to administer. Three deans passed relatively brief tenures: Noble C. Powell, a congenial Southerner, from 1937 to 1941; ZeBarney Phillips, who died from a pharmacist's error after a brief tenure; and John W. Suter, from 1945 to 1950, a liturgical scholar and custodian of the Book of Common

Prayer. All three were interesting personalities that left few traces of their presence on the institution.

Meanwhile, the cathedral's musical programs became clearly established. Paul Callaway began his long tenure as music director and organist in 1939, greatly expanding the cathedral's musical offerings. Two national church figures came to Washington in 1943, Theodore O. and Cynthia Wedel. Theodore soon became warden of the College of Preachers; Cynthia was to write on Christian educational themes and assume increasingly important leadership roles in the National and World Council of Churches. It was as if everything about the cathedral had moved to a new level. Construction was expanded, relevant issues were more forthrightly addressed, and the cathedral finally became an established national presence. The time of gestation was over.

Postwar America also represented a changing religious climate. Ecumenical activities were less suspect than before, and gradually the Episcopal Church became an active voice against racism. Gradually, through the patient work of educators like Cynthia Wedel, the inevitability of womens' ordination became a subject of public discussion. The Diocese of Washington grew in numbers with World War II's end, as did cathedral attendance, though funding to advance its construction remained modest. It would take until the mid-1970s before the walls were fully up, most stained glass windows were in place, the roof was on, and the towers were in place.

The Angus Dun Era, 1944–1962

Angus Dun (1892–1971), a well-known religious writer and national church figure, was Episcopal bishop of Washington for eighteen years. Dun spent twenty years as a teacher at the Episcopal Theological School in Cambridge, Massachusetts, before moving to Washington in 1944. Vignettes of his life and work are contained in a book written by his wife, *Catherine Whipple Dun: Life in Her Own Words*.[1] Material for the book was gathered from the collected letters of

---

1 Angus Dun, III, editor, *Catherine Whipple Dun, Life in Her Own Words* (Privately published. 164 Old Albany Road, Greenfield Massachusetts, 2012).

Mrs. Dun, prepared for a writing class she attended at Goodwin House, an Episcopal Church retirement home, in Alexandria, Virginia.

Like several other church leaders of his time, Dun had a strong interest in the ecumenical movement. In 1937 he attended the Edinburgh Faith and Order Conference, he was an active participant in the 1948 Amsterdam Assembly of the World Council of Churches, he spent ten years on the Central Committee of the World Council of Churches, and he attended international ecumenical conferences in Lund and Montreal, as well.

Dun's father was a founder of what became the Dun and Bradstreet credit rating firm. Angus was born with deformed limbs, and was severely afflicted with a deformed hand and a foot that required an amputation. He spent long periods in hospitals, and at age eleven contracted polio. A determined person throughout his life, he graduated from Yale University in 1914 as a member of Phi Beta Kappa. He Married Catherine Whipple Pew, a Radcliffe College graduate, on June 22, 1916, after which he entered the Episcopal Theological School in Cambridge, Massachusetts. One of his early parish assignments was at St. Andrew's Church, Ayer, Massachusetts, to which he was appointed in 1917 just as World War I was starting. Dun became chaplain to the large number of soldiers assigned at nearby Fort Devin, before leaving in 1919 for advanced studies in Oxford and Edinburgh.

For over twenty years the Duns lived in Cambridge, including several years in the spacious deanery of the Episcopal Theological School. "Those of us on academic salaries without private means lived a congenial village life within the School," Mrs. Dun remembered, and although formal invitations to meals decreased sharply during the war, there were always afternoon teas where faculty and students were welcome. Although the large house had five bathrooms and many small bedrooms, it was almost impossible to find servants. Mrs. Dun recalled their search, including hiring Albion, their Portuguese student butler, and Annie Wilson, "a shy girl and rather dumpy," who served briefly as cook.

"Albion did not confide in me that Annie was on trial leave from the Danvers Insane Asylum. She herself revealed that secret to me one night when a bishop was staying with us. It was all her own idea to tiptoe into the Bishop's room while he was asleep and clear out an extra closet where I hung some better dresses. She cut them into colorful strips with which to decorate the whole side of the house toward the chapel. It was conveniently covered with a vine from which she could weave them."[2]

In response, Albion, locked himself in a basement closet and said he wouldn't leave it until Annie was returned to Danvers, thirty-five miles distant. Mrs. Dun promptly arranged the journey. In Cambridge there was always a string of visiting bishops and seminary professors to attend to. One visiting English bishop from Hong Kong arrived during the winter without hat, coat, or gloves. As he was leaving by train for New York, Mrs. Dun asked if he had brought winter clothing. Unaffected, he replied, "I have a mitre in my luggage."

Dun as Bishop

Dun was hard-working, confirming more than 31,000 people and ordaining 105 deacons and 91 priests. He sometimes visited two or even three parishes on a Sunday where he preached, confirmed, and talked with as many people as he could. Dun also wrote nine books and spent a decade on the Central Committee of the World Council of Churches. His opposition to racial segregation in the church and society resulted in his being called "Black Angus" by opponents, but he was much admired in the Diocese of Washington for his steady clarity as a leader and for his interest in all sorts and conditions of people.

Despite his international and national church interests, he was first of all the active bishop in his home diocese, maintaining contact with Washington's eighty-some churches. E. Felix Kloman, rector of St. Alban's, said of him, "Bishop Dun is a clergyman's bishop because he's always frank and honest. He can be counted on to say to your face what he feels needs to be said. He says it to you, not to others."[3]

Life magazine ran a full story with pictures of his consecration, and President Franklin D. Roosevelt sent a telegram on April 18, 1944: "Let me add my sincere felicitations to those of your many friends on the day of your consecration as Bishop of Washington.

---

2 *Ibid.*, 59.
3 Louis Cassels, "An Indomitable Will . . . ," *The Washington Diocese*, Vol. 31, No. 5, May 1962.

Behind you are many fruitful years dedicated to the preparation of others for holy orders. Before you lies an even wider field of opportunity in which you can continue to exert an even stronger influence on the nation as a whole."[4]

Of the Diocese of Washington, Dun said in a 1960 convention address, "the City is our basic mission field, and retreat from it would be a betrayal of our mission. Without diminishing in any way our concern for new suburban communities we must not simply follow Episcopalians in their migration, or concentrate our efforts in the most comfortable and receptive neighborhoods."[5]

Of Jesus, he observed, "He looked steadily with open eyes on life and death, He rejoiced in the lilies of the field, which today are, and tomorrow are cast into the fire. He loved as we have not learned to love. Yet he never clutched anxiously at life. He spent it freely, with urgency but without panic haste. He had only a little time. He was not anxious about the morrow."[6]

Dun was not a self-promoter, seeking neither higher office nor headlines. He spent most of his time working on issues of the growing diocese and largely left administration of the cathedral in the hands of its various deans. The Duns occupied a large stone house on the cathedral close. The house's original donor, a widow, lived in an upstairs apartment for several years. After Dun's retirement, the entire house became space for diocesan offices.

The building's fourth floor originally held four bedrooms for servants, a bath, and "a speaking tube to somewhere" plus a "dumb waiter, the creaky rope-operated type (perhaps the cook sent early tea up to the butler)," Mrs. Dun wrote. The third floor contained seven bedrooms and four baths. There was also a lower main floor, and a garden-level set of rooms that housed the bishop's office, plus a bath, kitchen, laundry, maid's sitting room, and two safes.

The Duns had little interest in Washington social life, although President and Mrs. Franklin Roosevelt invited them to the White House on occasion. Mrs. Dun recalled receiving a hand-delivered pink, scented note from a prominent Washington hostess who offered to give a dinner party for the Episcopal couple, inviting any people they wished to meet and as many guests as they liked. "Thank

---

4 Franklin D Roosevelt, The White House, to Angus Dunn, Cathedral Close (telegram), April 18, 1944, NCA.
5 *The Washington Diocese*, Vol. 31, No. 5, May 1962, 19.
6 *Ibid.*, 21.

her," the bishop responded, "and explain that my evenings are taken up getting to know the parishes." The woman's chauffer returned promptly with a second note, this time asking the bishop to baptize her grandson. Bishop Freeman had been such a good friend, she wrote, and she hoped the new bishop would be like him. Dun replied that he preferred not to take baptisms or weddings and believed local parish clergy should perform such ceremonies.

Mrs. Dun recalled attending the 1944 diocesan convention where some of the clergy and laity were unhappy that the bishop announced to those assembled that colored and white people should sit and eat together at the same tables, a new experience for some participants.

The Duns had the habit of bicycling through Northwest Washington on Saturday afternoons, then stopping at a Howard Johnson's restaurant where they habitually ordered "3-Ds," double-decker hamburgers then popular with teenagers. Sometimes they took a winter bicycle vacation in Beaufort, South Carolina, and habitually they spent a month each summer at a family farmhouse in Heath, Massachusetts, which Mrs. Dun described as "a lovely little New England village where eleven clergymen have moved to get away from other clergymen," one of whom was Dun's friend, Reinhold Niebuhr.

In September 1967, long after retiring, Dun was invited back to preach on the sixtieth anniversary of the laying of the Foundation Stone of Washington National Cathedral, after which a delegation of fundraisers would visit prospective Washington-area donors. Dun recalled the original gathering of ten thousand people on September 29, 1907. "They came on foot, in trolley cars, in handsome carriages with purple ribbons tied to the drivers' whips, in horse drawn drays crowded with seats, in automobiles which today would look to us like comic antiques." Their purpose was "to build a towering holy place in the midst of our capital city." He continued, "Cathedrals from the beginning were not related to the private piety of men or to the private concerns of birth, and marriage, and death," but were tied into "the total common life of great human communities; tied in with the victories and defeats of a city and a nation." Dun rejoiced at the building's positive impact on the wider community around it despite the Great Depression, two World Wars, the Cold War, Korea, and Vietnam, and pervasive racism in American life. "Despite all this, Washington Cathedral has received a high measure of acceptance."[7]

---

7 Angus Dun, Sermon, September 24, 1967 (NCA 5.7.9).

Call: "Cleveland 3500"

By the early 1950s the cathedral and the schools had moved from a single telephone to over fifty lines and a busy switchboard, employing three operators. The changes followed the gradual expansion of its offices. The original cathedral office of the early 1900s, with one telephone, occupied a single room in the third floor of a large house diagonally across the intersection of Massachusetts and Wisconsin Avenues. Next a modest building was erected on the cathedral grounds, and by 1917, it contained four or five offices, each with its own upright telephone.

In 1924 the space was expanded to hold the cathedral campaign office, relocated from an office on K Street. Soon there were thirty phones in operation on the close (including the schools), a switch-board was added, and a changeover to the dial system took place. Soon there were three full-time operators and a relief operator: the board was open from 7:30 am to 10:30 pm seven days a week. During World War II a line was installed to an air raid warden's post in the cathedral crypt, in case of a German air attack on Washington.

Dun as Author

Dun wrote in the days when major publishers usually carried several religious titles, and universities invited Episcopal bishops to present lecture series. In such a setting, Dun gave several talks on Christian unity at the University of Chicago in 1945, and another on basic Christian beliefs at Yale Divinity School in 1956. He had a clear, compelling prose style and used language easily accessible to lay audiences, without ever talking down to them.

In *Prospecting for a United Church,* written in 1945 but published in 1948, he began by listing 232 different churches in Washington, DC, including 32 Roman Catholic, 41 Methodist, 38 Episcopal, 24 Presbyterian, 38 Baptist, 7 Congregational, 7 Disciples, 21 Lutheran, 4 Orthodox, 5 Adventist, and 1 Unitarian. This was in an era before the proliferation of independent and Pentecostal churches. Apparently there were no mosques in Washington, and Dun did not include synagogues.[8]

---

8 Angus Dun, *Prospecting for a United Church* (New York: Harper & Bros, 1948): 5.

"The presence in our world of the many, divided churches is so established a fact that most professing Christian people take it for granted—they have known nothing else," he concluded.[9] This is a world "burdened with its own tragic divisions of race and class and nationality" to which religious divisions are now added. For Dun, "in the deepest sense the Church is a hidden reality known only to God," a "secret society whose members cannot know one another with assurance. This hidden church can not be identified as part of any existing church, though its members may be part of an existing structure or alive and well outside them."[10] This was the mid-1940s, and a mainstream denominational leader writing of a wider, unknown, or secret church would have been highly unusual and suspect in an era of denominational triumphalism.

What does the future hold? Dun noted, "Without the will for unity there can be no progress, but the will cannot live and move unless the mind and imagination reach out ahead and point the way."[11] Despite claims to the contrary, there never has been a unified institutional church that satisfactorily combined spiritual and structural elements in the early centuries of Christianity, Dun told audiences. Part of the problem facing churches is their insistence on others accepting a total package of beliefs as a prelude to unity, he said, including accepting a particular leader and form of organization, creeds, and other statements of faith, and distinct denominational ways of interpreting scriptures. "The vociferous reiteration of what are in important measure the products of past conflict will not lead to peace and reconciliation," he reflected. "That can only come if there is recognition of important elements of truth and value in the witness and the inheritance of those divided from us" and the recognition that different traditions can demonstrate important religious truths until now largely misinterpreted or ignored.[12]

Envisioning the possibility of a united church was a bit like talking about the contents of a house for which no blueprint yet exists, the bishop continued. Such an institution should combine both Catholic and Protestant elements. Prophets, saints, and active

---

9 *Ibid.*, 8.
10 *Ibid.*, 15.
11 *Ibid.*, 95.
12 *Ibid.*, 107.

devout members do not arise out of thin air, but emerge from living communities aware of their roots and history.

He concluded, "The Church desperately needs the Spirit and must provide in its life for constant openness to that free, spontaneous, creative Spirit who is not always the Comforter but often the Distracter," he said. No single institution could capture the Spirit and claim it as an exclusive possession. Instead, a possible institutional response might be "a central structure with other structures gathered around it, all forming a unity and with the internal channels of communication wide open. Or, to use political language, perhaps we should think in federal terms."[13]

Noble C. Powell, Dean, 1937–1941

Three different deans served the cathedral in the 1937 to 1950 period. All had impressive resumes, but none left lasting impressions on its institutional life. Noble Cilley Powell spent an inconclusive four years as dean after the departure of G.C.F. Bratenahl. He was born into a Baptist family that attended a different church each Sunday in Lowndesville, Alabama, where he was born on October 27, 1891.

Years later he served as chaplain to the University of Virginia and rector and builder of St. Paul's Memorial Church, Charlottesville and as rector of Emmanuel Church, Baltimore, before being installed as dean of National Cathedral on May 7, 1937. Powell simultaneously held the post of warden of the College of Preachers, and was twice elected as bishop of Louisiana, although he had asked that his name be removed from the list of candidates. He declined the post, and was later elected bishop of Maryland, a position he held from 1941 to 1963.

Powell came to the cathedral at an unsettled time. He followed the seventy-four-year-old Bratenahl, who had been retired (he said "deposed") after a lengthy period of ill health. A popular St. Louis cleric, Karl M. Block, rector of St. Michael and St. George parish, had been named as Bratenahl's successor, but declined the post. Block later enjoyed a long tenure as bishop of Los Angeles. Bishop Freeman had also considered another candidate, a leading Evangelical, Samuel Shoemaker, longtime rector of Satterlee's old parish, Calvary Church in New York City.

---

13 *Ibid.,* 107–109.

Powell, who "spent his youth on the old plantation," was the son of an impoverished cotton farmer. He began his professional career as an entomologist, investigating the spread of the boll weevil for the U.S. Department of Agriculture before attending the University of Virginia, from which he graduated Phi Beta Kappa in 1917.

Ordained a deacon in 1920 and a priest in 1921 after attending Virginia Theological Seminary, "Parson Powell," as he was popularly known, spent a decade as Episcopal chaplain at the University of Virginia and builder of St. Paul's Memorial Church. With university students, he made periodic rounds of several rural preaching stations, walking over muddy or snow-covered mountain roads, sometimes holding services by a mountain fire or corncrib in the Blue Ridge Mountains.

In 1931 he moved to Emmanuel Church, a struggling historic downtown Baltimore parish, which revived under his enthusiastic leadership. While in Baltimore, he was a prominent member of several civic associations and the standing committee of the Diocese of Maryland, and he was a trustee of the Maryland Home for Friendless Colored Children.

After Powell had spent six years in Baltimore, Bishop James E. Freeman nominated him for the cathedral deanship. "Dr. Powell does not come to Mount Saint Alban as a stranger," Freeman said on February 5, 1937. "He has long been associated with the College of Preachers as student, adviser, and teacher for some ten years. His deep and sympathetic understanding of the Cathedral and its allied institutions, fits him in a particular way to undertake the large responsibilities that are being conferred upon him."[14]

Powell stayed only four years as cathedral dean. Focused leadership, energy, and an affable manner characterized his brief administration. In his first annual report, read at the 1938 diocesan convention, he noted that construction at the cathedral had ceased for lack of funds. Both the St. John's and St. Mary's chapels were virtually completed, and work had progressed on the north porch, through the efforts of the Women's Committee.

"It will be one of the most beautiful, if not the most beautiful porch in Christendom," he wrote with characteristic enthusiasm. The

14 Press release, "The Reverend Noble C. Powell, D.D., Accepts Election as Dean of Washington Cathedral and Warden of the College of Preachers" (Washington, DC: Washington National Cathedral, February 5, 1937): 1.

Canterbury Pulpit would be ready for use on Easter, and state-of-the-art acoustical equipment was installed in the cathedral, with special microphones for readers and musicians. Powell noted the steadily increasing number of tourists visiting the cathedral and called their presence "one of the truly fine opportunities on this continent for the doing of a truly great piece of missionary work." Also, the cathedral provided teaching opportunities, especially at its 9:30 am Sunday service. "While attendance is small, comparatively, it is growing and we look forward to the time when this will be one of the best attended of our services."[15]

Cathedral clergy were sometimes called on to fill in for parish clergy on short notice, he noted, and parishes were welcome to make more frequent use of the cathedral for baptisms, weddings, and funerals, and for visits. The report set the tone for most of Powell's sermons and writings: clear, positive, and affirming. While he hoped to make the cathedral a national church, Powell was not a political preacher, had no special interest in the fine arts, and had limited success as a fundraiser.

However, the cathedral's Aeolian-Skinner organ was installed in his time, and the children's chapel was dedicated. The stone tomb of Lt. Norman Prince (1887–1916), a founder of the Lafayette Escadrille, a group of American flyers who fought with the French army in World War I, was completed. At the same time, Powell welcomed an old friend, Presiding Bishop Henry St. George Tucker of Virginia, to the cathedral. Beginning in 1940, the Episcopal Church designated a special seat in National Cathedral for the PB, whose administrative office remained in New York.

Powell and his wife were active supporters of the Allied effort during World War II, especially of the Bundles for Britain program. The cathedral governing board had been expanded to include Methodist, Baptist, and Presbyterian members, including John R. Mott, a Methodist ecumenical leader and Nobel Peace Prize recipient, and William Adams Brown, a prominent Presbyterian theologian. Powell also served as warden of the College of Preachers at a pivotal moment in its history. He had been a participant in the first conference held at the college in 1925, and by the time he became

---

15 Noble C. Powell, "The Cathedral and Its Mission, Report Read at the Annual Convention of the Diocese of Washington, 1938." NCA (129.11.3.).

its warden in 1937, nearly three thousand participants had attended conferences there.[16]

In early June 1941 Powell announced "with sinking heart and distress of mind" he had accepted election as bishop coadjutor of Maryland. In 1943 he became diocesan bishop, retiring in 1963.[17]

Powell's preference was to work behind the scenes on contentious issues like racial integration, unemployment, and economic issues. David Hein, his biographer, said of Powell, "Devoted to the Bible and the Book of Common Prayer, Powell was an orthodox, Mainstream, Trinitarian, Christian thinker, one not usually typed according to any of the prevailing schools of academic theology."[18] Attractive as a person, and a representative church figure of his times, he was well regarded but left few traces of his time spent in Washington.

John Wallace Suter, Dean, 1944–1950

> O God of peace, who hast taught us that in returning and rest we shall be saved, in quietness and in confidence shall be our strength: By the might of thy Spirit lift us, we pray thee, to thy presence, where we may be still and know that thou art God: through Jesus Christ our Lord. *Amen.*[19]

John Wallace Suter (1890–1977) was the fifth dean of Washington National Cathedral from November 1, 1944, to mid-1950. At this point he resigned to return to a parish in New England and to teach in the religion department of St. Paul's School, Concord, New Hampshire.

Suter was the enthusiastic choice of Bishop Angus Dun, who had known him as a seminary student, and his credentials for the post were impressive. He was secretary of the Standing Liturgical Commission of the Episcopal Church and custodian of the Book

---

16 *Ibid.,* 74–75.
17 "Resolution" of Cathedral Chapter, June 11, 1941." NCA (129.11.1).
18 David Hein, *Noble Powell and the Episcopal Establishment in the Twentieth Century* (Eugene, OR: Wipf & Stock, 2007): 5.
19 *Prayer Book and Hymnal, According to the Use of The Episcopal Church* (New York: Church Publishing Incorporated: 1986): 832.

of Common Prayer. He had held rectorships in New England and New York, and he was the author of several books and articles on prayer.

A specialist in the history and form of liturgies, he had a dignified manner of conducting services, and a carefully cadenced, musical voice. His "Prayer for Quiet Confidence" (above) was widely used in the Episcopal Church, and was carved on the wall opposite the cathedral's Chapel of the Good Shepherd. His grandfather had been a clipper ship captain in the China trade who had been around the world seven times.

Suter attended Groton School and was a 1911 graduate of Harvard University, the son of an Episcopal priest who was custodian of the Book of Common Prayer before him. The custodian kept the official version of the Prayer Book and answered any questions about it in the period between General Conventions. Suter attended Union Theological Seminary in New York and graduated from Episcopal Theological School in Cambridge in 1914.

Ordained a deacon in 1914, he became a priest in 1915. He also served as rector of a Boston parish and became head of the Educational Department of the Diocese of Massachusetts, then head of the Department of Religious Education of the national church until becoming rector of the Church of the Epiphany on Murray Hill in New York City in 1932. Dr. Suter and his wife, Margaret Sturgis Suter, had three children. The first Mrs. Suter died in Washington in 1949, and a year later the dean married the woman who had been his secretary from 1945 to 1949, Alice Hoyt Elmer, at St. James' Church, New York.

Suter came to the cathedral at a difficult time in its history. His two immediate predecessors had served short tenures. Noble C. Powell had left to become bishop of Maryland. The next dean, ZeBarney Phillips, was a former rector of the Church of the Epiphany and Chaplain to the U.S. Senate. He died on May 10, 1942, after less than six months in office, from being given a wrongly filled medical prescription. Phillips, who suffered from kidney colic, had taken a morphine-like highly addictive drug, Dilaudid, which the pharmacist had erroneously compounded at fifteen times the prescribed prescription strength. The dosage called for fifteen grains, which the pharmacist misread as fifteen grams, a dose that killed Phillips after two days.

Suter's deanship took place in the final years of World War II and the immediate postwar years, which meant that fundraising possibilities were limited and much of the cathedral's programming was directed toward the military and their families. Shortly after his election, Suter presided over the funeral for Field Marshal Sir John Dill, head of Britain's Joint Staff Mission during World War II.

While at the cathedral, Suter saw work on the south transept progress, several stained glass windows installed, and work completed on a new office building. He was known as a careful, detailed administrator. A pension system for lay employees was instituted, the work of the Cathedral Choral Society advanced, and the society staged its first public concert, performing Verdi's *Requiem* in memory of Dean Phillips.

Suter retired from the cathedral at age sixty to become rector of St. Andrew's Church, Hopkinton, New Hampshire, and to teach at St. Paul's School in Concord. The dean was a reflective, thoughtful preacher and pastor. He was well liked by congregations, but not a forceful presence. He reportedly was highly disappointed that the cathedral did not designate him as dean emeritus, but carried on a lengthy and detailed correspondence with some cathedral clergy for several years over Anglican liturgies and worship customs.

Murder in the Cathedral Library: Catherine Cooper Reardon

Between eight and nine on the morning of March 1, 1944, an assistant librarian, Catherine Cooper Reardon, thirty-seven, was choked and beaten to death with a fireplace log in the cathedral library. Her partially clad body was discovered a day later, stuffed under steam pipes in a subbasement room, after colleagues spotted her purse and neatly folded sweater near her desk. She had lived with her parents in a nearby apartment building, at 3715 Woodley Road, and had failed to return home after work.

On March 3 police arrested cathedral handyman Julius Fisher, thirty-two, in "an obscure restaurant" in Northeast Washington. Fisher, who quit school in third grade, pleaded guilty to murdering Reardon. She had criticized him to the cathedral verger for poor janitorial work in the library, allegedly calling him a "black nigger."

He attacked her, first trying to choke her, and when she continued screaming, struck her repeatedly on the head with a piece of wood, fracturing her skull. Then he attempted to clean up blood droppings from furniture and carpets and stuffed the body in a basement closet under some heating pipes. There was no sign of sexual molestation. After a trial and a failed attempt to gain a retrial, Fisher was executed on December 20, 1946, in the District of Columbia's electric chair, the last person to be executed in the District of Columbia.

Reardon had graduated from the College of William and Mary in 1927, taught English and French at a Virginia high school until 1932, and then became an assistant librarian at St. John's College, Annapolis, until she began work as a volunteer librarian at the cathedral eight years before her death. Eventually she was given $20 a month as an honorarium and received excellent recommendations for other librarian positions for which she was a candidate.

The Supreme Court declined to grant Fisher a new trial.[20] The court's opinion denying a retrial was written by Justice Stanley Forman Reed; Justices Felix Frankfurter, Frank Murphy, and Wiley B. Rutledge argued that Fisher deserved a new trial, but it was not granted. The case attracted considerable attention in the legal community over the possible use or misuse of an insanity plea defense, and Richard Wright drew on it as the subject matter of his short story "The Man Who Killed a Shadow."[21]

Paul Callaway (1939–1977), Third Organist and Choirmaster, Director of the Cathedral Choral Society

Paul Callaway of Grand Rapids, Michigan, was named third organist and choirmaster at National Cathedral in 1939 after a widespread search. The diminutive bachelor was an organ student at St. Thomas', New York, with the renowned organist and church musician T. Tertius Noble, and had already played a favorably received concert

---

20 328 U.S. 463, *Fisher vs. United States*, No. 122, Rehearing Denied October 14, 1946.

21 Micheal Fabre, *The World of Richard Wright* (Jackson, MS: University Press of Mississippi, 1985): 108–122.

on the cathedral's Skinner organ during the spring of 1939. He had also studied with Leo Sowerby, whom he would bring to the cathedral as director of the College of Church Musicians in 1962, and briefly with Marcel Dupré in Paris. Callaway had an affinity for French organ music and made a recording of major French composers. Short of stature, he had wooden risers attached to the organ pedals so he could reach them with his feet.

Callaway (1909–1995) spent thirty-eight years at National Cathedral. An active musical entrepreneur, he founded the Cathedral Choral Society in 1941, and was first musical director of the Opera Society of Washington in 1956. At the cathedral he also conducted the choir, darting about the podium in his purple robe, sometimes jumping high off the ground to signal the entrance of a chorus.

Born in Atlanta, Illinois, in August 1909, he attended the Missouri Military Academy, then Westminster College in Fulton, Missouri, before heading to New York at age twenty to study with Noble and David McK Williams. Callaway had been at St. Mark's, Grand Rapids, when he was invited to Washington to take over the cathedral music program. His stated goal was "to make of Washington Cathedral a citadel for glorious church music," which he did.

As founding director of the Cathedral Choral Society, the entrepreneurial Callaway gave the first American performance of Britten's *War Requiem* and Bernstein's *Chichester Psalms,* brought concert operas to Washington, and improved the quality of Washington musical life through his widespread East Coast and midwestern musical contacts. At the cathedral, Callaway launched a continuing series of organ recitals, a spring music festival, and presented many choral works by American composers.

Initially his choir was composed of twenty choirboys and nine older male singers. "He was tough, remote, supremely dedicated, and he produced good results," former chorister John H. Shenefield recalled. "He would never have won a popularity contest—that was not his style—but he was an excellent musician, a complete professional, and he made us sing better than we thought we were capable of—and all of us admired him enormously."[22]

---

22 Quoted in Yang, 44. Yang devoted pages 39 to 62 of her dissertation to Callaway.

Then World War II came, and Callaway spent three and a half years leading an army band from August 1942 until March 1946, when he returned to the cathedral. Paul Hume, music critic for *The Washington Post*, recalled Callaway's initial concert on his return: "From the opening of the G Minor Fantasy and Fugue by Bach to the thunderous closing of Liszt's Fantasy and Fugue of 'Ad nos ad saluterem undam' it remains one of the great concerts of my experience."[23]

Gradually Callaway added boy and male choir members as funds allowed, and took responsibility for the senior choir, with his assistant, Richard Wayne Dirkson, directing the junior choir. Beginning in 1949 the cathedral launched a series of fifteen-minute Sunday morning radio broadcasts, and in 1953 started televising its Christmas and Easter services nationally. Church choirs and choral groups from high schools and colleges throughout America were invited to present Sunday afternoon programs at the cathedral. The Great Organ was rebuilt and expanded beginning in 1957 and in 1989 the console was rebuilt and a computer system installed to store various combinations of stops. Callaway was a leader in Washington music life, and in the 1971 opening season of the Kennedy Center conducted Handel's *Messiah* in the new concert hall. He retired as cathedral organist and choirmaster in 1977, stayed on as director of the Cathedral Choral Society until 1984, and died at his home of cancer on March 21, 1995. Upon his retirement, he was succeeded by his longtime assistant, Richard Wayne Dirksen, a skilled conductor and composer of hymn tunes and anthems, who later served in a number of program direction positions at the cathedral.

In the first half century of its evolution, the cathedral's music program expanded from a traditional English cathedral sound and repertoire to one programming major new works both by European and American composers. The organ moved from becoming a serviceable instrument to accompany hymns to one for concerts, and by the 1950s musicians were invited from America and abroad to perform as soloists or in worship services. The cathedral also attempted a long-dreamed-of project, creation of a college of church musicians that—should it work—would leave a permanent institutional base for musical advancement.

---

23 Quoted in Yang, 48.

Theodore and Cynthia Wedel, the Episcopal Church's Leadership Couple of the 1950s and 1960s

Theodore Otto and Cynthia Clark Wedel were the Episcopal Church's leadership couple of the 1950s and 1960s. From his base as warden of the College of Preachers at Washington National Cathedral, Theodore served three terms as president of the Episcopal Church's House of Clerical and Lay Deputies, and was a nationally known speaker and author of several books, including *The Coming Great Church* and *The Gospel in a Strange, New World*. Cynthia became president of both the National Council of Churches and the World Council of Churches and was the author of several carefully prepared adult educational studies for parish use. The topics ranged from the impact of Alvin Toffler's *Future Shock* to women's ordination, to the meaning of Thanksgiving for children, to the role of the church in public policy debates on women in the workplace.

Both Wedels were skilled at working with large organizations. He was a gifted writer. She was a trained psychologist, able to present unsettling issues in a nonthreatening manner. Between them, the Wedels raised most of the major issues confronting the institutional church in their time. Theodore Wedel (1892–1970) called his religious journey "A Pilgrimage to Canterbury from the Shores of the Black Sea."

Cynthia Wedel's (1908–1986) early geographic horizons were more distinctly midwestern American. Born in Dearborn, Michigan, she graduated from Northwestern University with a B.A. degree in 1929 and an M.A. in 1930, and held increasingly responsible Christian educational positions, moving to New York City in 1934 as the National Secretary for Youth Work. The occupant of the next office was a widower sixteen years older than Cynthia, the National Secretary for College Work, Theodore O. Wedel. After five years of collaborating on conferences and publications, they were married by Presiding Bishop Henry St. George Tucker in May 1939 in the chapel of the Episcopal Church's national headquarters at 281 Fourth Avenue.

Four years later they moved to Washington, where for seventeen years Theodore served in positions at the College of Preachers and National Cathedral. Cynthia, calling herself "the busiest volunteer in Washington," worked with both the Red Cross and the Girl Scouts and completed a doctorate in psychology at George Washington University (1957). She became a clear, measured voice for women's ordination, and a commentator on the moral aspects of public policy issues. Along with her friend Eleanor Roosevelt, she was a member of the Presidential Commission on the Status of Women from 1961 to 1963.

Theodore's Journey, "From the Black Sea to Canterbury"

The Black Sea part of Theodore Wedel's heritage was an all-embracing German-language Mennonite religious tradition. His father, a farmer and educator, was the first president of Bethel College, a Mennonite college in Newton, Kansas, where Theodore was born in 1892. But the Mennonite story began centuries earlier, in sixteenth-century Holland. Dutch Mennonites believed in a free church, pacifism, adult baptism, and the rejection of oaths.

Persecuted in Holland, the Mennonites moved to East Prussia, where they were offered asylum and large tracts of marshland they soon turned into fertile farmland. Again persecuted for their pacifism, in the 1780s the Mennonites moved to Russia, where they were welcomed and offered asylum by Catherine the Great. More than ten thousand Mennonites moved from Germany to Russia in the late eighteenth century, and built a thriving community near the Black Sea. But life in the Russian Empire became increasingly troubled, and by the late nineteenth century the Ukrainian Mennonites had sent an advance party to America. They had heard of an offer to settle along expanding railroad lands in Kansas, Nebraska, and Minnesota.[24]

Wedel's parents were among the sixteen thousand Mennonites that moved from Russia to "the new Canaan of America" in the 1870s and brought with them the "Turkey Red" winter wheat that was their staple in the Ukraine.[25] The industrious Mennonites were known for their entrepreneurial spirit, soil and water conservation methods, and willingness to adopt the latest farm machinery.

---

24 *Theodore Otto Wedel, An Anthology,* ed., William S. Lea (Cincinnati: Forward Movement Miniature Books, 1972): 11–13. An extensive source of information on the Wedels are the oral interviews conducted by John T. Mason, Jr. for the Bishop Henry Knox Sherrill Oral History Project, Oral History Research Office, Columbia University. A copy of the two-hundred-page transcript is contained in the National Cathedral Archives.
25 Lea, 13.

Theodore's father, Cornelius (1860–1910), was fluent in both German and Russian, learned English, obtained a college degree, and attended a German-speaking Presbyterian seminary in New Jersey.

In his thirties Cornelius was named president of Bethel College in Newton, Kansas, the earliest Mennonite college of higher education in America.[26] Theodore was one of three siblings who grew up on a college campus. He had a gift for languages and music. German was spoken at home, and Latin and Greek came easily for him. He also had a fine singing voice and skills as a pianist and organist.

The New Organist Discovers Anglican Chant and the Book of Common Prayer

It was the Anglican liturgy that quickly and unexpectedly brought Wedel to the Episcopal Church, a discovery that was not without cost. "It meant breaking ties with a church family deeply anchored in loyalty to a tradition . . . which had witnessed to a corporate community life of Christian brotherhood seldom . . . equaled anywhere," he wrote.[27]

The Episcopal Church in his small Kansas town needed a new organist on short notice. Wedel, age eighteen, volunteered and was given a quick course in Anglican worship by a church member. Here were prayers in cadenced English, musical responses and chants, and the celebrant in colorful vestments leading worship. "There arrived also a sudden illumination that I was experiencing something rich and strange, something which satisfied a long felt, though never consciously realized, hunger and need." Additionally, the church "was more than a sect. It was not easy for me at first to understand and appreciate the difference, since the little flock of Episcopalians in our Kansas town was . . . far from being the local habitation of a national, let alone a state Church."[28] In various writings over the decades ahead he drew on both the powerful sense of community experienced from his Mennonite heritage and the sense of mystery

---

26 Keith L. Sprunger, "Cornelius H. Wedel and Oswald H. Wedel: Two Generations of Mennonite Historians," *Mennonite Life* (December 1981): cover and 16–27.

27 "Theodore O. Wedel" in *Modern Canterbury Pilgrims, And Why They Chose the Episcopal Church,* ed., James A. Pike (New York: Morehouse-Gorham Co., 1956): 89–99.

28 *Ibid.,* 96–97.

offered in Anglican worship to raise possibilities for an ecumenical church of the future, to which he believed scattered Christendom was called.

Further Education, Ordained Ministry, a Move to New York

Wedel's father died suddenly of pneumonia in May 1910, leaving the youth with major challenges to continue his education beyond high school. Another youth from Newton, Kansas, had entered Oberlin College, and Theodore applied there, found a job waiting on tables, and sang in the glee club. With his gift for languages he majored in Latin and Greek, and graduated Phi Beta Kappa in 1914.

Next he took an M.A. in classics at Harvard University in 1915, and was confirmed in the Episcopal Church at the Church of the Advent, a high church bastion on Beacon Hill. Believing that jobs for classics majors would be hard to come by, he switched to English and Yale University, where he completed a Ph.D. in 1918. He lived a spartan existence in an unheated New Haven attic room, and subsisted on free soup, bread, and milk in the college dining hall. His doctoral thesis was on "The Mediaeval Attitude Toward Astrology, Particularly in England."[29]

Wedel was drafted into the U.S. Army in 1918. Commissioned a second lieutenant in the Coastal Artillery, he was sent to a base near San Diego and served as an instructor until the Armistice was signed in November 1918. Meanwhile, in 1917 he had married a young Mennonite woman who attended both Bethel and Oberlin colleges, Elizabeth Cornelia Ewert, the daughter of a successful banker from Mountain Lake, Minnesota. They had two children, Theodore Carl (b. 1919) and Gertrude (b. 1924).[30]

After leaving the army, Wedel held positions in the English departments at the University of Texas, Yale, and Carleton College. Theodore wanted to stay in the East, preferably at Yale. Elizabeth wanted to move back to Minnesota. Carleton, with its high academic standing, was their compromise location. While in Northfield, Minnesota, he resumed his leadership role in a small, struggling Episcopal community.

---

29 Theodore Otto Wedel, *The Mediaeval Attitude Toward Astrology, Particularly in England*, Yale Studies in English (New Haven, CT: Yale University Press, 1920).
30 Lea, 19–20.

In 1928 the bishop of Minnesota suggested that Wedel consider ordination. Wedel met with the diocese's examining chaplains, took the deacon's examination, and passed it with flying colors. Next he moved his family to Marburg, Germany, for a sabbatical year where he studied theology, after which he returned to Carleton, and was ordained in May 1931. Elizabeth died of cancer after a long illness during this time. Her husband now faced life alone with two small children.

A total career shift came Wedel's way in 1934 when he was offered the post of National Secretary for College Work for the Episcopal Church, headquartered in New York City. Wedel travelled all over the country, lecturing, meeting college faculty, and recruiting chaplains.

Warden of the College of Preachers, Canon Chancellor of Washington National Cathedral, President of the House of Deputies

The next and most productive phase of Wedel's church career came when he was offered the post of director of studies (1943) then warden of the College of Preachers in Washington, DC, where he stayed until retirement in 1960. At the same time, he was canon chancellor of Washington National Cathedral, loosely responsible for governance of the cathedral schools. He also was president of the standing committee of the Diocese of Washington for nearly twelve years and president of the House of Clerical and Lay Deputies of the Episcopal Church from 1952 to 1961.

The Wedel years were a golden age for the College of Preachers. The college was founded in the 1920s in attractive quarters on the cathedral grounds. Its intent was to elevate the standard of preaching in the Episcopal Church through weeklong conferences. Ten to twenty clergy would gather to hear leading preachers and theologians, and have their own sermons critiqued. A spacious commons room, monastery-like refectory, chapel, and large lending library were some of the college's features, plus houses for the warden and director of studies on the cathedral close.

Themed conferences were about Preaching the Liturgical Year, The Church and the Inner City, The Gospel and Main Street, and similar subjects. For decades the college was a catalyst of intellectual life within the Episcopal Church. But gradually, after Wedel's time, continuing education money for clergy dried up, conference times were shortened to a few days, and regional seminaries and universities offered competing programs. Eventually the College of Preachers closed its doors.

The 1940s and 1950s were also Wedel's most productive decades as a writer. He turned out volumes like *The Coming Great Church* (1945), *The Christianity of Main Street* (1950), *The Pulpit Rediscovers Theology* (1956), *The Gospel in a Strange New World* (1963), and "Exposition of Ephesians" in *The Interpreter's Bible* (1953). At the same time, he was much in demand nationally as a preacher, conference leader, writer, and editor.

Wedel saw his Episcopal Church work as integrally related to the then emerging ecumenical movement. He became chair of the department of evangelism of the World Council of Churches, a delegate to the Faith and Order Conference in Lund, Sweden (1952), a participant in the World Council of Churches assembly in Evanston, Illinois (1954), and an attendee at the international assemblies of the World Council of Churches in New Delhi, Uppsala, and elsewhere around the world.[31]

His work earned him the title "the Senior Presbyter of the American Church." His impressive leadership skills allowed him to moderate anything from a small clergy gathering at the College of Preachers to the larger church assembled in the House of Clerical and Lay Deputies gathering in Boston, Honolulu, and Miami Beach.

Sometimes his rhetorical flourishes obscured the details of his intended message. For instance, he saw the interaction of world religions as "a gigantic battle," one of conflict and confrontation among world religions. "Buddhism is on the march. Hinduism is on the march. So, also, is the great world of Islam. . . . I sometimes think that the whole of the Christian Church ought to go on a war-footing."[32] At times his hortatory style, peppered with rhetorical questions, made readers wonder where the author was headed. Still, his generosity of spirit was never lacking, nor the breadth of perspec-

---

31 *Ibid.*, 22–29.
32 Theodore O. Wedel, "Our Reason For Being," in *This Church of Ours, The Episcopal Church: What It Is and What It Teaches About Living* (Greenwich, CT: Seabury Press, 1958): 123.

tive demonstrated in his constant flow of books, articles, and conference presentations.

The Coming Great Church

It was the theme of "the coming Great Church" that wove its way into much of Theodore's later writing. He drew on the powerful sense of community that came from his Mennonite heritage, and the Anglican middle way, that had roots in both Catholic and Protestant traditions. This would be the Great Church of the ages, with its continuity of saints, liturgies, and symbols that were visible in the smallest, isolated chapel and in a large cathedral.

Reconciliation was a constant theme in Wedel's writing. There could be no prospects of church unity or the church making a deep impact in society without it. "One of the great word symbols of the New Testament can loom large on our horizon now—the word 'reconciliation.' Only as neighbor is reconciled with neighbor can men learn again to live with one another."[33]

He was an unabashed supporter of the ecumenical movement. For many Anglicans ecumenism meant cautiously inviting a Presbyterian or Methodist colleague to preach during the annual Week of Christian Unity, but Wedel wanted to move beyond that. He acknowledged that ecumenical theology was in its infancy and that "Reunion will be endlessly costly. None of us as yet fully want it despite generous lip-service to ecumenical ideals."[34] He summarized his position in words that could have appeared in any of his works:

> Modern nomadism has torn us from our moorings. We are, most of us, lonely and weak individual Christians, lost in the giant impersonal monopolies of economic and political imperialisms. We hunger, not merely for the Faith of our fathers, but for fellowship in that Faith. We hunger for brotherhood. We hunger for personal relationships. The Church has all these gifts. Where else shall we find them?[35]

33 Theodore O. Wedel, *The Gospel in a Strange New World* (Philadelphia: Westminster Press, 1958): 42.

34 Theodore O. Wedel, *The Coming Great Church, Essays on Church Unity* (New York: Macmillan Co., 1945): 3.

35 *Ibid.*, 11.

Wedel saw the entire church animated by the Holy Spirit, blowing like the wind among a crowd of people who could neither describe its origins or direction. To illustrate the point he spoke of esprit de corps, a telling example of which would be the crowd at a Yale football game. The whole stadium could be brought to its feet by a dazzling play, as if by a mighty wind exuding power and presence. Such spirit could not be called forth or generated, it came totally without the asking. An earnest outsider could not claim it, but an undeserving Yale undergraduate sitting in the stands would possess a portion of such spirit without trying to. Such spirit was given, not earned. Wedel was careful not to push the analogy too far, but it was one he often returned to.[36]

The problem of harmonizing Reformation ministries with the historic Catholic Church remained complicated, but not impossible, he believed. If the Reformation churches were part of the wider Church of Christ, then their ministries were priestly ministries, and must be respected as such, he argued, and invoked an image of the Little and the Great Church, both having distinct claims to ministry and sacraments. Wedel left it there.

He did not offer specific proposals for wider church unity, but offered a generously open reading of an ecumenical future that remained on the table and relatively little responded to a half-century later. But he did offer three suggestions: that the purely sacerdotal doctrine of the apostolic succession be abandoned; that recognition be given to the fullness of nonepiscopal ministries in the wider church; and that the historic episcopate be redefined and broadened in such a way that it would be acceptable to evangelicals.[37]

Revisiting Wedel's writings decades after they were published is to revisit most of the questions separating Catholics and Protestants, to which major questions of race and gender have been added. His generosity of spirit, while still adhering to what could be labeled an orthodox, historically and liturgically grounded Anglican viewpoint, left him as an important voice in ecumenical thought. "The coming Great Church" he wrote about is yet to arrive, but the markers Wedel laid down for its possible emergence remain as relevant today as they were when he first devised them.

---

36 *Ibid.*, 63.
37 *Ibid.*, 155–156.

The Contribution of Cynthia Clark Wedel

Cynthia Clark Wedel was trained as a psychologist and as a specialist in Christian education. She frequently employed the skills acquired in these disciplines as she rose steadily to become the most influential woman in the Episcopal Church during the middle decades of the twentieth century.

Born in Dearborn, Michigan, and the daughter of a civil engineer, she held two degrees in history from Northwestern University, and soon after graduation in 1930 became Christian education director at her home parish, St. Luke's, an active suburban church in Evanston, Illinois. A few years later she moved to New York City as first a field worker and then head of the national church's youth programs, a position she held after her 1939 marriage.

The Wedels moved to Washington, DC in 1943 and Cynthia became an active volunteer with the Girl Scouts and the American Red Cross. She also taught religion at National Cathedral School and later at American University. In 1957 she completed work on a doctorate in psychology at George Washington University; her thesis was on "A Study of Measurement in Group Dynamics Laboratories," reflecting her work in the group dynamics movement. Wedel also served as associate director of the Center for a Voluntary Society of the National Training Laboratories, and head of the Church Executive Development Board, a church management-training program.

Wedel was no stranger to controversy, and her leadership roles intersected with periods of major challenge in American life, including the women's liberation movement, the Vietnam War, and racial unrest. When she was elected president of the National Council of Churches in December 1969, her opponent was the black nationalist minister Arthur B. Cleague, pastor of the Shrine of the Black Madonna Church in Detroit, Michigan. Wedel received 387 of the 480 votes cast. Cleague asked her to withdraw in his favor. She replied, "I deplore discrimination against black people and have worked hard to eliminate discrimination, and I regard my election as a belated recognition of their importance."[38]

---

38 "Cynthia Wedel Loses Fight With Cancer," Episcopal News Service, Alexandria, Virginia, September 4, 1986, internet version.

Elsewhere she stated:

> As a psychologist I know very well that a fundamental
> human need is . . . security. . . . Because change is so
> threatening to many people who found their security
> in familiar places, people, customs, and behavior, it is
> no wonder there are strong coalitions . . . who oppose
> changes in family life, the role of women, education, eco-
> nomic arrangements and other areas of both personal and
> common life. There is only one source of hope in this
> situation—and that source is God . . . It is my belief that
> God—who is love—wanted love in God's creation.[39]

On the then-controversial issues of women's ordination, her
approach was to stress that the church's ministry would gain from
the contributions of ordained members of both genders, without
neglecting the equally important ministry of the laity. "As far as
we know, from the earliest days of Christianity, men and women
received precisely the same baptism," she once observed.

In addition to serving as the first woman president of the
National Council of Churches from 1969 to 1972, she also served
as president of the World Council of Churches from 1975 to 1983.
In the time before the Episcopal Church accepted women's ordination, she held every position available to a laywoman, including president of the Episcopal Women of the Diocese of Washington from
1955 to 1961, and as a member of the national church's Executive
Council.

In 1961 President John F. Kennedy appointed Wedel, along
with her friend and fellow Episcopalian Eleanor Roosevelt, to the
Commission on the Status of Women, where she served until 1963.
She was also one of three Protestant women invited to attend as
observers at Vatican II by the Roman Catholic Church's Secretariat
for Promoting Christian Unity.[40]

---

39 "A Moment in Ecumenical History, Wedel's September Song: A Wise and
     Gentle Voice," National Council of Churches U.S.A. internet website.
40 "Cynthia Wedel Dies; Directed Church Councils," August 30, 1986, From
     Times Wire Services, internet version.

The Church and Social Action

Among the church's most consistent voices in raising issues about health and welfare needs, women's employment, citizenship, and civic participation, Wedel wrote and lectured extensively on these subjects for over three decades. Some people might criticize the church as being "too political," but Wedel answered such issues frontally in a 1970 article entitled "The Church and Social Action."[41] She began by noting the changes she recognized in herself in considering the church's role in political life since she graduated from college in 1929 during the Great Depression.

The issues then were basic survival, employment, and finding food, but they changed in the 1930s. Public health care and preventative medicine, education and job creation, and decent housing—government responsibility for basic human welfare—was now seen as more important than simple survival. She noted that the contemporary generation of church members were far better educated than their predecessors, but spent too much time on intra-church feuds. This was costly, for it left mainline churches divided and ineffective, and gave the field on many public policy issues to fundamentalist and radical right wing voices.[42]

For the wider church to be an effective voice on social issues, its members needed to be both better informed on policy questions and more effective as activists, a topic she addressed in "Citizenship—Our Christian Concern." She urged Christians to identify the root causes of slums, juvenile delinquency, substandard schools, and inadequate health care. Speaking out on local issues, attending meetings of governmental bodies, supporting officials that do their jobs well, and removing corrupt and incompetent officials were all part of responsible Christian citizenship.

Political power, she continued, began in the smallest local units, specifically in the 150,000 local precincts, where most governmental business was transacted. Register to vote, know the elected representatives of government and their voting records, and be in contact with representatives, she urged. "Any measure which has the

---

41 Cynthia Wedel, "The Church and Social Action," *The Christian Century*, LXXXVI, No. 26 (August 12, 1970): 959–962.

42 *Ibid.*, 961–962.

enthusiastic backing of some citizens has a very good chance of being written into law," she wrote. "The problem arises when groups of people who represent a rather narrow segment of society, of a very special self-interest, organize and make their wishes known to legislation, while others, whose interests may be more broad, or less selfish, do nothing."[43]

In 1954 she laid out a comprehensive statement on "Health and Welfare Needs of the Nation and the Place of the Church Agency" in a talk for the Department of Social Relations of the Episcopal Diocese of New York. Despite America being the world's richest, strongest nation, millions of its citizens were unable to maintain a decent standard of living and have access to basic health care. The handicapped, blind, deaf, and crippled faced additional burdens. She cited as especially important the problems of rising juvenile delinquency, the rehabilitation of the physically handicapped, a rapidly aging population, and the problems of the mentally ill.[44]

She positively cited the Episcopal Church's support of more than two hundred health and welfare agencies nationally with annual budgets totaling more than $40 million, serving over twenty-five thousand people daily. While encouraging of such church service agencies, she also noted that many had outmoded organizational structures and failed to keep current with medical and social welfare developments. The church, she continued, should keep constant ties with such agencies and not allow them to sink or swim on their own.

A few years later, she introduced the issues of *Employed Women and the Church* (1959) in an adult educational unit published by the National Council of Churches of Christ. This study focused on two special issues, "The Situation Today" and "The Changing Family." Noting that by 1957 the word "womanpower" had been added to "manpower," she wrote that one-third of all women fourteen years of age and over were employed. Better health and increased longevity of women meant that the largest group of women in the labor force was women over forty years of age, many of whom worked from economic necessity. Additionally, women were moving increasingly into

---

43 Cynthia Wedel, *Citizenship—Our Christian Concern* (New York: United Church Women, n.d.): 7–10.
44 Cynthia Wedel, *Health and Welfare Needs of the Nation and The Place of the Church Agency,* Department of Christian Social Relations, Diocese of New York (New York: Diocese of New York, 1954): 5.

professional fields beyond what was traditionally described as "women's work"—nursing, teaching, office work, and food services.[45]

Such change brought with it changing roles for men and women, and for the family, but the sense of freedom enjoyed by women was also marked by tensions. "The real answer probably lies in the mutuality of the decision for the wife to go to work. If both agree about it, and face honestly the hazards in the situation, the two-income home can be as happy as the traditional one. If either husband or wife enters into the plan reluctantly at the insistence of the other, it can be fraught with peril for their relationship."[46]

The Ordination of Women, "Not 'If' But 'When'"

During the early 1970s Cynthia Wedel emerged as a leading mainstream voice for the ordination of women in the Episcopal Church. As on other issues, like race and social justice, she was a consistent voice, steady, but without bitterness or a confrontational manner. Her basic position was that the entire church and its ministry gains from the ordination of women; it is not an either/or question, but one whose time has come.

She first raised the issue in a carefully crafted forward to a 1973 book on *Women Priests in the Catholic Church?*[47] In it she said that a way must be found for Anglicans and Catholics to seriously confront the issue, mindful that both traditions share the historic orders of bishops, priests, and deacons, even if the Roman Catholic Church denies the validity of Anglican orders. She also acknowledged an Anglican desire to proceed cautiously because it might disrupt relations with Rome. But since Rome proved to be implacable on many questions, the position failed to gain traction. At the same time she noted that while the Roman Church has appealed to history to oppose the ordination of women, in fact there was ample documentation that a contrary view was sometimes voiced. "Even in the early times and among Church Fathers, there was far less unanimity

---

45 Cynthia Wedel, *Employed Women and The Church,* Study and Discussion Guide for Church Groups (New York: National Council of the Churches of Christ in the U.S.A.: 1959): 8, 15.

46 *Ibid.,* 35.

47 Haye van der Meer, *Women Priests in the Catholic Church? A Theological-Historical Investigation,* trans., Arlene and Leonard Swidler (Philadelphia: Temple University Press, 1973).

than is assumed. Many of the often quoted statements against women were made in debates attacking heretical groups and not at all in the context of discussions on the place of women."[48] If the church is the Bride of Christ, she suggested, what does that say about the place of women in its structure? "Men and women are more than simply biological entities—they comprise body, mind, and spirit" and should be dealt with in their fullness."[49]

A few years later, she and coauthor Robert Kevin revisited the historical and biblical arguments on women's ordination, citing Archbishop William Temple's 1916 remark, "Personally I want to see women ordained to the priesthood." As for Jesus, "He showed amazing respect for women. They were included among His followers; were the first witnesses to His resurrection; and are frequently mentioned by St. Paul as his fellow-workers in the early Church."[50] "No one who favors the ordination of women wants women to *replace* men in the priesthood. It is the wholeness of the Church, the fullness of the image of God, which many feel can come only when all of us—male and female—are truly one in Christ Jesus."[51]

The Hale Memorial Lectures at Seabury-Western Theological Seminary, Evanston, Illinois, represented her most extensive discussion of the subject. In the talks, Wedel drew on her training in both history and psychology. She challenged readers:

> If the Church, especially in the Western world, could witness to the possibilities of a new fellowship of human kind on a world-wide scale through its words and actions, instead of being absorbed in looking backward and fighting to preserve its old institutional forms, it might indeed become a powerful instrument in God's hands. The church needs to proclaim and demonstrate the rightness of pluralism and of an equality which does not require conformity or sameness.[52]

---

48 *Ibid.,* viii.
49 *Ibid.,* viii.
50 Robert Kevin and Cynthia Wedel, *The Ordination of Women:* Cincinnati: Forward Movement Publications, 1975, 3–4.
51 *Ibid.,* 5.
52 Cynthia C. Wedel, *Reflections on Ministry, Implications of Personhood, Gender, and Vocation,* The Hale Lectures for 1976 (Cincinnati: Forward Movement Publications, 1976): 11–12.

What does the ordination of women bring to the church? It means moving beyond an outmoded and fundamentally unchristian idea of authority and hierarchy, and a distorted idea of ministry, basically alienated from its potential global constituency. Also, the meaning of lay ministry would be enhanced and would no longer be limited to "women's work," but would result in a shift in the church's understanding of what constituted ministry. Men and women would bring different gifts, but they would complement and supplement one another and enrich the life of congregations and the wider church.[53] She saw no rush toward ordination once the priesthood was opened to women, because it would take time for discernment and preparation for ordained ministry. (Ordination was not a goal she ever sought for herself.)

The collective contributions of Theodore and Cynthia Wedel to national and international church life included major leadership roles in denominational and ecumenical groups. Deeply probing gospel and theological issues, both wrote with clarity for wider popular audiences; Cynthia especially was skilled at raising controversial issues like racism, technological change, and the place of women in ordained ministry in a cogent but nonthreatening way.

Both were tall and impressive in bearing. Theodore had the finely chiseled features of a cleric whose portrait could have come from the walls of an old university. Cynthia was statuesque with the sure demeanor that resembled that of her friend and contemporary Eleanor Roosevelt. For the Wedels, nothing in creation was outside the purview of a loving God; good, engaged theology could speak to any problem and any aspect of human society, and the pull of the future, the coming Great Church, needed to focus on both its wider structural dimensions and smallest components, like the small struggling churches of the American Midwest.

Later Years: 1960–1970

In 1960 Theodore Wedel retired from his College of Preachers position and spent an active period as a visiting professor the Ecumenical Institute, Evanston, Illinois; Episcopal Theological School, Cambridge, Massachusetts; Union Theological Seminary,

---

53 *Ibid.*, 18–19.

New York; and at Virginia Theological Seminary in Alexandria, Virginia. Gradually, his health failed and in 1969 he and Cynthia moved into an Episcopal Church retirement community in Alexandria, Virginia. He died on July 20, 1970. Cynthia remained at Goodwin House, active in numerous leadership roles, until she died of cancer at age seventy-seven on August 24, 1986.

Washington's first Episcopal bishop, Henry Yates Satterlee (1843–1908) (center), and the lay and clergy trustees of the Washington National Cathedral Chapter, c. 1906.

President Theodore Roosevelt (center, standing) spoke at the laying of the foundation stone for what would become Washington National Cathedral, September 29, 1907, at Mount Saint Alban, Washington, DC.

The original 1907 George F. Bodley architectural drawing for the West End of Washington National Cathedral. The fourteenth-century English Gothic design was later altered: the towers were made higher, aisles and doors widened, and three large rose windows added.

A view of the proposed Washington National Cathedral from the south side, by the prominent English architect George F. Bodley. The baptistery (near the front tower) was never built. Bodley died in 1908, and his successor, Henry Vaughan, died in 1917, after which Philip Hubert Frohman (1897–1972) became principal cathedral architect: the resultant building was largely his work.

American architect Ernest Flagg (1867–1957) envisioned Washington National Cathedral as a French Beaux-Arts style building. Flagg's plan was originally accepted by the cathedral's backers before Henry Yates Satterlee was elected first bishop of Washington in 1895. Flagg's budget overruns and testy relations with donors, and Satterlee's strong preference for English Gothic architecture, cost Flagg the cathedral project.

A sketch of Flagg's unrealized proposal for the National Cathedral which, in addition to the building, included the girls' and boys' schools, a chapter hall, Episcopal college, offices, clergy housing, and a hostel for visiting clergy and returned missionaries.

William Temple, archbishop of York, and James E. Freeman, third bishop of Washington, at National Cathedral during Temple's 1936 visit to Washington.

Canon Anson Phelps Stokes (1874–1958) was a staff member of Washington National Cathedral from 1924 to 1939. A pioneer in cathedral urban work, he is best known for his early advocacy of racial integration and his support of the 1939 Marian Anderson Easter concert at the Lincoln Memorial after the famous contralto was denied use of the D.A.R. auditorium.

Bishop of Washington from 1944 to 1962, and his wife, Kitty, some-times took Saturday afternoon bicycle rides from the bishop's house on the Cathedral close out Wisconsin Avenue to nearby Bethesda, Maryland. Dun integrated the cathedral schools and diocesan parishes during his tenure and was an early voice for closer interfaith cooperation.

Washington National Cathedral in the late 1940s. Construction originally began with the Bethlehem Chapel in 1908. The central tower was not com-pleted until 1964, and the remaining work was completed on September 29, 1989, eighty-three years to the day after construction started.

Dean Francis B. Sayre near the scaffolding of Washington National Cathedral. Sayre, a skilled amateur wood carver, knew the cathedral stonemasons and construction workers by name and frequently spoke with them on his daily rounds. The former Navy chaplain was dean from 1951 to 1978.

Senator John F. Kennedy and Dean Francis B. Sayre. Kennedy sought Protestant clergy support for his presidential bid in 1960. Sayre endorsed the idea of a Roman Catholic running for president and sought the senator's support to complete the cathedral's Woodrow Wilson Bay.

Dean Francis B. Sayre and President Richard M. Nixon (both smiling) encounter one another at National Cathedral, c. 1970. Sayre was sharply critical of Nixon's conduct regarding the escalating war in Vietnam. Nixon withheld releasing a seven-gram piece of moon rock from the July 20, 1969 Apollo 11 spaceflight scheduled for inclusion in a cathedral window until urged to do so by NASA administrator Thomas O. Paine. After agreeing to the moon rock's release, Nixon reportedly told the NASA administrator, "Don't tell Frank."

Canon Michael Hamilton was a staff member of National Cathedral from 1964 to 1993, where he held forums on religion and science issues, women's ordination, the arms race, the Vietnam War, poverty, and racial integration. Hamilton, a former university chaplain, published several books and conference reports on his cathedral conferences.

Dean Francis B. Sayre, Attorney General Robert F. Kennedy, Bishop William F. Creighton, Chief Justice Earl Warren, and British Ambassador Lord Harlech at the May 7, 1964 dedication of the Gloria in Excelsis Tower of Washington National Cathedral.

John M. Burgess was the first black canon at Washington National Cathedral, from 1961 to 1966, while he was also Episcopal chaplain at Howard University. He later headed the Episcopal City Mission in Boston and was the first black bishop elected in the Episcopal Church in the United States, serving as bishop of Massachusetts from 1970 to January 1976.

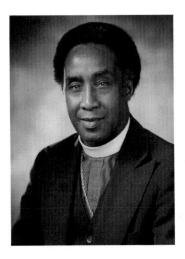

John Thomas Walker (1925–1989), a canon missioner at National Cathedral from 1966 to 1971, was elected suffragan bishop of Washington in 1971 and became diocesan bishop of Washington in 1977 and cathedral dean as well from 1978 until his death in 1989. He was also a candidate for the position of presiding bishop of the Episcopal Church in the USA.

John and Maria Walker were married on June 23, 1962, in St. Paul's Cathedral, Detroit, where Walker was rector of St. Mary's Church, a small multiracial parish in downtown Detroit. Walker was a graduate of Wayne State University and Virginia Theological Seminary, and later taught American history at St. Paul's School, Concord, New Hampshire, where one of his students was John Kerry, later senator from Massachusetts and secretary of state.

Then Canon John T. Walker with Dr. Martin Luther King, Jr., and John C. Chapin, communications officer, at National Cathedral on March 31, 1968, shortly before Dr. King preached his last sermon. Four days later the civil rights leader was assassinated in Memphis, Tennessee.

Archbishop Desmond Tutu (r.) and Bishop John T. Walker (l.) at Washington National Cathedral in the 1980s. Walker actively supported Tutu, a Nobel Peace Prize recipient, and visited him and churches in South Africa during its apartheid era.

Jane Holmes Dixon (1936–2012), the second female bishop in the Episcopal Church. Dixon was elected as suffragan bishop of Washington in 1992. From 2001 to 2002 she was bishop pro tempore of the Diocese of Washington and frequently preached or participated in cathedral services.

Frederick E. Hart (1943–1999) created a three-part tympanum, the semi-circular decorated space above a church door, for the West End of Washington National Cathedral between 1978 and 1984. The center panel of the tympanum is shown here. Hart began work at the cathedral as a mail-room clerk in 1961, became an apprentice sculptor, and eventually one of America's best-known public artists. His West End work included *Ex Nihilo (Out of Nothing), Creation of Day, Creation of Night*, and statues of Adam, Saint Peter, and Saint Paul. He also created the bronze statue of three soldiers at the Vietnam Veterans Memorial (1984).

West Nave Creation Rose and nave clerestory window, twenty-six feet in diameter, is one of the cathedral's visual treasures. Designed and made by Baltimore stained glass artist Rowan LeCompte (1926–2014) with assistance from master German artisan Dieter Goldkuhle, the window contains over 10,500 pieces of white or colored glass abstractly arranged by LeCompte to depict the creation of the universe. The window is set more than fifteen feet back from the West End façade, requiring LeCompte to employ chipped nuggets of prism-like colored glass instead of actual symbolic figures. The project took several years to complete and was dedicated in October 1977 by President Jimmy Carter in the presence of Queen Elizabeth II.

Associate Justice Sandra Day O'Connor, the first woman jurist appointed to the U.S. Supreme Court in 1961, was an active member of the National Cathedral Chapter. O'Connor spoke at the state funeral of President Ronald Reagan and on other occasions at the cathedral, where she was also a lay reader. She described her experiences at the cathedral in the book *Living Stones*.

Presiding Bishop Katharine Jefferts Schori (b. 1954), formerly bishop of Nevada, was elected as presiding bishop of the Episcopal Church on June 18, 2006, and invested on November 4 of that year at National Cathedral, and seated in the presiding bishop's stall the following day. She was the first woman elected as a primate in the Anglican Communion. Preaching at an Earth Day service at the cathedral on April 21, 2013, Schori called on Christians to become "effective shepherds and pasture tenders for the whole creation."

CHAPTER FIVE

The Cathedral in the 1960s and 1970s

At almost any point in the story of Washington National Cathedral, the question would arise, "How did the dean get along with the bishop?" This, however, was not an issue in the relations between Bishop Angus Dun or Bishop William F. Creighton and Dean Francis B. Sayre, whom Dun had brought to Washington in 1951 as cathedral dean.

The Dun and Sayre families had been neighbors in Cambridge, Massachusetts, and Creighton and Sayre had a longstanding cordial relationship. Creighton largely left the running of the cathedral to the dean and was mainly present at Christmas and Easter at the dean's invitation, as well as other exceptional services, such as a presidential funeral, the visit of British royalty, a diocesan convention, or at a periodic multi-parish confirmation service.

Sayre was left largely on his own to articulate the cathedral's mission and in nearly a quarter century addressed many public policy issues in his sermons, from McCarthyism to the Vietnam War, from civil rights to world poverty. He was largely a one-man show. There never was a question of who was in charge and Sayre's was a highly successful operation until his former deputy, Canon John T. Walker, became bishop, and decided to combine the two positions, as had sometimes been historically the case.

Sayre had hired Michael Hamilton as a canon and program planner, and it was Hamilton, through sermons, symposia, and publications, who provided an exploration of the religious aspects of many public policy issues as well. Sayre also decided to push ahead with completion of the cathedral's main tower, incurring a debt of over ten million dollars in the process. Cathedral music also moved to a new place with Paul Callaway, who after his return from World War II greatly expanded its program of organ recitals and choral concerts, bringing a steady program of concerts to the cathedral, beginning with a 1943 performance of Verdi's *Requiem*. Sayre, aided by Callaway and his assistant, Richard Wayne Dirkson, engaged the leading American composer-church musician Leo Sowerby to launch the College of Church Musicians in 1962. Support for the program was strong, but it never found the critical mass of funding needed to continue beyond Sowerby's death in 1968. Seen in retrospect, the 1960s represented a watershed moment in the life of Washington National Cathedral. Sayre's hard work paid off.

William Forman Creighton: Bishop Coadjutor, 1958–1962; Diocesan, 1962–1977

Realizing that he would be retiring in 1962, and that the demands on a bishop in a growing diocese were also expanding, Bishop Dun called for the election of a second bishop in 1958, for the first time in the history of the Diocese of Washington. A special convention met in November 1958 and elected John B. Coburn, a leading Episcopal cleric, who surprisingly declined the offer. Coburn at that time held Dun's old post as dean of the Episcopal Theological School, Cambridge, Massachusetts. He later became rector of St. James', New York, and bishop of Massachusetts.

Washington tried again in January 1959: the two leading candidates were William G. Pollard, an Episcopal priest and well-known atomic scientist in Oak Ridge, Tennessee, and William F. Creighton, the popular rector of St. John's, Norwood Parish, a suburban

Washington church. Creighton was elected and consecrated bishop on May 1, 1959 at the cathedral.

The son of a missionary bishop to Mexico, he was born in Philadelphia on July 23, 1909, and graduated from the University of Pennsylvania in 1931 and the Philadelphia Divinity School in 1934. After graduation he served churches in North Dakota and Minnesota and was a decorated navy chaplain before coming to Chevy Chase in 1946. Creighton had served as a member of the standing committee of the diocese and as a delegate to the General Convention. He also held several national church positions, and took a strong stand on racial issues and for the ordination of women.

A low churchman, his temperament was precise and determined, he was cordial in personal relations, and was known as a focused problem solver. During his busy episcopate he had only minimal contact with the cathedral. He and Sayre had a warm personal relationship but the bishop left management of the cathedral totally to the dean.

Francis Bowes Sayre, Jr., Dean, 1951–1978

> Come, Labor on, Who dares stand idle
> On the harvest plain, while all around us
> Waves the golden grain? And to each servant
> Does the Master say, "Go work today."[1]

The choir and congregation in the partially completed nave sang this hymn on May 6, 1951 at the installation of Francis Bowes Sayre, Jr., as fifth dean of Washington National Cathedral. It was the start of a twenty-seven-year relationship that defined the cathedral and its mission in its time and also proved controversial. Sayre (1915–2008) soon developed clear ideas of what he wanted the cathedral to be. He would listen attentively to others who held differing views, but would rarely act on them unless they fit with his own inclinations of what would be appropriate or possible for the cathedral. Sometimes, if a problem was bubbling toward the surface, Sayre would extract a sherry bottle from a desk drawer and order a special dinner in the Saint Alban's School refectory, at which the usual suspects—cathedral

---

1 Hymn 541, Episcopal Church hymnal, 1940.

clergy, builders, and benefactors—would spent a convivial but inconclusive evening of camaraderie and discussion of issues facing the cathedral community.

Early Years

Sayre was born in the White House on January 17, 1915. His mother, Jessie, was the second of Wilson's three daughters, and his father was a high-ranking government official who held several overseas and domestic diplomatic or public policy postings. Sayre's fund of Wilson stories was limited, however, for Wilson had left the White House by the time the child was three. Also, the Wilson connection could work both ways. The former president of Princeton University was among the most moral, idealistic, and articulate of American presidents, but someone whose rigidity, especially toward Republican Senator Henry Cabot Lodge, was largely responsible for America not joining the recently formed League of Nations.

Sayre as a young person lived and went to school in Thailand, France, and Switzerland, where the family accompanied Francis B. Sayre, Sr., on his overseas assignments. The youth also spent a year working on a family ranch in Montana. He attended the Belmont Hill School in Belmont, Massachusetts, a recently founded private school for boys, when his father was teaching at Harvard Law School. Like his father, he graduated as a political science major from Williams College, *cum laude* in 1937. Sayre originally attended Union Theological Seminary in New York before transferring to the Episcopal Theological Seminary, where he sought to learn more about the Episcopal Church.

After two years as an assistant at Christ Church, Cambridge, he entered the U.S. Navy in August 1942 as a chaplain. Assigned to the Pacific theater, his duties included ministering to military personnel in the Philippines and to Japanese prisoners of war. The recipient of seven battle stars, he rose to the rank of lieutenant commander.

After discharge from the navy, he became an industrial chaplain in Cleveland, Ohio, a new form of ministry for Episcopalians. His assignment was to build bridges between labor unions and the church and to work for better relations between workers and management. Sayre also spent 1947 to 1951 as rector of St. Paul's, an East Cleveland parish in a working-class neighborhood.

Sayre's time spent among blue-collar industrial workers, he later said, was good preparation for work with the large number of cathedral masons and construction workers, each of whom he knew by name and with whom he often spoke on his daily rounds.

Sayre's wife was Harriet Hart, whom he married in 1946. She was the daughter of Admiral Thomas C. Hart, commander of the American navy in the Pacific before the attack on Pearl Harbor. An attractive presence and a good listener, she could mix easily with any of the audiences with which Sayre interacted.

Bishop Dun, Sayre's former professor at ETS, persuaded Sayre to accept the Washington position. The new dean's salary was $9,000 a year, plus housing. During his early years at the cathedral, Sayre explored different avenues for programming, in addition to fundraising, "To be an influence on public affairs," he reflected, "I had to learn how and why to be influential. What was I dean of this Cathedral for?"[2] Part of the answer was to provide a moral voice on questions of public policy. He had been exposed to political activism at an early age. While still a college student, Sayre was an eager participant in the Roosevelt First Voters' League, with offices in New York run by James A. Farley, a longtime Roosevelt insider. He flew to a youth rally in Kansas City on a DC-3 to introduce Roosevelt, an experience he long remembered.

Although the cathedral was officially the mother church of the Diocese of Washington, Sayre had little interest in diocesan affairs. He rarely visited or spoke at Washington parishes, although he accepted preaching invitations all over the United States and abroad. He and his wife were much in demand for embassy invitations, and his diary shows that in 1975 he turned down invitations for receptions honoring the Kissingers, a dinner at the Smithsonian for the outgoing secretary, a reception at the British Embassy to commemorate publication of the works of Richard Hooker, a tulip reception at the Dutch Embassy, and the institution of a new president of Georgetown University. The possibilities for such encounters grew steadily through their Washington years.

The Sayres were a close family. His uncle, John Nevin Sayre, was a pacifist, secretary to the International Fellowship of Reconciliation,

---

2 Margaret Shannon, "God's Emissary, The Prophetic Voice of a Cathedral Dean," *Cathedral Age* (Winter 2008): 10.

and editor of *The Witness*, an Episcopal Church political and social issues commentary magazine. The two exchanged several letters of nuanced polite disagreement, while reassuring each other of their familial affection.

The dean was welcoming of other religious groups using cathedral worship space. By 1958 four different liturgical languages could be heard in the cathedral on Sunday mornings: the Russian Orthodox in Old Slavonic, the Ukrainian Orthodox congregation worshiping in Ukrainian, and the Polish National Catholic Church holding their mass in Polish. Until recently the Syrian Orthodox had held services in Arabic and on Friday evenings the Temple Sinai Jewish congregation had been holding Friday evening services in Bethlehem Chapel until their new temple was completed. Eventually, as their own churches were built, the congregations moved into them. As a thanksgiving the Ukrainians gathered at the Episcopal Christmas Day evensong and sang a selection of traditional Central European carols.

Sayre was tall, rail thin in his early years, and had the chiseled features of a Roman sculpture. Impeccable in dress and manner, he had a carefully modulated, mellifluous voice and could look with full concentration into the face of those moving through a receiving line, while grasping their hand warmly, and then slowly moving them on.

Although he knew the names of each cathedral worker (the Italian masons threw him a party in a Bethesda restaurant when he retired), he guarded his personal space and kept a certain distance from most people. The voluminous correspondence he left after retirement seems scripted, even in what pass for personal observations. If he divulged personal information, it was usually in a carefully crafted anecdote that illustrated a point.

He left a large collection of sermons and lectures, yet there is a repetitive quality to many of them. Rhetorical questions opened many sermons, and words like "tis" were used frequently, as were period phrases. Many of the verbal illustrations were soon dated. His positions on Watergate, the Vietnam War, civil rights, racism, ties with Great Britain, and opposition to Senator Joseph McCarthy were often repeated, with language that changed little across the years.

There is nothing on the place of women in the church, nor about Prayer Book or worship service reform. Although he spoke about many public policy issues, such as the plight of refugees, and testified before Congress, his remarks and sermons rarely suggested someone who was currently tracking issues in their nuanced complexity.

There was nothing that ever rang false about Sayre: he was who he was, and often came across in a carefully prescribed way as a preacher. Although he interacted with power brokers and congressional leaders, his relations with most were formal and somewhat detached. With colleagues, he was collegial with many, intimate with few. He left a personal library with the books of most major religious figures of his time, including Paul Tillich, Reinhold Niebuhr, and prominent British and German writers, but after seminary he did not appear to stay current with what they were writing, nor seek them out when he traveled. "This is someone caught in a groove," one might say of his sermons, "someone who stayed in the same place too long."

Sayre's political activism addressed a wide range of issues. Shortly after his arrival at the cathedral he named a black man, John W. Burgess, as a cathedral canon. A difficulty arose when Burgess, chaplain to Episcopal students at Howard University, and his wife were included in a 1952 invitation to the National Cathedral Association's annual dinner at the Chevy Chase Club.

Sayre said in a letter to Burgess, the club "was guilty of race discrimination and so we are in the terrible situation of not being able to invite you and Mrs. Burgess if we are still to have the dinner at the Club." Sayre was not a club member but was reluctant to make a public controversy over the issue because "it would probably divide our own Cathedral group and probably would not help toward the understanding that we both are striving to promote."

He asked for Burgess's opinion, adding, "If you think this is the place that we ought to fight side by side then I will reconsider the decision and fight with you, if that seems to be the right thing." Burgess thanked Sayre for his frankness, which he called "a great advance in church circles, for the usual procedure is either to say nothing at all or to rationalize the action with pious nothings." He approved of Sayre's course of action: "I believe I do understand and approve what has been done, and also have utter confidence in your motivation and am grateful for your friendship."[3]

---

3 Francis B. Sayre, Jr. to John M. Burgess, Washington, DC, April 14, 1952;
John M. Burgess to Francis B. Sayre, Jr., April 23, 1952, NCA (104.6.17).

Public Controversies

One of his most controversial sermons was a 1972 Palm Sunday meditation in which he criticized Israel's treatment of Palestinians in occupied territories as a "moral tragedy of mankind." Sayre called the Israelis "the oppressed becoming the oppressor." He set his remarks in the historic context of Christ being acclaimed as he entered Jerusalem, only to be crucified a few days later, adding, "Arabs are deported; Arabs are imprisoned without charge; Arabs are deprived of the patrimony of their lands and their homes; their relatives may not come to settle in Jerusalem. They have neither voice nor happiness in that city that, after all, is the capital of their religious devotion, too."[4]

The Washington Post responded in an editorial on April 4, 1972, that Sayre had "committed an error of a particularly serious character." The sermon produced a firestorm of responses, mostly from the Washington Jewish community, that took issue with the dean. One writer said, "As our Passover approaches I want you to know that at our Seder we will offer a special prayer for your well being and pray that your heart will be cleared of hate, bigotry and prejudice you carry as a heavy burden for we Jews. . . . All of us at our Seder, Jews, ministers and converts to Judaism will think of you, along with Hitler and other anti-Semites and hope that with time the curse you bring will disappear."[5]

His May 25, 1952 baccalaureate sermon at George Washington University also attracted considerable public attention. In it he began by drawing a sharp contrast between a view of humanity that links humans with God and those that put a premium on worldly success. "What is it you ask of life?" he asked the senior class, "For what do you choose to strive? Is it merely a job? To be fashioned into the world's plebian likeness? Or the likeness of God which gives scale and grandeur to life?"

Next he cited a *New York Times* article that said more than two hundred top Hollywood stars were being examined for their political loyalty at the request of the American Legion. "Such is the degree to which our current hysteria is pitched that now even great corporations

---

4 William Willoughby, "3 DC Clergymen Rap All-Jewish Jerusalem,"
  The Evening Star, Washington, March 27, 1972.
5 Dr. Arnold Krochmal to Reverend Francis Sayre, Jr., March 22, 1974, NCA.

allow themselves to be dictated to by private groups of self-appointed guardians of patriotism. No charges made public, no hearings held, no process of law: just the threat of a boycott of the moving picture house is used." The dean quickly added he was "neither defending nor attacking the movie stars. I know nothing about them. Nor am I here to stand in judgment upon the American Legion." The real question is, in whose image do we believe we are made, God's or the American Legion's? "To force men to answer for their thought and livelihood to the secret opinion of any private group seems to me to be only the next worst thing to being accountable to Moscow itself or to any other posse of self-constituted hundred percenters."[6]

On February 19, 1973, the cathedral hosted a concert for peace. Leonard Bernstein and a volunteer chorus of over a hundred voices prepared by choral conductor Norman Scribner sang Haydn's *Mass in Time of War*, with brief remarks by Senator Eugene J. McCarthy before the performance, and a short prayer by Dean Sayre following it. Almost fifteen thousand people gathered for the event, most of them standing in the rain outside the building once the cathedral was full. The cathedral staff worked hard to present the concert as a cultural event and not a political protest, but still received a large number of letters pro and con treating it as such.

Groups and individuals that supported Sayre's positions sometimes tried to co-opt Sayre and use his support or that of the cathedral to back their causes, and those who opposed him were equally vocal. The dean was adroit at courteously answering them all, without personally joining forces. There was an exchange with Billy Graham that was laudatory about Graham but did not result in the cathedral hosting a Billy Graham crusade as Graham wanted, and another with Caesar Chavez who sought a bell for his farmer's union headquarters in California, for which the dean found funding.

Dean Sayre and Senator Joseph McCarthy

The dean's early tenure coincided with one of the most highly charged eras in modern American political history, the period of

---

6 Excerpts from the sermon preached on May 25, 1952 at the baccalaureate service, George Washington University, NCA (Sayre collection). At the time this chapter was written, the cathedral archives had received a large number of Sayre sermons that had not been catalogued.

influence of Senator Joseph McCarthy and his unrelenting tirades against supposed communist influence in government and national life. "It comes mighty close to 'tempting God,'" Sayre cautioned, "when anyone operates on the assumption that they are the divinely constituted guardians of other men's consciences or thoughts."[7]

From 1950 to 1954 Senator Joseph R. McCarthy was a front-page name throughout America. The Wisconsin Republican rose to prominence following a February 7, 1950, Wheeling, West Virginia, speech where he said that 205 communists were working or had recently worked in the State Department. He never produced the list—he said it was in his luggage—but capitalized on a climate of fear, especially toward foreigners. The government, as a counter-measure to McCarthy, introduced a loyalty oath program, and summarily fired many employees, especially those with Eastern European family or political connections.

McCarthy never tried to build a consolidated political movement. He was essentially a headline-grabbing loner, a skilled self-publicist who knew how to provide journalists and broadcasters with vivid copy, even if it was refuted the next day. He was also no respecter of senatorial protocol, and although he could be charming, he could be dismissive of colleagues as well, once calling another senator a creature living "without brain or guts." In 1954 his senatorial colleagues passed an act of censure on McCarthy, after which he was largely shunned in public life. He died on May 2, 1957 at the Bethesda Naval Medical Center, in part from the debilitating effects of sustained alcoholism.

Sayre had periodic interaction with President John F. Kennedy and his wife. He had asked Kennedy's help when the Woodrow Wilson Bay was being constructed in the cathedral. Kennedy sought Sayre's support during the 1960 presidential primary when he was being attacked as a Roman Catholic running for president. Sayre responded with an open letter to "fellow pastors in Christ" supporting the legitimacy of a Roman Catholic running for president. Sayre was also one of the three religious leaders asked to walk in front of the horse-drawn caisson at Kennedy's funeral, as it moved from the White House to St. Matthew's Roman Catholic Cathedral.

---

7 NCA (Sayre collection).

Civil Rights, the Vietnam War

Both the civil rights movement and Vietnam War were major topics of Sayre's sermons. On March 25, 1965, he and Canon Michael Hamilton joined twenty-five thousand others on the last leg of the march from Selma to Montgomery. He was instrumental in having Martin Luther King, Jr. preach at National Cathedral on March 31, 1968, four days before King died from an assassin's bullet.

The King sermon drew a congregation of three thousand people, and another thousand listened through loudspeakers outside or at nearby St. Alban's Parish. King had flown in that morning and the sermon's content was drawn together from his recent speeches in several cities. The press was especially interested in a King remark after the service that he might call off his planned Poor People's Campaign march on Washington if he received a concrete commitment from President Lyndon B. Johnson and Congress to aid the nation's poor people. "We are not going to tear up Washington," he said, but would instead hold a massive outpouring in June of hundreds of thousands of people pressing Congress for "jobs or income now."[8]

Sayre reflected:

> One of the terrible sins of America has been the perennial abuse of human rights, often for whole races of people. In his march on Washington, Martin Luther King said, "I have a dream," and he spoke at Lincoln's tomb. I went down to that. And then, later, I and three of the Cathedral's canons went to Selma. But one trip wasn't enough for us to make a dent. So I proposed to all the canons that we go in a series that week. And we did. I was the first, and then they followed. And as each of us came home, we preached in the Cathedral on the travesty of democracy and the racial sin that was going on in Selma and Montgomery.

Sayre had first met Martin Luther King when the latter was a student at Boston University. "I was glad to invite him to speak at Washington Cathedral and come to our house to have a meal with

---

8 Ben A. Franklin, "Dr. King Hints He'd Cancel March if Aid Is Offered," *The New York Times* (April 1, 1968).

my family. That was just a couple of days before he was killed. King left my house to go to Memphis where he was killed."[9]

After the Pentagon Papers were published in 1972, Sayre began a series of sermons castigating the nation's leaders for pursuing the Vietnam War. He recalled one particularly poignant meeting with Secretary of Defense Robert McNamara. Sayre believed that America was not sure who it was fighting: the communist government in Hanoi, or countries beyond Vietnam. President Nixon, he believed, was confused, and Sayre became increasingly critical of Nixon and his policies. "I remember being in McNamara's office and discussing that with McNamara. McNamara was, I could see, going the same way I was. He was distressed and upset and he resigned because of that. He told me about that man outside his window,"—Norman Morrison, a thirty-one-year-old Baltimore Quaker, who had burned himself to death over the Vietnam War. "McNamara protested it himself. That was when I went to see him. I needed to know how he felt about it. . . . He cleared out everybody and he talked to me frankly and personally and tearfully, almost. But he was obliged to act as Secretary of Defense. It made a deep mark on me."[10]

Recalling his meeting in McNamara's office, he continued, "My heart went out to the Secretary, for I knew him then to be in the wilderness himself, of which the prophet spoke. He must have known in that instant, the exile of Israel and her sorrow. I loved him for his tender conscience."[11] The passage Sayre cited in his sermon was from the King James Bible, Jeremiah 31:2, "The people that were left of the sword found grace in the wilderness."

The dean regularly had the cathedral's public information officer issue a press release summarizing his key sermons on public issues. For example, on June 27, 1972, he preached on the Pentagon Papers: "How can any of us hope to ever win this awful war, if history is conceived of as the toy of such shallow arrogance as has characterized this nation's leadership?" He said the tragedy of Vietnam was triggered by Allied arrogance at the end of World War II when the British returned unchallenged to Hong Kong, and France to its

9 Oral interview, Robert Becker with Francis B. Sayre, Jr., Vineyard Haven, MA, November 10, 2000, NCA (63.5.5): 4–5.
10 *Ibid*.
11 Francis B. Sayre, Jr., sermon, "Pentagon Papers," June 27, 1971, NCA (104.13.3).

former colonial possessions unchallenged. "We have lost the meaning of history," he observed.[12]

In a sermon on the Pentagon Papers, he said:

> It has been a disturbing experience for me, as for many of you, reading [the papers] to realize to what complete extent the principal actors in our history have been oblivious of any sense of God's purpose or leading. I have known virtually all of them personally here in Washington, but I did not perceive in those years the extent of the infection by which my friends were led to think of themselves almost as God, and therefore could excuse in themselves the callous disposition of other people's lives, the cynical bamboozling of the body politic, scorn of law and lawmakers alike, and the abuse of truth.

Sayre also visited South Africa to meet with Dean Gonville ffrench-Beytagh of Johannesburg Cathedral who was being tried for subversion for his anti-apartheid activities, and arranged a speaking tour for the dean in American cathedrals. While in South Africa, Sayre preached in a small African church in Johannesburg, surrounded by a ghetto that held eight hundred thousand black Africans. It was 1971, when non-Europeans were "sequestered in sub-human poverty. They may not move without a permit; they may not move on land on which they dwell; they may not marry outside their group, they have no rights at all that may not be wrestled from them at any hour of the day or night by the grim authority of officials that need answer to no court, nor any justice, for their arbitrary action."[13]

An amusing exchange took place with Vice President Hubert Humphrey. Sayre wanted an on-camera interview in the vice president's office for a film about the cathedral in the nation's capital. Humphrey agreed to film the interview and then invited the Sayres to the vice president's residence for drinks, and tried to enlist the dean's help in getting his nephew admitted to St. Alban's School. Sayre finessed the request, for the boy's test scores were far from being

---

12 G. James Hibbard, National Cathedral press release, June 27, 1972, NCA (104.13.3).

13 Francis B. Sayre, Jr., sermon, "Marvel not," June 6, 1971, NCA (Sayre collection).

competitive. Meanwhile, Sayre in return invited the Humphreys to look at their home from the tower of the National Cathedral, an invitation the vice president never acted on.

Sayre's sermons were sometimes thin on substantive content and read more like topical op-eds from a progressive-minded news magazine. He was more the writer of set pieces than a spontaneous preacher. He published a book of poetic prayers, which some readers found maudlin. For example, Sayre wrote this entry on South Dakota:

> Red man, white man,
> Who shall sing for thee
> Of the great ocean of grass, thy tawny home?
> Of badlands, draws and lookout hills?
> Of coyotes and bison and friendly beasts of the
> barn?[14]

Welcoming the Queen

Sayre exemplified the strong pro-British orientation that has always been a part of Anglicanism. He welcomed the queen to National Cathedral, kept in frequent touch with the British embassy, and on the fiftieth anniversary of the English-Speaking Union, spoke of the power of language:

> The savor of our society is not merely that we have the same language but that that language is ENGLISH. When the African in distant Ghana learns this language, he learns with it the Rule of Law. When the Australian plants his cockney accent in a frontier town in the Outback, you know that fair play is also rooted there. . . . And here in America it was English that was broadest to them all, into which the other tongues would merge, so preserving the democratic union that would otherwise lie in bits. For Magna Carta is in her stream, and Shakespeare, and Lincoln's words at Gettysburg, and Milton, and Frost and Sir Winston.[15]

---

14 Francis B. Sayre, "For All the States," (Washington, DC: National Cathedral Association, 1972): 46.

15 Francis B. Sayre, Jr., sermon, "50th Anniversary of the English-Speaking Union," Washington Cathedral, November 8, 1970, NCA (Sayre collection).

Sayre regretted not holding more interfaith encounters in his time at the cathedral. He said later of Buddhists:

> At bottom, beneath their customs and habits and dress and race, they're saying exactly the same thing that we are, that is what the Cathedral is trying to say. Some of them have parishioners in their Buddhist temples and some don't. But that doesn't matter, what matters is that they are in a society where there's a need for somebody to see through the common morays of mankind, whatever they are, and they are very different around the world. But seeing the common bodies we have, the common spirits that all men and women have, and the violations of those in so many ways.

He regretted that in twenty-seven years at the cathedral he did not do much more to promote interfaith dialogue.[16]

The Moon Rock Window

One of the cathedral's treasures was an actual seven-gram rock fragment from the moon set in a west aisle stained glass window. The window, a gift of NASA administrator Thomas Paine, was designed to commemorate the unity of faith and science. It had been completed, but there was a hole where the 3.6-billion-year-old moon rock should be. The problem was Dean Sayre had fallen out with President Nixon, who would not answer his letter requesting the moon rock that remained stored in a government warehouse. The director of the space agency, whom Sayre knew well, said he would handle the request in about a year's time, along with other matters he needed to discuss with the President. Sayre asked the administrator to stress to the president that both the Vietnam War and exploration of the moon were national events that transcended personality differences.

> He went to see the President not only about that. He was careful not to make that the only thing, and the President

---

16 Oral interview, Robert Becker with Francis B. Sayre, Jr., Vineyard Haven, MA, November 10, 2000, NCA (63.5.5); 1.

said "Well, I won't tell Frank about it but you have my permission." So I got it and it's in there now. When the window was finished and installed the astronauts helped to dedicate the window. Every one of the men who went there and brought this back helped dedicate the window and its meaning. Faith penetrates even space, that's what we tried to say, and it's true.[17]

The window was dedicated on June 2, 1974, the fifth anniversary of the first steps on the moon by astronauts Neil Armstrong, Buzz Alden, and Michael Collins, all of whom participated in the cathedral service.

A magazine profile described Sayre as central casting's idea of a cathedral dean. A senator said Sayre's sermons were "clear Wilsonian prose: precise, objective, yet at the same time lofty and inspiring."[18] Others found them repetitive in their commentaries on public issues. And there was always the building to complete. Should the cathedral next finish construction of its central tower or complete the nave? That was a central question facing the dean. Sayre favored building the Gloria in Excelsis Tower, although the cathedral debt soared in the process.

Sayre also had strong interests in music and supported the cathedral's music programs. The long-planned College for Church Musicians that opened in 1962 was his project, as was support for organist–conductors Paul Callaway and Richard Wayne Dirkson, two leading figures in the cathedral's musical life for over three decades.

Walker and Sayre, Differing Views on the Cathedral's Role

It was Canon Michael Hamilton who suggested hiring an African American seminary friend, John T. Walker, to be a resident cathedral canon specializing in urban ministry, the first full-time black canon on the staff. John Burgess, though a cathedral canon before becoming bishop of Massachusetts, had been resident at Howard University.

Walker would, within a few years, become Sayre's boss as bishop of Washington, which precipitated a clash of generations,

---

17 Oral interview, Robert Becker with Francis B. Sayre, Jr., Vineyard Haven,
   MA, November 10, 2000, NCA (63.5.5): 4.
18 *Ibid.,* 13.

personalities, and policies. Walker had grown up in conflict-ridden Detroit. He was active in community groups and deeply involved in racial and civil rights issues. After he moved from being a cathedral canon to suffragan bishop in 1971 and diocesan bishop in 1977, he announced that he would be dean of the cathedral as well, a historic role some earlier bishops had assumed, but one that challenged Sayre's carefully cultivated power base.

Richard T. Feller, clerk of the works and a keen observer of cathedral politics, said that:

> [Walker] knew that Sayre had gone his own way, done his own thing and that his predecessor [Bishop] Creighton had nothing to do or say about the Cathedral and he knew that over the years, the deans and bishops had always had conflict over the operation of this cathedral. Walker . . . knew what he wanted done, how it was to be run, and he wasn't about to have some dean in his way. That's why he did it.[19]

Sayre highlighted "that thorny old subject of the relation between Cathedral and Diocese" in a letter to another dean. "I think I have a good set-up," he said, adding, "any set-up will depend almost entirely on a good personal relationship of bishop and dean. I thank God for my happy friendship with Bill Creighton, but I must say that I dread the day of his retirement, whenever that might be."[20] It came three years later in 1977.

In 1977 Sayre distributed a paper for the Cathedral Chapter on his objections to Bishop Walker's plan to be both bishop and dean, noting that the cathedral had a life of its own "not to be defined in terms of a single Diocese, nor even of the National Episcopal Church. The leadership of the Cathedral ought to reflect this unique opportunity. I have been at a loss to understand why Bishop Walker first submitted his proposal to the Diocesan Council, which cannot be expected to envision this role, much less mobilize from the Diocese,

---

19 Robert Becker, oral interview with Canon Richard T. Feller, September 8, 2000, NCA (163.5.2): 11.
20 Francis B. Sayre, Jr. to Allen L. Bartlett, Jr., June 26, 1974, NCA (104.5.17). Bartlett was dean of the cathedral in Louisville, KY, at the time, later became bishop of Pennsylvania, and later in retirement an assisting bishop in Washington.

the kind of financial backing that is so badly needed."[21] What Sayre missed was Walker's intention to shift power from the Cathedral Chapter to the diocesan council.

"Leadership of this great Cathedral is far too important and demanding a responsibility to be entrusted either to the part-time care of a Bishop, however fine he is, or to the subordinate discretion of a surrogate, however efficient he may be," Sayre wrote. "It required the full-time and unceasing care of the ablest and most dedicated man we might find."

Two additional major issues for the Episcopal Church in the mid-1970s were revisions and reforms of its liturgy and the ordination of women. There is no record of Sayre having preached or spoken out on either subject. He was no liturgical innovator, although he did not object to Hamilton instituting a Sunday morning guitar mass that was highly attractive to students of the two cathedral schools, who were required to attend church on Sundays. Bishops Creighton and Walker, both strong supporters of women's ordination, announced in 1975 that there would be no further ordinations in the Diocese of Washington until the 1976 General Convention of the Episcopal Church, meeting that October in Minneapolis, acted favorably on the ordination issue.[22]

Sayre alluded to the question in a September 14, 1975 sermon, a week after several women clergy had been illegally ordained at a Washington parish by retired or resigned bishops. Bishop Creighton had specifically asked the other bishops not to enter the diocese for that purpose. Sayre said the action posed "the danger of fatal division" because of "the loss of charity and loving patience that has characterized events of these latter days." He concluded "the defiance of Bishop and church law makes mockery of the sacred rite which only the unbroken family can administer in Christ's name, and not

---

21 F. B. Sayre, "The Future Leadership of Washington Cathedral," October 20, 1977, NCA (Sayre Collection).

22 Barbara R. Rathell, Press Release, Office of the Bishop, April 1, 1975. See also Bishop William F. Creighton's Statement to the Press Regarding the Proposed Unauthorized Ordination Scheduled for September 7, 1975, including a press conference transcript, NCA (6.13.3). General Convention affirmed the ordination of women, and an ordination service for women and men was held at the cathedral on January 7, 1977. Although Bishop Walker preached and several participants spoke with the press after the service, Sayre, though vested, was not among them.

some rump of the divinely impatient claiming the superior authority of the Holy Spirit for the rebel act."[23]

Retirement

The differences over how the cathedral would be run precipitated Sayre's retirement in January 1978, on his sixty-third birthday. After retiring he had a brief tenure as head of international programs at the Woodrow Wilson Center for Scholars housed in the Smithsonian Institution, but eventually the Sayres moved to Vineyard Haven, their longtime Cape Cod retreat, and for a decade. Sayre then took on the role of chaplain to the local hospital. He rarely returned to Washington, one exception being for the installation of Nathan Baxter as the cathedral's seventh dean in 1982. The large house built on the cathedral close for the dean was renamed Sayre House in 1988, although by then it had become cathedral administrative offices.

When he retired in 1978, Sayre was the cathedral's longest serving and most visible dean. He was a national and international presence who had spoken out on major moral issues of his day, including McCarthyism, the Vietnam War, the Arab-Israeli conflict, and civil rights. He had also worked hard to build the cathedral and expand the National Cathedral Association and broaden its donor base.

If he could be somewhat distant and formal, Sayre's achievements still were major for over a quarter century. Perhaps he stayed too long at the cathedral, and when the bishop combined the cathedral and diocesan leadership positions into one person, Sayre took it as a personal loss and brooded about it, diminishing the impact of his considerable accomplishments over a long incumbency.

Canon Michael Hamilton (1964–1993)

For almost thirty years, Canon Michael Hamilton was a major public policy voice at National Cathedral. Dean Francis B. Sayre hired him in 1964, and he served under four different cathedral leaders. When he retired as senior canon emeritus in 1993 he had served longer than any other clergy in the cathedral's history.

---

23 Francis B. Sayre, Sermon, Washington National Cathedral, September 14, 1975, NCA (Sayre collection).

Hamilton organized a steady stream of seminars and lectures on civil rights, interfaith, environmental, church-state, and poverty issues. Prior to joining the cathedral staff, he had worked for six years in an experimental ministry to faculty and graduate students at the University of Southern California in Los Angeles. "It was actually a good prelude to my work at the Cathedral because there I discovered the interdisciplinary nature of all major thoughts and questions in our century, something universities didn't know. They still were very narrow, one part of the university dealt with medical things, another with engineering, and I used to get them all together at lunch and ask them awkward questions."[24] At the cathedral, Hamilton "looked at the city of Washington and, indeed the wider nation, rather like sort of a university, where all these ideas were bubbling around but not necessarily connected, and very seldom related to the Christian faith."

Hamilton remembered a long lunch with Sayre at a secluded restaurant. "I don't know why the hell he hired me, to tell you the truth. I didn't meet anybody else at the Cathedral, I wasn't interviewed by anybody else, but Frank was his own boss, and there I got the job. Frank said, 'I want you to explore what's going on in relation to what a National Cathedral might do about the big issues, the political issues.'" Sayre was drawn to such issues, but he didn't have time to implement any program in relation to them. "So when he said 'think big', it really helped me." Both Hamilton and Sayre were deeply interested in public policy issues and their moral implications, including, in scientific endeavors, which would be a new departure for the Cathedral.[25] On Civil Rights:

> I had been demonstrating, was nearly killed as a matter of fact, down in Georgia when I was demonstrating in front of a segregated Episcopal School and some bastard with a huge truck came roaring down this country road and went square at us. I jumped as fast and hard as I could and landed in a ditch where his truck couldn't follow me. I was always concerned for not just talking about things but if possible, acting them out in some way.

---

24 Robert Becker, interview with Canon Michael Hamilton, November 3, 2000, transcript in NCA (163.5.3): 1–2.
25 *Ibid.,* 3–4.

Reflecting on his civil rights work, Hamilton said, "I always had an ally in Frank, but he was cautious, a little more conservative than I am as a generation." Civil rights:

> was just one of a lot of problems that were going on in the country, and slowly its importance became apparent. The Cathedral did not take a leading part in organizing the public on civil rights because there were other organizations that were doing it. Our role was to do what we could at the Cathedral. We had some big services on it and I was very much restricted by Bishop Creighton's concern that there not be rallies in the Cathedral.

Hamilton was part of the cathedral's group that marched on Selma and Birmingham, Alabama, in March 1965:

> It was a very large march . . . I remember walking through the streets of Birmingham and the people on the sidewalk shaking their fists screaming abuse at us. Frank stood tall and looked ahead and bravely marched on, but once he got into the spirit of it he was great, and he's a natural leader in the sense that he has the right word for so many of these things. We went up to town hall and the state building and heard some speeches, marched back, got on the planes, and came home, and then Frank had an idea. We're going to have a witness to it, and got all four of us in the pulpit, the two from Selma and the two of us from Birmingham. It must have looked odd, There must be a photograph of it somewhere. All of us in the pulpit, each talking for five minutes talking about our experiences. Cannon Sharp and Canon Workman went to Selma and Frank and I to Montgomery.[26]

At the cathedral, Hamilton organized an annual Christmas pageant for young people from the cathedral schools. Well respected as a pastor and counselor, he also published more than fifty articles in religious and secular journals, edited or co-edited numerous books and conference reports, and was active with the Diocesan Peace

---

26 *Ibid.*, 16.

Commission and the Washington hospice movement. He retired in 1993, and joined his wife, Eleanor Raven-Hamilton, a foreign service officer, in Brussels, where he also served as Anglican chaplain.

The bishop was insistent that the cathedral be a place for worship, and for educational and cultural programs, but not a site for political rallies. Additionally, Hamilton's resources were limited. His office was himself and a secretary, and he felt he could contribute to the unfolding of various movements, but not much more. On some emerging issues like genetics, there were moral and genetic issues in what they were doing affected wider segments of society. He wanted to bring scientists out of their laboratories to explore such subjects with different audiences. He was "also very concerned about the church's attitude toward science." The Christian churches had a centuries-old history of condemning scientific discovery, "Copernicus, Freud, whatever. I was trying to get the church, through publications in church journals, to be open to these new events rather than having a traditional 'no, no, no' attitude."

In the 1960s, both Hamilton and Sayre preached frequently on the moral issues raised in public policy debates. During a sermon on the Vietnam War:

> in the middle of the sermon a general stood up, in full uniform. He walked sideways out so that he got out of his seat into the middle of the aisle, he saluted the high altar, turned around, kicked his heels and marched the whole way down the nave to the West door. I would love to have met that man. It was such a glorious piece of dramatic protest. I'm in the pulpit seeing this going on thinking "I'm in trouble here." Thirty-nine people walked out on me in that sermon . . . I had more people walking out on me in my sermons than anybody else . . . But Frank Sayre supported freedom of the pulpit. Now that must not have been easy for him, as some members of his staff, like Canon Leslie Glenn, was a hawk on Vietnam. Sayre gradually became a dove.[27]

Hamilton was opposed to expanding the cathedral's social activist ministry into the city of Washington. "Why did I object to it?

---

27 *Ibid.,* 21.

Because I thought basically those were things that the parishes could and should do. The Cathedral could do some things that the parishes couldn't, which was deal with the big national and international issues, and scientific issues. A parish doesn't have the resources" to address such issues.[28]

Hamilton recalled how John T. Walker came to the cathedral:

> I got him to the cathedral. There was a vacancy, the Dean had fired a couple of canons, and Frank wanted a black. We needed a black. I knew John had just finished a time in Africa and was looking around. He went from school to Africa and just by pure luck I said, "Frank, what about this great guy John Walker whom I know?" So he explored him, he probably had a lunch with him as he had with me and he was hired on the spot.

Hamilton reflected, "I knew him in seminary. He was personally so winsome a guy, so nice, so genuine, that he had that reputation, and also everything he had done he had done well. So it was a very good choice of the Dean's."[29]

Hamilton also had a growing interest in interfaith encounters that intersected with the Diocesan Peace Commission's work. In a May 6, 1990 sermon on "'Other Sheep Have I': The Destiny of Non-Christians," he raised the challenging question of what Christians should think about non-Christians. After reading the works of Raimundo Pannikar, a brilliant Jesuit writer who was born a Hindu. Hamilton asked the often-posed question: What is the destiny of devout Hindus, Buddhists, and Muslims? "Are they forever to be deprived of God's heavenly kingdom because they never met a missionary, or for good reason, did not respond positively to one?"[30] Most of his hearers were probably Christian because they were born in and grew up in Christian homes, he continued, but for a Muslim to become Christian there would be severe restraints, including a death penalty for apostasy in some countries.

---

28 *Ibid.,* 36.
29 *Ibid.,* 17.
30 Michael Hamilton, "'Other Sheep Have I': The Destiny of Non-Christians," sermon preached on May 6, 1990, *Cathedral Age,* Fall 1990.

Still, Christians might find "lesser aspects of the truth about God" in other religions. Hamilton said other religions reflect "gifts that God has given them" and hoped "we can stand and worship together and, in silence, know that God is with all of us." "Not all on earth will come to this table, but we hope, pray, trust and believe that all shall share in the heavenly banquet. 'Other sheep have I that are not of this fold; I must bring them also, so that there shall be one flock and one shepherd.'"

Of his own faith journey, Hamilton described himself as "a nasty little rational agnostic for ten years" who wasn't "going to believe in God unless God conformed to my intellectual and rational expectations for his existence." From an active Christian woman with whom Hamilton was living, he realized, "We're not as important as the sins of the mind, prejudice, pride, greed and all those things. So it was by the love of a woman I got back into the church. . . . I was humbled. God gave me exactly the kind of experience that I personally needed for my own growth."

Although he was born in Northern Ireland, Hamilton served in the British army for three years, and then worked his way through the University of Toronto, entered Virginia Theological Seminary in 1952, and graduated in 1955. His decision to study for the ministry was not difficult or dramatic, he recalled. Once he became an active Christian it was a logical next step. Always interested in social issues, including poverty, his initial parish assignment was to a Cincinnati slum, where he worked with Appalachian migrants.

Hamilton in the second half of the twentieth century and Anson Phelps Stokes in its earlier decades were both cathedral canons of long tenure that probed social and political issues beyond the usual fare of sermons. Stokes had little encouragement from Bratenahl, who was dean during most of the time he was there. Hamilton had the backing of Sayre, who himself often selected public policy issues as topics of his own sermons.

Lay Ministry: Drs. Lee and Charles Tidball

Although bishops, deans, and canons were the cathedral's most visible personalities, numerous laity also advanced the cathedral's work. No names are more associated with lay ministry at the cathedral than those of Drs. Lee and Charles Tidball, who were regulars at the

Wednesday early morning Eucharist in Bethlehem Chapel for over thirty years, alternating roles as lay readers and chalice bearers since the mid-1960s. Both sang in the Cathedral Choral Society and contributed substantially to the rebuilding of the cathedral organ and other projects, including four of the lancet windows in the cathedral tower.

Lee served as a board member of the Cathedral Choral Society, the College of Preachers council, and the Cathedral Chapter. Until retirement, she was a professor of physiology at George Washington University Medical Center, after serving as a postdoctoral fellow at the National Institutes of Health. Her husband retired as a professor of computer medicine and neurological surgery in 1992, after spending thirty-five years at George Washington University Medical Center in a wide range of teaching, research, administrative, and medical practice roles. He spent several years not only as a lay minister, but in building a computer database listing information about over five thousand artworks gathered at the cathedral.

For many years, the Tidballs lived within a short walk to the cathedral, and their apartment was often crowded with former students and their families, the Tidballs having no children and few immediate relatives of their own. "Perhaps the Cathedral provides a balancing force in our careers," Lee once remarked, adding, "It's impossible to define precisely the immensity of the Cathedral for us. It is both intimacy and grand space. It is music, art, and the liturgy, opportunities for service and for giving, people both known and unknown. In sum, it is the holy, guiding us toward our wholeness and shalom."[31]

Vincent Palumbo, Master Carver (1936–2000)

Numerous Italian stone carvers and masons, many from the same village or region, worked on the cathedral that once employed fourteen carvers at the same time. Vincent Palumbo, a fifth-generation stone carver, was named cathedral master carver in 1978. He came to America with his father in 1961 and spent nearly forty years on Mount Saint Alban, beginning as a carver of flowers, leaves, and

---

31 Sherwood Harris, "Lee & Charlie Tidball," *Cathedral Age,* Summer 1995,
    Vol. 2, 16–20.

birds, progressing to gargoyles and angels, then to larger sculpted figures, like Martin Luther King, Jr., and the cathedral's pulpit. He also carved ninety ceiling bosses, the large, decorative ceiling stones placed where vaulted ribs intersect. Palumbo did much of his work in a wooden shed in front of the cathedral's West End, but was often seen high, moving about on interior and exterior scaffolding.

The workers often gathered for lunch at a communal table in Vincent's shed, the meals laced with camaraderie and red wine. A 1984 documentary film about their work, *The Stone Carvers* by Marjorie Hunt, won an Oscar. It focused on Palumbo's life and work, and was based on an earlier book by Hunt and Paul Wagner. Palumbo's shed had a large window where he could look out at streams of tourists as they walked by and they, in turn, could watch him and other carvers at work. He worked closely with the well-known sculptor Frederick Hart, whose "*Ex Nihilo*" center tympanum, and "Creation of Day" and "Creation of Night" were major artistic components to the cathedral. "The sculptor creates it, but we give it life," Palumbo told an interviewer in 1998, describing the process as being one of creation in the original design, death in the plaster model, and resurrection in the final carving.

Palumbo was a voluble personality, given to lively banter with whomever he encountered. Once when Dean Sayre admonished him for whistling appreciatively as a young lady walked past, the sculptor responded with a carving of himself dangling from a scaffold, whistling, while a tall angel, not unlike the dean, stood nearby, finger raised in admonition. At a memorial service for the sculptor, Dean Nathan D. Baxter spoke of the "ministry of the fabric," the work of artists and artisans, and remarked, "Vince was Vince. He was opinionated, ambitious, frank, stubborn, and even stone headed. Yet, he was loving, funny, romantic, forgiving, creative, spontaneous, brilliant, passionate and contagiously expressive. What can I say? He was Italian!"[32]

Frederick Hart's "Ex Nihilo" Sculpture

Frederick Hart's gripping *Ex Nihilo*, three bas relief sculptures of "Creation," "Night," and "Day" on the cathedral's west façade, are

---

32 Nancy Montgomery, "Building for Eternity," A Master Carver, Vincent Palumbo, 1936–2000, *Cathedral Age* (Spring 2011): 20.

among the cathedral's best known artistic works, along with Rowan LaCompte's west end rose window and the Space Window. Many critics consider Hart's creation work the major piece of American religious sculpture of the twentieth century.

Hart (1943–1999) began his cathedral career as a mailroom clerk in 1961. He tried to join the cathedral's tightly knit Italian stone carvers community as an apprentice, but they initially refused. Eventually master carver Roger Morigi took Hart on as an apprentice, and Hart graduated from floral and geometric carvings to gargoyles. Morigi encouraged him to enter the 1971 national competition to make the creation sculpture on the western façade, and Hart won, although the cathedral building committee rejected his first proposals.

He was living at the time in an unheated P Street garage with his two German shepherd dogs and asked a beautiful woman walking through Dupont Circle, Lindy Lain, if she would be his model. She agreed, and they married a few years later and had two sons. His cathedral commission took Hart thirteen years from inception to completion.[33]

Hart was penniless and totally unknown as an artist in the early 1970s, but the creation sculpture and accompanying statues of Adam and Saints Peter and Paul brought him professional acclaim, and he was asked to make a bronze sculpture of three soldiers to accompany Maya Lin's Vietnam Memorial, a V-shaped black granite wall with the names of the fifty-seven thousand American dead. President Ronald Reagan dedicated the work on Veterans Day in 1984.

With the cathedral and Vietnam sculpture, Hart's career trajectory rapidly moved from obscurity to fame. The theme of his cathedral work was the journey from darkness and primal chaos to light, joy, and exuberance. He saw the cathedral work as representing the victory of the creative forces of the universe proclaiming a loving God. The Jesuit thinker Teillard de Chardin's *The Cosmic Life* and other writings influenced Hart's perspective.

Despite his spotty formal education, Hart was widely read, became a Roman Catholic convert, and was married at St. Matthew's Cathedral. Commissions regularly came his way during the last two decades of his life, and Hart bought a large hunt country property in

---

33 Frederick Turner, *Frederick Hart, Changing Tides* (New York: Hudson Hills Press, 1995).

rural Virginia. His work was both representational and naturalistic, while fully employing the advances of modern technology. It often included works of a patented new technology he called acrylic light painting. His health was problematic and he died at Johns Hopkins Hospital on August 13, 1999, two days after it was discovered he had cancer. Major collectors still seek his work decades after his death.

Leo Sowerby, Dean of American Church Music

Leo Sowerby, who built his reputation in Chicago and spent his final years in Washington, DC as head of the College of Church Musicians at National Cathedral, was a skilled keyboardist, choral director, and the composer of over 550 works, several of which are still performed regularly by church musicians.[34] Sowerby (1895–1968), sometimes called "the dean of American church music," was a quintessential midwestern American composer.

Born and raised in Grand Rapids, Michigan, where his father worked at the post office, he was once too poor to afford the twenty-five-cent cost of organ lessons, so he made a replica of the organ pedal stops from heavy brown butcher paper and practiced his footwork on them. Following the death of his parents, he moved to Chicago at an early age, began composing at age ten, and in 1913 had a violin concert premiered by the Chicago Symphony Orchestra, for whom he wrote several works over the next two decades. At the American Conservatory in Chicago he studied musical theory with Arthur Olaf Anderson, a composer and pianist, but otherwise was largely self-taught. In 1913 he became summer substitute organist for a suburban Chicago Episcopal Church, where he played three services and held a rehearsal each week for four dollars, which he considered good pay. During World War I he enlisted in the U.S. Army, became a second lieutenant, and bandmaster of the 332nd Artillery

---

34 The Music Division of the Library of Congress contains a large collection of Sowerby scores, and the Washington National Cathedral Archives has several files of Sowerby-related material. Other works on Sowerby include Michael Patrick Guiltian, "The Absolute Music for Piano by Leo Sowerby," Ph.D. dissertation, University of Rochester, 1977 (microfilm; Ann Arbor, MI: University of Michigan); and Ronald M. Huntington, "The Musical Contribution of Leo Sowerby," Master's thesis, University of Southern California, 1957 (microfilm; Ann Arbor, MI: University of Michigan). There are several newsletters of the now-defunct Leo Sowerby Foundation.

Band that served in France and England in 1918 and 1919. Sowerby was the first American composer to receive the Prix de Rome (1921) and in 1946 was awarded a Pulitzer Prize for his cantata *Canticle of the Sun,* written around words attributed to St. Francis of Assisi.

The world of leading church musicians was not large in early twentieth-century America, and Sowerby taught several generations of accomplished musicians in Chicago. One of his students, Paul Callaway, had been organist and choirmaster at an Episcopal Church in Grand Rapids, Michigan, and later was named head of the Washington Cathedral music programs in 1939.

Some of Sowerby's other Chicago students included William Ferris, Norman Luboff, Ned Rorem, and David Van Vactor, and he was a contemporary of American composers like Samuel Barber, Howard Hanson, Walter Piston, and William Schuman, all of whom he knew. During his lifetime several recordings were made of his music, and individual works of his were included in many recorded anthologies. The influence of French Romantic composers was strong and Sowerby carefully studied the works of Franck, Widor, Vierene, and Dupré. His 1964 hymn tune "Rosedale" remains popular with the Easter hymn "Come Risen Lord." He knew jazz and wrote two pieces for the Paul Whiteman orchestra, plus regional-related tone poems like "Prairie," "From the Northland," and smaller works based on folk tunes like "The Irish Washerwoman" and "Pop Goes the Weasel." Sowerby also wrote a commemorative work for Carl Sandburg based on several of the midwestern poet's works.

The cathedral performed six or seven Sowerby works a year in the early twenty-first century. Michael McCarthy, head of cathedral music programs in 2012, described Sowerby's compositional style as "deeply southern fried Vaughan Williams," comparing him as well to British composers like Herbert Howells, a minor but distinctive figure.[35]

To listen to some of his works is to listen to the compositions of an American original, trained in a classical tradition. His works remained within the constraints of composing technique as taught in his time. He would not be considered revolutionary or pathbreaking in more modern times, but an accomplished regionalist

---

35 Oral interview, Michael McCarthy with Frederick Quinn, Washington, DC, August 2, 2012.

within the tradition of Western church music. Additionally, Sowerby rarely talked about his music, unless someone asked him a question about it. When he came to Washington, he was given a house on the cathedral close, within easy walking distance of the College of Preachers and the cathedral. As a member of the Episcopal Church's Joint Commission on Church Music, he was one of the music professionals responsible for *The Hymnal 1940*. E. Power Biggs recorded his *Symphony in G* for Columbia Masterworks in 1955, but the recording was never released.

Sowerby gained his national reputation for work as organist-choirmaster at St. James' Episcopal Church, Chicago, which became the Chicago Cathedral in 1955. Prior to that, he was associate organist at the Fourth Presbyterian Church, a major Chicago institution. Sowerby kept a small summer cottage in Palisades Park, Michigan, where he spent much of his spare time. He was a sincere church member, who joined the Episcopal Church after he moved to Chicago, and took communion once a month, which would have been the norm for many Episcopalians of the 1920s and 1930s.

He retired at age sixty-seven from the Chicago cathedral, when he was asked to become founding director of the College of Church Musicians, a position he held until his death in 1968. Dean Sayre enthusiastically backed the college with prodding from Callaway and Dirksen, in an attempt to enhance the impact of the cathedral's music program.

The college opened on September 13, 1962, with six of the seven original fellows present. Sowerby said the fellows represented several denominations and came from churches all around the country. Each man (there were no women) was asked to present a recital on the large cathedral organ during the year. Beginning with the first year's report, the need to raise funds for an endowment was a constant concern, so that the CCM would no longer "depend entirely on ringing doorbells and telephoning our friends" to survive. But the college was competing with university departments of music, conservatories, and seminaries. Musicians and churchgoers welcomed it, but financial support was never adequate for its needs.

Sowerby was of medium height, a bit overweight, with a serious face, as if he was perennially worrying about something, which was not the case. He never married, was a chain smoker of Fatima cigarettes, and began most evenings with a pitcher of martinis, often shared with musician friends, choir, or students. He was generously hospitable, and choir members were frequently invited by "Doctor Leo" or "Uncle Leo" to his Chicago apartment for home-cooked dinners or choir parties, where the wine and conversation flowed freely. He was generally attired in white shirt and tie. "Formal" is an adjective that would easily describe him.

He could quickly read and comment on a student's score and was direct in his critical comments. "Let's see if we can't improve on that," he often said, and began to pencil-in changes. Sowerby conducted choirs with a No. 2 pencil, knew exactly what he wanted, and was a precise director. The impression, after listening to several of his works, is this was an American composer from the Midwest, a traditionally trained musician, often writing in a regional idiom. Their religious content was heavily drawn from biblical phrases and psalms. The best works, like the hymn tune "Rosedale" and some of the anthems, like "I was Glad," will endure, but he also churned out a lot of less memorable service music, often for next Sunday's service.

Sowerby also wrote several cantatas. *Forsaken of Man,* a Passion setting completed in 1939, was performed annually for many years at the cathedral. *The Throne of God* was written in 1956 to commemorate the fiftieth anniversary of the laying of the cathedral's cornerstone. His production included anthems like "Love Came Down at Christmas," "I Will Lift Up Mine Eyes," and "Christians, to the Paschal Victim," and organ works like *Come Autumn Time* (1916), *Carillon* (1917), and *Arioso* (1942). Popular mid-century, they eventually fell out of favor, although are witnessing a revival in the twenty-first century.

One of Sowerby's most remembered events was the daylong dedication service for the Gloria in Excelsis Tower that took place on Ascension Day, May 7, 1964. Five services were held in the cathedral throughout the day, beginning at 7 am. Sowerby, Dirksen, Samuel Barber, and Ned Rorem composed special music. The actor Basil Rathbone read commemorative material on the cathedral's history at each service. His remarks summarized the cathedral's aspirations. The tower was complete now:

> Flood-lit in white radiance it stands, a sentinel, a sign of God's eternal glory. Its light-reflecting limestone pinnacles will, for ages, remind men of the glory of reverent and

determined dedication on the part of thousands who built for its long future. Its illumination is revealing, not only of the perfection of its fabric, but of the countless bene-factions of those who served well and with ample sacrifice to raise it on Mount Saint Alban. They are remembered, those faithful and devoted souls now departed. Their memorial is the Cathedral ideal, a living ideal, beckoning us onward . . . It reminds us of Him who said, "I, if I be lifted up, will draw all men unto me."[36]

A week-long festival of his own music was held in April and May 1995 honoring the hundredth anniversary of Sowerby's birth. "His works are not easy to sing," Douglas Major, director of cathedral music at that time, reflected in 1995. "They often go to an unex-pected place." Major described Sowerby's style as a "personal, chro-matic, jazzy/bluesy dialect driven by solid, majestic rhythms."[37]

The College of Church Musicians lasted from 1962 to 1968, and although it was carefully designed and enthusiastically backed, it never gained the financial support needed for survival. During the college's six active years, Sowerby was charged with introducing participants to the intricacies of Anglican church music and liturgical services, plus providing lessons in composition and organ playing. It trained twenty-four persons during its existence, but with Sowerby's death in 1968 there was no possibility of the program holding its own. Dean Sayre, who in 1953 had first launched the college idea at a conference of church musicians and composers at the cathedral, incorporated what remained of it into the cathedral music depart-ment. The cathedral continued its impressive music programs, but the college was no more.

---

36 Richard T. Feller and Marshall W. Fishwick, *For Thy Great Glory* (Culpeper, VA: Community Press, 1965): 76.
37 Douglas Major, "Leo Sowerby and Washington National Cathedral," April 1, 1955, NCA (125.18.9).

CHAPTER SIX

The Building Is Completed, Toward New Times (1977–1989)

The episcopate of John Thomas Walker, from 1977 to his death in 1989, was as distinctive an epoch in the life of the cathedral and Diocese of Washington as any other. Provost Charles A. Perry, who also worked hard to complete the cathedral's building, aided him and sought to expand the cathedral's programming in music and the arts. It was also a time of social change: women clergy were added to the cathedral's ranks, and the cathedral sought to increase its witness in interracial and interfaith Washington.

Walker, who had emerged from the unrest of Detroit, had become a major voice in urban ministry in Washington and elsewhere. He was a friend of Desmond Tutu, and became a significant international presence in anti-apartheid efforts in South Africa. All of these interests he brought to the cathedral, first as a canon on Dean Sayre's staff, then as his boss. When Walker combined the positions of dean and bishop in 1978, he brought with him an institutional management specialist, Charles A. Perry, as cathedral provost from 1978 to

1990. Walker died literally at the same hour as the final pinnacle was being placed on the cathedral's central tower, but the issues he dealt with continued in full force.

The cathedral became a steady presence for women's ministry, beginning with a historic ordination service on January 8, 1977, at which Bishop Walker preached and several women clergy were ordained. The cathedral also added several women priests to its clergy ranks, and expanded the ministries of lay women and men.

Walker was the first African American resident canon of the cathedral from 1966 to 1971, and then was elected suffragan, or assistant bishop, of Washington in 1971, then coadjutor, with right of succession when bishop William E. Creighton retired in 1977. Technically, Walker had begun church life in Washington by working for Sayre, but when it was evident that the dean, who had been in place for over two decades, would now be working for his former assistant, Sayre's retirement was inevitable.

Other issues surfaced, fueled by the generational and life experience differences of the two church leaders. Sayre had told Walker that the dean ran the cathedral and the bishop came to the cathedral at the dean's invitation, principally to preach or celebrate services at Christmas and Easter, and he intended to continue that practice. Walker responded, "It's the other way around Frank, the bishop is head of the Cathedral and can participate in services any time he wants to, and that is what I intend to do."

Walker then announced in late 1977 that he would assume the dual positions of bishop of Washington and dean of the cathedral, assisted by a provost, or chief administrative officer, Charles A. Perry, to run the day-to-day operations of the cathedral. Perry had strong managerial credentials. An economics and government major at Cornell University, he had spent seven years with the U.S. Atomic Energy Commission before attending Virginia Theological Seminary. He had also conducted over forty midlevel and senior management training seminars as a consultant to International Business Machines and other corporations.

Sayre rejected the new alignment, and spoke out against it until Walker asked him not to, as it might be regarded as an open fight between bishop and dean. Sayre muted his criticisms, but the differences remained. Canon Richard T. Feller, who supervised cathedral construction work from 1953 to 1978, when he retired as Clerk of the Works, said, "I knew at the time when Walker rose to be bishop that Sayre was not going to work for one of his former canons. Sayre had too big an ego for that. As soon as it was announced that Walker had been elected diocesan bishop after being suffragan bishop, I knew in my heart that spelled the dean's resignation or that he would retire, and he did."[1] "John Walker was a very savvy guy," Feller continued, "he was trusted by whites and blacks and that's a heck of an achievement back in his day, not now. He was trusted implicitly," Feller continued.

"I had never thought about becoming a bishop," Walker once wrote a young man who had asked him what it was like to have his job. "It is easier to be a priest and work with one congregation." A bishop must "celebrate the Holy Eucharist at least one hundred times a year. I have weddings, baptisms, funerals, and meetings beyond imagining. If that were not enough, a bishop must do work for and with the National Church and the Church worldwide."[2] A committee of laity and clergy had nominated him for the new position of suffragan bishop, and he was consecrated at a special convention held at the cathedral on June 29, 1971. He held the assistant's post for five years, until Bishop William F. Creighton announced his retirement plans, and on September 29, 1977, Walker was installed as diocesan bishop at age fifty-two.

He was a modest person but a public figure, and from 1970 to 1977 hosted a weekly television show called *Overview*. The program was never simply a forum to promote the cathedral, its art and music, but focused on wider civic questions and issues like drug prevention, crime, voting rights, education, nutrition, and job opportunities for women. Walker was an activist community leader as well, and frequently sought out by the media for his opinions on policy issues.

On March 13, 1985, he invited the public to join him in a protest march from the cathedral to the South African embassy, a short walk down Massachusetts Avenue. The hundred-some protesters were arrested, and Walker said:

I submit that those who have not seen how black South Africans are treated may indeed misunderstand what we

---

1 Richard T. Feller, clerk of the works, interview transcript, with Robert Becker, September 2, 2000, Washington, DC, NCA (163.2.4): 4.
2 Robert Harrison, *Transformed by the Love of God, John Walker, A Man for the 21st Century* (Cincinnati: Forward Movement, 2004): 100.

do here. I have been to South Africa. I've seen and heard
the abuse heaped on Christians, many of whom are members of the Anglican Communion. I am led, I trust, by
our Lord Jesus Christ, to bear witness in support of our
Christian brothers and sisters in South Africa who though
created in the image of God, are treated as things and
animals by other Christians. They live lonely and isolated
lives. Frequently they must wonder if God cares for them
at all.[3]

Walker constantly raised the issue of South Africa with Congress,
the White House, the State Department, and with the South African
embassy.

Early Years: Georgia, Detroit, St. Paul's School, Uganda

Walker arrived at the cathedral in 1966 as canon missioner with wide
exposure to both urban problems and international life. Born in
Barnesville, Georgia, in 1925 of an itinerant sharecropping family, he
was schooled in Detroit where he witnessed the growing Southern
migrant population of blacks seeking World War II defense industry
jobs in the overcrowded city. Detroit in the summer of 1943 experienced a thirty-six-hour riot during which property was looted, cars
were burned, and thirty-four people died. His high school graduation was canceled for fear of violence.

Walker later graduated from Wayne State University in 1951 and
hoped to be a librarian, a safe vocational goal for someone emerging
from abject poverty. The Walker family had strong church ties, which
in Detroit Walker transformed by attending a neighborhood Episcopal
Church instead of the African Methodist Episcopal (A.M.E.) church
that was the family's habitual place of worship. Michigan bishop
Richard S. Emrich supported Walker's desire to enter the ministry,
but insisted he attend Virginia Theological Seminary in Alexandria,
Virginia, the first African American to do so.

When he was at Virginia Theological Seminary, Walker left
campus infrequently, except to attend an integrated parish, or one
of two Washington eating-places that welcomed African Americans:
Old Ebbitt's Grill and the Old Europe. Decades later, he spoke with

---

3 *Ibid.*, 190.

fondness of the Old Europe, a German restaurant on upper Wisconsin Avenue within walking distance of the cathedral, which welcomed diners of all races.

After three years in seminary and two years in parish ministry at St. Mary's. Detroit, Walker spent eleven years at St. Paul's School, Concord, New Hampshire, as an administrator and teacher of American history. Following a sabbatical year teaching at a seminary in Uganda, in 1966 he left the prestigious New England Episcopal boarding school for a position at National Cathedral.

He arrived in Washington in 1966 as the city's racial crisis was deepening, and the sermons he delivered between 1967 and 1969 reflect his growing concern over the relationship between the white power structure and the realities of life for most black Americans. Crime was a serious problem in Washington, fueled by the lack of adequate housing and educational opportunities for many black residents, plus the perception that the police and city government were not on their side. This was Walker's working environment, his responses to it were clear, he was compassionate, and never histrionic or self-serving. At heart he was a careful listener and wise counselor whose responses were generally brief and to the point, but he always saw the gospel as action-oriented and transformative of society.

The problem of Walker's unclear role as canon was illustrated In a late 1960s letter to Sayre. Walker said he understood his ministry as a cathedral canon to be participation in regular cathedral worship services; inner city work, "which helps keep the Cathedral in touch with the so called Black Revolution"; and sustained contact with schools and young people, the "Youth Revolution." Noting Sayre's concern that Walker was out of town too often, Walker said that many of the events he attended or chaired were on Mondays, his nominal day off. "I am one of a few clergy that still has entrée with the rebellious young, and one of a rapidly vanishing breed of black clergy still working in an otherwise white institution who still has credibility . . . with a large segment of black people." He next turned to his decreased participation in Sunday services. While he had once had a significant part in all the Sunday cathedral services, he now felt like "black window dressing."

> As you know, Frank this is a difficult matter for me. . . . It
> is very difficult for me to walk in with no function except

sometimes to carry the chalice. . . . To black visitors (and some have said this to me) I appear to be a useful tool and willing to be used. Several times Cathedral employees (Black) have asked me why I am so seldom involved at the 11:00 am on Sundays. It is difficult to be convincing when I answer.

Walker added that he was not being super-sensitive, "but I also believe that we should all have regular priestly functions here (Sundays and weekdays). This is of considerable importance to me."[4]

By 1971, when he was elected suffragan bishop of Washington, Walker had been active in Washington urban ministry, including helping found Inter/Met, an interracial, interdenominational downtown seminary for students who still worked at their regular jobs. In 1972, shortly after the massacre of a group of Israeli athletes in Munich, Walker was asked to speak at a memorial service at Washington's Lincoln Memorial Reflecting Pool. He began his remarks by praising the efforts of the Jewish community to share with the wider world their collective grief over the massacre. In both cathedral and diocesan positions, Walker made a concerted effort to welcome Jewish and Arab leaders.

As a teacher, Walker had a strong interest in American history, especially the larger issues of the Civil War. In a 1981 meditation he reflected on a recent visit to Civil War battlefields, especially in Virginia. "It was not the fact of it being All Hallows Eve, that turned my mind . . . to thoughts of the dead," he wrote after visiting Chancellorville and Fredericksburg:

Rather, it was the deep sense of history and presence that momentarily captured my thoughts. Looking at the ground all around and at the arrows pointing toward the battlefield, I could not help identifying with the dead of that war. The still, green earth is enriched by the blood of so many of the young men of a nation. The thought then came that it didn't matter on which side they had fought. Each side had fought what it believed was an

---

4 NCA (7-3-3). The letter is undated, but was probably written in Walker's third or fourth year as cathedral canon, probably in 1969 or 1970. Sayre did not reply in writing.

honorable war for justice and truth, and liberty. Both sides believed that they were doing God's will. In what is for us an incomprehensible way, both believed that they were fighting and dying as Christians for human freedom.

He concluded, "Each time I drive past such a battleground, I relive that important time in American History. On each occasion, I have a dramatic experience of anamnesis (recall and remembrance) and of the meaning of the communion of saints. Later that night, I found myself reciting the names of family, friends, students, and others who had died in recent wars (many in their youth)."[5]

Methodically, as cathedral canon and bishop, Walker expanded his civic contacts. He became an active member of the Council of Churches of Greater Washington, a participant in a monthly meeting of Protestant judicatory heads, and chair of the board of Africare, an African-related economic and social development program. He also was a member of the police chief's Citizens Advisory Council; a delegate to the fifth assembly of the World Council of Churches in Nairobi, Kenya in 1975; and a frequent speaker at the U.S. Naval Academy and State Department. From the time he took over as diocesan bishop in 1977, Walker urged an expanding list of community leaders to work together on racial, gender, and other community issues. He was one of the founders and a longtime officer of the Urban Bishops Coalition.

During 1975 Walker convened a cathedral summit of forty representatives of various faith traditions who agreed to work together for continued dialogue, provide a budget of $71,000, and support an interfaith conference that would both provide a forum for interfaith contact and develop action programs to address issues affecting the quality of human life in the Washington region. Clark Lobenstine, a Presbyterian cleric, was hired as executive director of the group.

The Interfaith Conference of Metropolitan Washington brought together representatives of twenty-four different institutions including Jews, Muslims, and Christians that focused on questions of the aged, human rights, criminal justice, peace, and interfaith cooperation. It soon added representatives of the Latter-Day Saints, Jain, Baha'i, and Hindu religions. The IFC actively supported a food bank, housing

---

5 Harrison, 220–221.

programs, summer camps for children, lectures, concerts, and joint prayer services.

Walker was not by inclination a joiner of organizations. He encountered the region's religious and civic leaders regularly as part of his job, and was not drawn to the trappings of power. Besides, he had a young family, a wife and three children, with whom he wanted to spend time, a cathedral foundation and chapter to run, and a large diocese that covered the District of Columbia and part of Maryland that required constant attention. It was a full-time job and then some. He was fully encouraging of the ministry of the laity within the Episcopal Church, was an early advocate of the ordination of women, and was active in strengthening the national and international ministry of the Episcopal Church. He also became a candidate for the post of presiding bishop in 1985, but lost by ten votes.

"Even as his power and authority increased, he was utterly without pretention," Harrison wrote, adding:

> [O]ver the years, he and Maria and their three obliging children took in many strays—not dogs and cats . . . but stray people. Crime victims found a refuge in the Walker's home until they felt safe enough to start rebuilding the security of their own. Friends of friends passing through stayed over for a few days. Family from Detroit or Limon, Costa Rica, was frequently in residence. Folks who were between houses or waiting for a job came to dinner and left a few months later. Diplomats who had been called back home dropped their children off to stay with the Walkers while they finished their school term.[6]

Their Cleveland Park home, not far from work, was in an attractive middle class neighborhood. The Walkers lived an unpretentious, family-centered life; John ironed his own shirts. His manner was low key and conciliatory, but uncompromising on basic issues, he stayed in contact with people whose viewpoints were sometimes polar opposites from his own, and he never took such differences personally.

In 1983, in a Martin Luther King, Jr. Day sermon, Walker joined the growing number of commentators who rejected the concept of the melting pot as representing American society. "Slavery for

6 *Ibid.,* xix–xxx.

African-Americans continued even after it was ended, transferred into the powerful Jim Crow. Native Americans lived and died on reservations. Orientals were excluded. Jews and Catholics were suspect. The idea of a great American Melting Pot was a dismal failure." A prophet was needed to proclaim a new vision of Christian society, and King represented such a prophetic voice. "Martin was such a prophet. He marched, he preached, and he went to jail. He was single-minded in his devotion to the dream." Part of honoring his memory is to annually evaluate "how far we have travelled along the road that leads to the dream's fulfillment. Do our laws recently passed, does our economic activity, does our public behavior help to build the new Jerusalem?"[7] This was not a vague poetic concept for Walker, but meant the actual changes required in society to make communities free of racial and gender inequities.

After five years at the cathedral, he was elected the assisting bishop of Washington, a galvanic event in his life and that of the diocese and cathedral. In his final annual report as a cathedral staff member, he wrote, "As suffragan bishop I hope to continue to serve this Cathedral Church and to support what it struggles to become— a House of Prayer for all people; a symbol of hope for all who are without hope, and a sign that faith lives on in the human heart."

Walker was keenly aware of the interplay of religion and politics, especially at the cathedral. He kept in frequent contact with his friend Desmond Tutu in South Africa and followed the work of liberation theologians in Central and South America. Although the cathedral's charter identified it as "a great church for national purposes," any service or meeting it held with political overtones produced strong pro and con reactions. When President Ronald Reagan decided to hold a prayer service marking his second inaugural at the cathedral, his staff insisted that Jerry Falwell, head of the Moral Majority, be the preacher. Walker rejected the possibility, and eventually a compromise was reached. The preacher would be Billy Graham, but Walker got to review his sermon in advance. "The incident throws in sharp relief the relationship between politics and religion that Walker held in such creative attention," Harrison observed, "He masterfully balanced the distinct halves of the Cathedral's mission. Guided by his own convictions, Walker saw that televangelism

---

7 *Ibid.,* 59.

and partisan agendas were not going to be confused with the procla-mation of the Gospel."[8]

The bishop was much in demand as a speaker on the intersection of religion and politics. As commencement speaker at the University of Maryland in 1986, he urged listeners, "to help protect the prin-ciple of freedom of religion which also includes freedom *from* reli-gion and the inherent right of religious bodies to call governments to responsibility and restraint in all matters but certainly on those issues that are rooted in morality, e.g., poverty, feeding the hungry, pro-viding shelter for the homeless, matters of war, peace, and of human rights. These are precious rights always to be protected against any who would raise government above the rights of the people. This is a legacy which we have received and I ask you to protect it and carry it on to those who follow in your footsteps."[9]

Women's Ordination

Walker was a strong proponent of the ordination of women, and preached at the landmark service of several women ordinands on January 8, 1977, shortly after the Episcopal Church voted for the full inclusion of women in its ordained ministries. He told those gath-ered for the service, "I am aware and acknowledge that there are those in this diocese and throughout the Anglican Communion who are opposed to the inclusion of women in this church's ministry and priesthood." Yet "the notions of exclusiveness were rejected by our Lord and by those who have passed on the Gospel message to us. Further, I am convinced that though we are often tardy in under-standing the secret this does not mean that the secret must forever remain closed." At the service, two women whose extracanonical ordination in 1975 had not been recognized were accepted and three additional female and three male deacons were ordained as well. The women included Elizabeth P. Wiesner; Carole Crumley; and Pauli Murray of Boston, the first black woman to become a priest in the Episcopal Church, an attorney and civil rights advocate, ordained by Bishop Creighton for the bishop of Massachusetts.

---

8 *Ibid.,* xxvii.
9 John T. Walker, "Church, State, and Civil Disobedience," commencement address, University of Maryland, May 27, 1986.

The Growing Debt of National Cathedral, an Expanded Role for the Bishop

In 1977, just before he became diocesan bishop, Walker elaborated on his ideas of what the cathedral might be. He noted that the Diocese of Washington had always been at the forefront of justice and political reform issues. He called on Protestant, Catholic, Jewish, Islamic, and other faith bodies to work even more closely than before toward four basic objectives, much better communication within the interfaith community, for it to represent a unified voice in times of moral crisis, for it to be a force for moral and social transformation, and to create an interfaith community that would be "a sign, a visible witness to the Oneness of all the peoples of this community—and of this earth—under the Fatherhood of God."[10]

An enduring question for Walker as bishop was what to do about National Cathedral and its growing debt. More than a half century after its construction began the building was still not finished, and was over $12 million in debt, although the exact figure was not certain. Construction on the building was suspended during the summer of 1977 for lack of funds, and resumed in late September 1980 after a capital campaign was launched. The front towers were completed in 1983, and by January 1984 the building's current debt was paid off. The impressive bronze entrance gates were in place by 1987, the last of 106 gargoyles had been carved, landscaping of the space in front of the cathedral was undertaken, and the bishop met one-on-one with potential donors around the country.

A flash point came as the United States Bicentennial approached. Sayre saw it as the ideal occasion to complete construction of the nave, and by 1977 the cathedral's construction debt had risen to $12.5 million. Walker, now bishop of the diocese and dean of the cathedral, wanted to see the building debt-free. He also announced that he would be both bishop and dean of the cathedral. This put him in immediate conflict with Sayre, who had run the cathedral largely uninterfered with for over two decades.

On November 15, 1977, Walker brought the question to a head in a letter to Sayre in which he took issue with the direction Sayre said he wanted to take the cathedral in the next decade. Walker did

---

10 Harrison, 22.

not openly challenge Sayre when the dean publically presented his plan to the Cathedral Chapter, but had told Sayre it would conflict with cathedral fundraising possibilities. He asked Sayre not to publish the plan in *Cathedral Age*. He, in turn, would not publish his refutation of it. Walker added, "Your response was that you did not intend to fight me and that you wanted our friendship to remain intact, . . . Yet your statement prepared for the Chapter did not reflect that desire. It did not offer me any alternative plan. Rather, it was an attack on the plan I had offered. . . . It also questioned whether Canon Perry and I could do the work I had carved out for us." Walker concluded, "Throughout this past year I have been at a loss to understand the nature of your animosity toward me or the precise reasons for it. I am aware of your depression over the revelation of the financial crisis. I remind you that I was in no way responsible for the financial crisis." But he concurred with Bishop Creighton making a general announcement of the multimillion-dollar cathedral construction debt. He concluded, "I deeply regret all that has happened but as I said a month ago I can not wait until you are gone to begin the work of building for the future." He asked Sayre to join him in the effort to erase the cathedral's indebtedness and raise funds for its future, and to help "bind the community here on Mount. Saint Alban together. If you cannot join me then I ask you to remain silent. The battle in which you are engaged is suicidal. It will destroy what you have built and your reputation with it." Finally, the next two months could be a time of drawing together, of unity, or "a time of bitterness and recrimination. It is up to you. Which will it be? I await your response when we meet Thursday at 3 PM."[11]

Sayre did not frontally attack Walker but displayed the cool reserve that could be a feature of his dealings with others. Earlier in the year, he had declared his position and had lost. He still maintained that no one person (or two people) could manage the diocese and the cathedral, even with the best intentions. It was left for Sayre to retire with dignity and with the good wishes of many people with whom he had worked. He remained distant, though, from bishop and diocese, and rarely had anything more to do with the institution where he had spent over a quarter century.

---

11 Letter from John T. Walker to Francis B. Sayre, November 14, 1977, NCA (7.3.5).

The life experiences of Bishop Walker and Dean Sayre were quite different. For Walker, issues of justice, peace, education, race, and gender became increasingly important, and he spoke out on them, and believed the cathedral and diocese should be active agents for change and reform. It is not that Walker and Sayre publicly disagreed: that rarely happened, but as Walker's authority as bishop became increasingly clear, Sayre's influence as dean waned, and the dean announced his retirement set for January 17, 1978, his sixty-third birthday. He would have liked to stay on, even after twenty-seven years at the cathedral, but Walker had assumed the dean's role as well as being bishop: Sayre's time had come and gone. Bishop Ronald H. Haines, Walker's successor, said, "I'm almost certain that John, as Canon Missioner, felt that Dean Sayre was less than friendly to him and that it was perceived in racial terms. So when John became bishop, Sayre left very quickly. So maybe John felt he wasn't going to go up against another dean and would just be dean himself."[12]

The Bishop, the Diocese, and the Cathedral: New Directions

On September 15, 1977, Bishop Walker had issued a carefully crafted statement entitled "Mission and Ministry of Diocese and Cathedral." It represented a different understanding than the dean's of what the relationship of the two bodies should be, based on different understandings of their respective histories. It was not a personal disagreement with Sayre, but an expanded, different perspective on Washington diocesan history.

Walker saw the bishop as a "boundary person standing between the church and society. As a witness of God's judgment on both, he is required to remind the church of its calling to work diligently for a just society and to remind society that without justice it will perish."[13] For Walker, the parish would be the front line of ministry, and relations between the bishop and cathedral would be different. The cathedral would be the chief mission church of the diocese,

---

12 Ronald H. Haines, Bishop, with Robert Becker, interview transcript, December 14, 2000, Washington, DC, NCA (63.5.2): 6.

13 John T. Walker, "Mission and Ministry of Diocese and Cathedral," September 15, 1977, NCA (8.1.12). I am grateful to David Booth Beers, former chancellor of the Diocese of Washington, for providing a copy of this document.

and would have an important national mission due primarily to its unique location. It would become a leader in the ecumenical movement and in the development of closer ties with other faiths as well, all under the bishop as chief pastor. "In the bishop and through his authority can the Cathedral and its institutions be brought into a common ministry with the Diocese."[14] When the dean's resignation becomes effective, January 17, 1978, "I will not nominate a successor. As bishop and dean, I will function as chief liturgist and spokesman of the Cathedral and am already scheduled to participate in every season of the church year and at all major festivals."[15] Perry, at that time executive officer of the diocese, would become provost, or executive vice president, of the Cathedral Foundation, the bishop's manager of both diocese and cathedral. Walker said that the bishop assuming such a joint role harmonized with the earlier history of diocese and cathedral, and that what he was doing was restoring a basic relationship that had fallen out of use in recent decades.

"While Walker was bishop, Perry met weekly with him," Bishop Ronald H. Haines, Walker's successor, observed:

> They had a standing meeting and Perry went over everything that was going to be done and what was coming up and Walker was approving or disapproving of what Perry did. John didn't take any issue with iconography or anything like that. He left that entirely to Charles. I think John wanted to decide who was going to use the cathedral. Charles knew when he took the job that this was Walker's decision. Charles had already worked for [Bishop] Creighton and he knew that the dean did whatever he wanted and never consulted Creighton at all. Walker knew it too.[16]

A commission appointed to review the cathedral's mission roundly supported Walker as being "uniquely suited to remind both church and society" of their spiritual and ethical needs, and the mission and ministry of the bishop and of the Cathedral and its institutions are a natural extension of the mission and ministry of the

---

14 *Ibid.*, 3.
15 *Ibid.*, 3.
16 Ronald H. Haines, Bishop, with Robert Becker, Interview Transcript, December 14, 2000, Washington, DC, NCA (163.5.2): 11.

bishop and the Diocese of Washington. The power of combining the two most important symbols of the Episcopal Church in Washington cannot be overestimated and the times call for such a combination, John W. McTigue, the commission's chairman wrote, adding, "Harnessing the rich resources of Mount Saint Alban in common task under a single leader offers opportunities for service to church and community as envisioned by the founders of the Cathedral."[17]

In January 1978 Walker announced a capital campaign for the cathedral to both pay off the debt and expand its programs. He personally visited many potential donors. By August 31, 1989, the cathedral's construction debt was paid. A festive celebration was planned for Michaelmas, September 29, 1989, when the last tower stone was blessed and put in place. This was exactly eighty-two years after construction had begun.

As the skilled workers were completing the tower, John Walker lay dying in nearby Sibley Hospital from complications after a heart operation. The bishop had originally planned to preside at the day's festivities. News of his death was announced at the evensong that followed the tower dedication. Five thousand people gathered the following Thursday for his funeral, and the mortal remains of the sixth bishop of Washington were placed with those of his predecessors.

Charles A. Perry, Cathedral Provost (1978–1990)

Charles A. Perry spent twenty years on Mount Saint Alban, as executive officer of the diocese and as provost of National Cathedral. For much of that time he was in the shadow of Bishop Walker, for whom he worked from 1977 to 1989, but he still emerged as very much of a thoughtful, independent voice. As both a teacher and administrator, Perry was a strong and stabilizing presence in cathedral life in the turbulent 1980s.

Perry was born in White Plains, New York, on November 5, 1928, and graduated from Philips Academy, Andover, Massachusetts. He left Cornell University in 1950 with a B.A. degree in economics and government, and spent seven years in the congressional liaison and public information office of the U.S. Atomic Energy Commission

---

17 John W. McTigue to William F. Creighton, "The Cathedral Mission" (Commission Report), April 27, 1977, 3.

in Washington before attending Virginia Theological Seminary, from which he graduated with honors in 1961. He also held an advanced degree in public administration from the University of Minnesota in public administration, completed an executive development program at Cornell, and later gave numerous intensive seminars for midlevel and senior corporate officials on improving institutional management.

Perry served as Episcopal chaplain at Indiana University and to students at the University of Virginia before joining the diocesan staff as executive officer in 1971. When Walker became cathedral dean in January 1978, he brought Perry with him as provost, the day-to-day administrator of the cathedral and its multiple activities, although Perry kept the position as diocesan executive officer as well for several years.

Perry also wrote a book on the Resurrection, and published many of his sermons and reports on the cathedral. In his 1978–1979 report he wrote, "Awesome in dimension, the magnitude alone hushes the garrulous visitor and lifts the eyes and hearts of all who enter. The Cathedral educates by being there. Preachers, musicians, and guides may proclaim and interpret the word but a Gothic cathedral, in stone and glass, enshrines it." In the previous year, more than a quarter of a million people had visited the cathedral and a hundred and fifty volunteer guides provided tours and answered questions. Noting that more than half the visitors were children, Perry said their numbers indicated, "We are responsible for the education of more children than are enrolled in all the Episcopal Sunday schools in fifteen dioceses the size of our own."

During Perry's tenure, the cathedral maintained its strong commitment to public programs. It sponsored a hearing on infant mortality in the District of Columbia, established a cooperative pastoral ministry with St. Alban's Church, assisted the Washington Hospice Society, and held over fifteen hundred services attended by more than two hundred thousand people. In 1978 and 1979 the cathedral also hosted fifty-nine guest musical groups and sponsored organ recitals by thirty different visiting musicians. About eighteen thousand donors raised over $600,000 in the annual campaign, helping to reduce a $10 million debt, which also carried $800,000 a year in interest costs. Perry wrote:

I close on a personal note. I am sure of our mission.
I believe I know what the Cathedral is called to be and

with more funds available would be prepared to announce new program initiatives. I am confident in the skills and commitment of key staff. I trust we can continue to increase operating funds to keep up with inflation. My principal worry is that we must raise capital funds very rapidly before the interest eats us alive. In 1979 we used the last of our unrestricted capital. Now we are totally dependent on the Capital Campaign to pay interest.[18]

Though skilled as a detailed-oriented executive, Perry was also a constant voice on public religious issues. In a 1983 sermon on "The Prodigal Son" he wrote, "We have exploited our democratic heritage by dividing up into a proliferation of petty single issue self-interest groups, each grasping for its piece of pie at the expense of those too weak to organize and at the expense of the larger purposes of the nation. We are spending our political inheritance with reckless abandon pretending that no sacrifice is required to maintain and develop it." National reorientation, he continued, was far different that personal turning to God. He found the efforts of prominent evangelists, like Dr. Billy Graham, to be misdirected and have no lasting impact on the nation as a whole. "I do not blame the evangelists, although I personally believe that many of them have underestimated the depth of our sickness or offered primarily individual and personal solutions when only a massive national change of heart would suffice." Perry acknowledged that he might be long on diagnosis and short on solutions: "I see myself both at home with the Father, feeling the security of his gracious and forgiving welcome, and at the same time part of a people alienated and apart from him." This dualism means "I do not judge my people . . . Nor do I pretend that all is well with the world because my eyes and ears tell me differently."[19]

In October 1990 he left the cathedral to become president and dean of the Church Divinity School of the Pacific. He left Washington, listing his achievements as an expansion of the cathedral's school outreach programs, elimination of its massive debt, and

18 Charles A. Perry, "A Report from the Provost, 1978–1979," *Cathedral Age* (Winter 1979): 2–5.
19 Charles A. Perry, "The Prodigal Son," March 13, 1983. *Cathedral Age* (Summer 1983): 20–22.

a dramatic increase in the number of volunteers. This led to an only partly fulfilled goal, to make the cathedral an adult education center for the Episcopal Church. "The Episcopal Church has not always done a good job of raising the theological I.Q. and sophistication of its otherwise highly educated community. And we have the chance in this place to provide educational opportunities across the board." He saw the cathedral as "a place where the semi-churched and the unchurched drift in," adding, "We don't have to make them into Episcopalians, but perhaps we can help them grow as Christians." In addition to fundraising and completion of most building projects, Perry's twelve years at the cathedral included increased relations with the church population in South Africa and expanded numbers of visits from clerics from the Soviet Union.

As a former diocesan executive officer and provost, he was well aware of "a necessary tension between the great church for national purposes and the chief mission church of the diocese. We can't be all of one. We have to be some of both. The question is how." He also affirmed the work of his wife, Joy, in providing hospitality at Bratenahl House through a steady number of luncheons, dinners, and receptions. "Joy sees this as a real ministry. As a result of her hospitality, many people feel that their work and contributions have been appreciated."[20]

Bishop Ronald H. Haines on Cathedral-Diocesan Relations

Bishop Ronald H. Haines (1934–2008), Walker's successor, took a different approach to cathedral relations. He did not have time to be both bishop and dean, he believed, and instituted a search for a new dean to replace the acting provost, Sanford Garner, former rector of Christ Church, Georgetown, who had succeeded Perry in 1990.

Haines explained the complex relationship between the two institutions:

> When I came to the Diocese of Washington as Bishop Walker's suffragan, my Cathedral role was very unclear.

---

20 Lindsay J. Hardin, "Twenty Years on the Hill: An Interview with Charles Austin Perry," *Cathedral Age* (Summer 1990): 31–33.

In those years, Bishop Walker was both dean and bishop with Charles Perry as provost. It was an unusual situation further complicated by a set of old by-laws. Bishop Walker ordered the rewriting of the by-laws that was completed just about the time that he died. His untimely death created a time of legal confusion. In most dioceses, when the diocesan bishop dies, it is not a suffragan who becomes the ecclesiastical authority but rather it is the Standing Committee. The Diocese of Washington has a canon specifically to the contrary. Thus, as suffragan, I became the ecclesiastical authority. By extension, I then took Bishop Walker's chair on the Foundation Chapter. It was during that time that the new by-laws were ratified which clarified the roles of diocesan bishop, the dean, the canons and, by specifically not mentioning the suffragan bishop.[21]

Elsewhere, Haines wrote another bishop who asked about cathedral–diocesan relations:

The total personnel list and budget for the Cathedral Foundation which includes not only the Cathedral itself but the three schools, the College of Preachers, etc, is five times larger than that of the diocese. The tension we have is that the diocese likes to think of 'our Cathedral.' However, the diocese does not contribute any substantial amount towards the upkeep of the Cathedral. In fact, the Cathedral treats itself as a parish and supports the diocese. About eighty percent of the income for Washington National Cathedral comes from outside of the diocese. We are always aware of that pull between serving the diocese and serving our national constituency.

It was 1991 and Haines wrote that "the Cathedral is looking more towards the diocese than it has at any time in recent memory. We are now working so that Cathedral programs and diocesan programs are mutually compatible. The Cathedral is very careful that we do not see it as an agent of doing the diocese's work."[22]

---

21 Ronald H. Haines to Mrs. Lloyd Symington, April 20, 1994, NCA (8.1.12).
22 Ronald H. Haines to Robert H. Johnson, March 12, 1991, NCA (8.1.12).

"The key to unity is the bishop. It cannot be anywhere else," John R. Frizzell, Jr., Perry's successor as executive officer of the diocese, wrote in a 1989 study called "Diocese and Cathedral" written shortly after Walker's death. Referring to Walker's combining the bishop's and dean's roles in one person, Frizzell concluded, "That idea clearly did not work out and, in my judgment, clearly did not work out due to the time demands on both positions. I do not think that those demands will lessen in the future if both diocese and Cathedral are to move forward as we all hope that they will."[23]

"We cannot ignore the fact that there is a reservoir of hostility in the diocese toward the Cathedral which was made very clear in the recent Pinnacle Campaign," a funding effort to obtain contributions from diocesan churches for one of the cathedral tower pinnacles. "There are a great many factors which have contributed toward that hostility," Frizzell concluded: a topic that should be a high priority for a new bishop and dean. Frizzell also pointed out that the cathedral's annual contributions to the diocese and national church were small, despite the cathedral's being called "the Chief Mission Church of the Diocese." In 1988 the major parish of St. John's Church, Lafayette Square, gave the diocese $110,370, the cathedral $55,000. In the same year, St. John's income was $809,350, the cathedral's $4,066,099. "In the current budget year the Cathedral will spend $1.2 million on outreach yet there is no definite knowledge in the Diocese that I am aware of as to how the money is spent. At the same time, the Diocese will spend $1.6 million in outreach and I suspect that the Cathedral's knowledge of that effort is no better than ours. Common sense alone . . . demands that there be better coordination in the future."

Women Clergy at National Cathedral

One of the innovations Bishop Walker and Provost Perry made at National Cathedral when Walker became cathedral dean was a greater inclusion of women, lay and clergy, in public roles in the cathedral. Walker had long been a supporter of the ordination of women, and, like Bishop William F. Creighton, he wanted the measure to be approved by the Episcopal Church, which happened on September

---

23 John R. Frizzell, Jr. Diocese and Cathedral, November 24, 1989, NCA (8.1.12).

16, 1976 at its General Convention in Minneapolis. Then on January 8, 1977, an ordination service took place at National Cathedral of several women and men, and two women who had previously been irregularly ordained in September 1975 were recognized as legitimate clergy. Walker was preacher at the service, and noted its historic nature. Parenthetically, there is no record of Sayre ever voicing favor (or opposition to) the ordination of women, although he did criticize the earlier illegal ordination conducted in a Washington parish by several retired or resigned bishops whom Bishop Creighton had specifically asked not to hold the ordination without proper authorization. Like the issue of updating the Book of Common Prayer of 1928 or the 1940 Hymnal, major efforts within the Episcopal Church, Sayre's position appeared ambiguous, neither supporting nor vocally opposing them. They appeared not to be major concerns to the outgoing dean.

Gradually, several women joined the cathedral staff ranks. Elizabeth P. Wiesner was a volunteer clergy member for several years; Carole Crumley was hired as a full-time staff member after a hiring freeze was lifted in 1981; R. Carter Echols, a lay canon, became Canon Missioner in 1987; and Bishop Jane Dixon frequently preached and took services when she became suffragan bishop of Washington in 1992 and bishop pro tempore in 2001 and 2002, following the retirement of Bishop Ronald H. Haines. The cathedral had no specific plan for more inclusive women's ministries, but this was a movement gaining momentum throughout the Episcopal Church, one Walker, Perry, and their successors actively supported.

Elizabeth P. Wiesner (1917–2011)

Elizabeth Phenix Wiesner was one of the first women to serve as volunteer clergy at National Cathedral. She was ordained in January 1977 by Bishop William F. Creighton. Her main role was to serve as a weekday pastoral counselor and to provide local referrals to those who came to the cathedral seeking a church home.

A graduate of Stanford University, she joined the American Red Cross during World War II, then transferred to the Office of Strategic Services (OSS) where she served as secretary to Allen Dulles in Switzerland, and married a Foreign Service Officer, Louis A. Wiesner, in June 1950. From 1976 to 1982 she served as a part-time non-stipendiary clergy person at the cathedral, and she also served as an assistant at St. Margaret's from 1973 to 1976 and at All Souls from 1982 to 1984, both parishes in Washington. Then she served parishes in Boston, Massachusetts, and in North Conway, New Hampshire, where the Wiesners kept a summer home, to which they retired and where she died on September 6, 2011 at age ninety-four.

She was the author of two short books, *Between the Lines: Years with the Red Cross and OSS* (1998) and *Pilgrim and Pioneer, a Journey with God* (1989), and was a member of the National Association for the Self-Supporting Active Ministry. Wiesner was one of four women who attended the 1978 Lambeth Conference of 440 male Anglican bishops at Canterbury, where women were admitted only as accredited press representatives. "Our presence gave a certain poignancy to the situation," she wrote. "One of the issues Lambeth addressed itself was the ordination of women to the diaconate, priesthood, and episcopacy. And of all those there, the four who were most intimately and personally concerned were present only as spectators." She saw her role as a ministry of presence, reminding the bishops that women's ordination was not just an abstract theological issue, but affected "real live human beings who were seeking to be obedient to their feeling of vocation."[24]

Canon Carole A. Crumley (1944–)

Carole Anne Crumley was the first woman priest hired by the cathedral as a full-time clergy staff member after the cathedral lifted its hiring freeze in 1981. Born in Johnson City, Tennessee, in 1944, Crumley was a graduate of Duke University (1966) and held an M.A. from the University of North Carolina (1969) and a Master's of Divinity from Inter/Met Seminary (1976), a multi-denominational seminary that functioned for several years in Washington.

A former high school teacher of English and French, she was one of several women ordained at the January 8, 1977 cathedral service. Her cathedral work was as canon pastor and educator, specializing in spirituality, pastoral contact, and ministry to single persons and young adults. She also was a founder of the Cathedral Center

---

24 Elizabeth Wiesner, "Reflections on Lambeth," *Cathedral Age* (Winter 1978): 27–28.

for Prayer and Pilgrimage, directed the Cathedral Volunteer Service Community, through which young adults engaged in inner city service projects, and managed the cathedral's expanded clergy volunteer program.

In a 1983 Epiphany sermon, Crumley laid out an agenda for the church in the century's remaining years: "It involves new ways of relating between men and women: a letting go of the way women are held as stereotypes" and "a recreating of each other as friends and teachers." Additionally, "it reveals the relationship between our humanity and the created order so that we can claim again as brother, sister, father, mother, sun, moon, sky and earth." Such a unity requires the examination of old prejudices "journeying to new places in unfamiliar company."[25]

R. Carter Echols, Canon Missioner (1997–2000)

Canon R. Carter Echols served as missioner and director of metropolitan ministries at National Cathedral from 1997 to 2000. As lay canon missioner, she was responsible for cathedral outreach to the Washington metropolitan area, for liaison with nonprofit community organizations, and for relations with national social ministries. She held a B.A. in religious studies from University of Virginia and an M.B.A. in the management of nonprofit agencies from William and Mary, and spent over twenty years with nonprofit service organizations, including almost nine years as executive director of Samaritan Ministry of Greater Washington, which included the social service programs of thirty-seven congregations. Echols was a member of a provincial coordinating team for Justice, Peace and Integrity of Creation ministries.

Well known as a preacher, in a March 1, 1998 Lenten sermon she explored the concept of powerlessness. "No matter how much power we have, each of us knows the feeling of powerlessness," she said. "We have felt powerless at the possibility of war. . . . Powerless to make someone else stop drinking or smoking or to make them love us. . . . Powerless in the face of poverty and natural disasters. Jesus in the wilderness, tempted in every way as we are tempted. Perhaps we

---

25 Carole A. Crumley, "God's Transforming Power," *Cathedral Age* (Spring 1984): 1.

are most quickly hooked by the ways Jesus' temptations reflect our desire to be in charge."

Echols summarized, "Through reflection and remembrance, we stop viewing the story through a reflected mirror and we become actors in the scene. In the context of this great story, it becomes clear that none of us will ever be powerless, nor will we ever be all-powerful. But whether we acknowledge it or not, we will always be God's beloved creations, valuable enough to God to receive the gift of Christ's death and resurrection."[26]

Jane Holmes Dixon (1937–2012)

Washington's Jane Holmes Dixon was the second woman bishop elected in the Episcopal Church and third woman consecrated a bishop in the Anglican Communion. She was a frequent presence in the cathedral from her election as suffragan bishop on November 19, 1992 until she retired in August 2002. Additionally, she was ecclesiastical authority, bishop pro tempore in the diocese from January 2001 until June 2002, in the period after one diocesan bishop retired and until a successor was elected.

Issues of justice and inclusion were important to her ministry. Following the 9/11, terrorist attacks, at a September 14, 2001 cathedral service, she told President George W. Bush and a packed cathedral, "Those of us who are gathered here—Muslim, Jew, Christian, Sikh, Buddhist, Hindu—indeed, all people of faith—know that love is stronger than hate and that love lived out in justice will, in the end, prevail." Referring to the cathedral as a house of prayer for all people, she urged those present "to be united so that we will make that message of love the message that the world needs to hear in this time of great tragedy."[27] Her preaching was always biblically grounded: in an Easter Sermon in 2002, she said, "This Easter Sunday morning in Washington the biblical truth still propels you and me to live our lives as lovers and risk takers. For if Jesus broke the bonds of death, then death is not the final word and life is lived

---

26 R. Carter Echols, Sermon, March 1, 1998, National Cathedral website.
27 Jane Holmes Dixon, "Remembrance Greeting," September 14, 2001, Washington National Cathedral website.

not to preserve life but to risk it. To risk it by living as if love matters most and that love is stronger than hate."[28]

The chapter and foundation, while updating their governing bylaws, presented Bishop Haines and Bishop Dixon with a document that removed the bishop of Washington from his or her traditional role as head of the chapter and foundation. Dixon pointed this out to Haines, who voiced his objection to the drafters: the draft bylaws were revised to retain the long-established role of Episcopal oversight.

A native of Mississippi, Dixon attended Randolph-Macon Women's College and Vanderbilt University, where she met her husband of fifty-two years, David, an attorney with the Department of Justice. At age forty, after being an eighth-grade teacher and mother of three children, she "stepped out of the kitchen into a new and different world" by attending Virginia Theological Seminary, from which she received a master of divinity degree in 1982 and a doctor of divinity in 1993. After work at the Church of the Good Shepherd, Burke, Virginia, and St. Alban's, Washington, DC, she became rector of St. Philip's Church in suburban Laurel, Maryland, until she was elected a bishop. By custom each newly elected bishop chooses another bishop as mentor, but Jane picked long-time friend, Verna Dozier, an African American teacher and author who had first suggested ministry as a career possibility to her. Preaching at Dixon's consecration in May 1973, Dozier said, "Die to your need to have everyone like you. You have a great capacity for friendship to which this Cathedral tonight bears eloquent witness, but there will always be those who choose to stand outside that circle. Be sure the choice is theirs. Resist the temptation to seek for the fault in you. As you rejoice in the mystery that there are many who love you, rest in the mystery that there are some who do not."[29]

From March 2001 to June 2002 Dixon engaged in a closely followed legal case in federal courts with the vestry of Christ Church, Accokeek, a historic southern Maryland church that challenged her decision not to license their controversial choice as rector, a cleric who would not recognize the authority as bishop. The vestry was

---

28 Jane Homes Dixon, "Easter Sermon," March 31, 2002, Washington National Cathedral website.
29 Vera Drozier, "Sermon preached at the Ordination of Jane Holmes Dixon as Suffragan Bishop of the Diocese of Washington, November 19, 1992."

also controlled by a handful of families that opposed the ordination of women. They found a supportive candidate who said his skills included an ability "to gum up the works" in the Episcopal Church. He was backed by breakaway church bishops in Texas and Pittsburgh.

The case was decided in Federal District Court by Judge Peter J. Messitte and sustained on appeal in the Court of Appeals, Fourth Circuit.[30] The decisions reaffirmed the Episcopal Church's hierarchical nature, the authority of diocesan bishops, and the right of bishops to license clergy in their dioceses.

Following her retirement, Dixon became a mentor to young clergy and senior advisor for interreligious relations for the Interfaith Alliance, where she had been board chair. In 2011 she received the organization's Walter Cronkite Award, along with broadcast journalist Jim Lehrer. "Throughout her ministry as priest and bishop, she was a champion for reconciliation and justice," her successor, Bishop Mariann Budde, said in announcing Dixon's death on December 25, 2012, adding, "Called to serve at a time when some refused to accept the authority of a woman bishop, Jane led with courage and conviction, and sometimes at great personal cost."[31]

The pioneering work of women clergy and lay leaders of the final decades of the twentieth century reflected the evolution of Washington National Cathedral, and at the century's turn women in widespread leadership roles was an accepted part of cathedral life.

Across the span of its history, the cathedral has reflected several tendencies that interfold, but do not blend together in any predictable unity. It is, first of all, "A House of Prayer for All People," but how inclusive the term "all people" is depends on the decade. Likewise, it has always been a national church, where presidents are celebrated or buried, where national tragedies are wept over, and triumphs, like landing on the moon or winning World Wars I and II are celebrated,

---

30 Dixon v. Edwards, 172 F. Supp 2nd 702 (D. Md. 2001) and Dixon v. Edwards, United States Court of Appeals, Fourth Circuit, No. 01-2337, Argued Jan. 24, 2002–May 24, 2002. The cases were later cited nationally in many disputes between the Episcopal Church and breakaway congregations.

31 Mariann Edgar Budde, December 25, 2012, letter to the Diocese of Washington, Washington National Cathedral website. Bishop Budde also said, "Bishop Jane Dixon died in her sleep early this morning after spending a joyful Christmas Eve with her family. Her death comes as a shock to her beloved husband of 52 years, Dixie, to their children and grandchildren, and to all of us blessed to have known Jane as friend, mentor, and colleague."

or events like the Vietnam War or conflicts in the Middle East are prayed about and explored in their larger implications. Through art, music, and worship, it is a welcoming place of prayer, where people worship God in different languages and represent different denominations and faith traditions. Those who built and maintain the cathedral structure realize it is sacred space, where individual and collective pilgrims encounter the *mysterium tremendum*, and where divine mystery intrudes on even the most carefully planned activity or gathering. It is not difficult to chronicle the building's construction or to report on what a preacher has said about a particular subject, but the builder's intentions, and those of its occupants, have always been to create something more, a setting where human quest and divine reality meet one another, and where, as was Bishop Satterlee's hope, in the King James translation of the Bible "the Word became flesh and dwelt among us" (John 1:14).

Appendix: Four Documents in National Cathedral's History

Four documents important to National Cathedral's history are excerpted below: the 1907 original architects' report, written by George F. Bodley and Henry Vaughan, their most extensive written statement of their understanding of Gothic architecture as a desirable building style centuries after it was conceived.

Second is the 1939 pamphlet by Anson Phelps Stokes on *Art and the Color Line*, challenging the Daughters of the American Revolution's refusal to allow the negro contralto Marian Anderson to present a concert at Constitution Hall, a leading Washington concert venue of that era.

Third is the September 1977 statement by Bishop John T. Walker explaining his reasons for combining the positions of bishop and dean in a single office, a practice that had fallen out of use in recent decades, and was especially challenged by the incumbent dean, Francis B. Sayre, resulting in his resignation.

Finally, stained glass artist Roland LeCompte in 2001 discussed his work in conceiving and crafting some of the cathedral's renowned stained glass windows, including the 10,500 piece Rose Window on the West Front. Collectively, these documents highlight four continuing aspects of cathedral life, architecture, race, church governance, and beauty, all of which appear and reappear throughout its history.

Bodley and Vaughan on Gothic Architecture and the New Cathedral (1907)

This 1907 report accompanied the initial architectural designs of architects George F. Bodley and Henry Vaughan which were for a fourteenth century English Gothic cathedral, but which were subsequently modified. Bodley died in 1908, Bishop Henry Yates Satterlee in 1908, and Vaughan in 1917. For example, the red brick recommended in the 1907 document was replaced by a lighter hued Indiana limestone in Cathedral construction, the towers were made taller, the West End reconfigured, and a detached Baptistery building was never built.

The New Cathedral
Washington
A.D. 1907

Gentlemen,

In laying the drawings of our design for the new Cathedral before you we would offer a few explanatory remarks, calling attention to the general character of the building, and to some of its distinctive features.

In style it is, as was widely desired, "Gothic" of the fourteenth century—a style of architecture, as we think, the most beautiful that the world has ever seen. In its dimensions it will be larger than most of the Cathedrals in England, or on the Continent. The total length is 476 feet, and the total width 132 feet. These are the external dimensions. The height of the ridgeline of the roof is 130 feet; while to the internal apex of the vaulting it is 93 feet.

The Central Tower will rise 280 feet from the ground. The plan is that of Nave and Aisles, Transepts, Choir and two Chapels. Double Aisles are planned for the Nave. These latter will be especially useful for Monuments and memorial windows and tablets. The Choir terminates in an apsidal Sanctuary. The building will be vaulted in stone throughout.

The lighting of the interior is designed to have fine effect, being lit by ample Clerestory windows. The light, thus coming from so high a level, will, in your bright climate, be striking and uplifting. There are lower windows in the Aisles: but they are quite subordinate. Then there will be a striking effect of light in the "Sanctuary," or eastern part of the Choir. For there is to be a large window both on the north and south sides, coming lower down, but much out of sight, being in the depth of thick walls. These windows will be 65 feet long. Light will be given by them to the Apse, in an especial and striking manner. It is for this important effect of light that we propose to have no Chapel at the far eastern end, in the more usual position when a Choir-aisle runs round the east end.

This plan has the advantage, too, of giving an interior of which the whole length is seen on entering at the West End; thus, adding to the perspective, and to the impressive effect of the building.

We propose two Chapels at the ends of the Choir-aisles, the south one could be the Lady chapel and the other of SS. Peter and Paul, who give title to the Cathedral; or the north Chapel could be the Chapel of St. John the Evangelist, the two Chapels thus symbolizing the scene of Calvary. As aisle terminating in a mere wall always has a poor and unsatisfactory effect. It will be a great advantage to have Chapels here at the eastern ends of the two aisles, for light there would take the eye and have a disturbing effect. The Apse with the effect of light there we have spoken of, should be the leading and the impressive feature. The two long windows will not be seen until one gets opposite to them, while their effect of light-giving, as we have said, will be exceedingly good. The exterior of the Apse, unhidden by a further building, will be commanding in its lofty proportion, and will make a very conspicuous landmark eastward, crowning the hill with its cluster of many pinnacles.

The Chapels at the ends of the aisles would be used for people during Choir services, and will thus afford accommodation. An isolated Lady Chapel would be a place per se and not useful for those attending the services conducted in the Choir, nor would it add to the internal effect. It is for these reasons that we have planned the Chapels where shown, and no separated Lady Chapel. The Chapel in the position shown will be bright with its south window. There will be a gleam of light from it.

Another feature to which we would call attention is, that it is proposed to have a broad soffit, 9 feet 6 inches wide, forming the eastern arch of the central tower. This deep sweep of soffit, or underside of the arch, we propose to have carved with figures of Angels. Arranged in a suitable design. It would be, as it were, an Angelic canopy over the Rood and will be an effective treatment. It would recall the words "which things the Angels desire to look into," and the words of the old hymn, "Inter Angeles laudamus Te," "We praise Thee amidst the Angels." The Angels could each hold a scroll with the words, "Sursum corda," [Lift up your hearts] the keynote, as it were, of the whole building.

Beyond this arch would be the Choir and the sanctuary. In the latter, could be represented our Lord, in glory, blessing, in the upper part of a lofty and dignified Reredos.

The stained glass Clerestory windows, as they could be placed, should consist of single figures, for they are too high up to contain "subjects." The glass should have finely colored figures on a light, silvery ground. These windows could set forth the history of religion in the world, beginning, in the Nave, with some of the Old Testament worthies, Prophets and Kings; and so on to Malachi, the last of the Prophets, and St. John the Baptist, and then to the Apostles and saints of the New Testament, and to many of later Christian years. We think, however, that all represented should be worthies of the Old Testament or Christian Saints, recognized as such. The great Church, however, will not have any very especial need of colored glass. It would be desirable, however, to have it in the south windows of the Lady Chapel, or the sunlight may be too strong there. It would be well, too, to have it at the east and windows of the Apse. But there are other things for which gifts would be more desirable, before the glass, in point of time. There are many stone statues desirable, and many carved subjects.

We have alluded to the outer aisles as being available for monuments. Here there could be placed mural tablets as memorials, and Brasses round the walls; and indeed "altar-tombs" with effigies, one in each space, could be placed as opportunity occurs. The Bishop reminds us that as Washington Cathedral is at the Capital of the Nation, and will inspire combined religious and patriotic feelings, it would be well, in some parts of the Cathedral, if place could be made for statues, bas-reliefs and other works, commemorating great American heroes and statesmen of the United Sates, and historical incidents of Colonial times and after the Revolution, which are dear to the hearts of American people. This could be easily arranged and suitable places found.

The site is a remarkably fine one, very commanding and beautiful. The Cathedral will be a conspicuous object from the Capitol and other parts of the city. When complete, with its surrounding buildings, it will be "as a city set on a hill."

Approaching the West End by a triple avenue of trees, those visiting the Cathedral will find three lofty open arches, the central one wider, and much higher, than the other two. These lead to three wide vaulted spaces to be used as large porches or porticoes, and so on to the three recessed west doorways. The central portico could be treated richly internally with arcading and many statues and carved subjects. These statues would be such as the Major and Minor Prophets, etc., etc. David and other worthies, all Old Testament characters, ending with St. John the Baptist, who could be turning to the central entrance, where, in its midst, there could be the figure of our Lord blessing those who enter. Below could be inscribed "Lux Mundi," or "Salvator Mundi." St. John the Baptist could hold a scroll inscribed with his "Ecce Agnus Dei." The two subordinate side entrances at the west could have statues of St. Peter and St. Paul, one in each, and, possibly, some scenes from their lives, at the sides of these porches internally.

While the exterior surroundings of this lower part of the west end are massive (the richer part being kept for the top of the Towers, "whose glory is in their height"), the interior of this central portico can be rich and stately, and be made beautiful with its many figures and pictorially carved subjects. It may be a very "Testament in stone," beginning with Adam and Eve in the Garden of Paradise, and ending with St. John the Baptist preaching in the Wilderness. Other statues, outside this great porch, and in different parts of the Cathedral, could be many and various Christian saints and heroes and worthies, and possibly some few modern ones, e.g., and more especially, Washington and Penn. (FN: Such modern figures would be better as statues, or in subjects, than in stained glass where modern costume is so incongruous, and indeed almost impossible.) Suitable statues may be added to the building as time goes on. Brackets could be provided for them from the first. In passing, we may say that all and every gift should not be in kind, but that the money should be given for each gift, and that all things given should be approved by the Architects. Incongruous things may be given, with the best intentions, that may be out of character and without harmony with the surroundings. This is most important. It is astonishing what harm a single note out of harmony will do; and so with every detail of furniture, or color; everything must be in keeping and manifest the same intention, drawn from the same inspiration.

Passing along the north side of the Cathedral externally, we would speak of the height of the walls, the interest of the window tracery in the Clerestory, the massive, but not too heavy, flying buttresses and pinnacles: of the light and shade given by them, and the bands of rich work in the outer aisles, of the molded plinths and windows and niches and the carved Canticles of the Church's Matins and Evensong, and the traceried parapets. Then, passing these, we get to the North Transept, with its protected entrance up many steps, and its high turrets and Rose window. Then to the vestries for Bishop, Clergy, and choir, and so to the lofty east end, with its apsidal termination and its bold flying buttresses and pinnacles. "Sanctus" will be carved on each of the three sides of the Apse parapet. (FN: The small places round the Apse would be of use for extra vestry rooms and for keeping books, etc., in, and one a verger's vestry, another with a safe.)

Coming round to the south side we see the outside of the Lady Chapel, and a somewhat similar to the northern, but varied, South Transept, with its different Rose window, Doorway, with figures set round it, and its many steps necessitated by the fall of the ground. Then to the Baptistery, a lofty stone octagonal erection, with its seven windows and high roof, surmounted by a metal Cross. The effect of this Baptistery, externally, will be good. It will be varied in its light and shade, being octagonal, and it will stand out from the great mass of the great Church, with its gilded Cross at the Apex, catching the light, and its many flying buttresses and its connecting passage.

Such will be the leading features of the exterior, all of commanding proportions.

And now to enter the Cathedral at the west, through the great portice we have spoken of, and through the shelter of an internal oak lobby.

The first impression will be the continuous height of the main, or central part, namely, the Nave, Choir, and Apse. The next, and nearly as powerful a one, will be the width; for with the outer aisles and the double range of columns on either side, and the Transepts, the effect of the width will be very considerable. Then, as we hope and think may be confidently anticipated, will be the uplifting proportion of the whole—the tall piers and arches, with the Triforium and the lofty Clerestory, and the rich and full tree-like, branching vaulting, springing from soaring vertical shafts, rising from the floor, and of slender diameter. For pains have been taken to make the interior effect a striking and an aspiring one. Then the eye will be taken up to the Rood and to the broad enriched soffit of the east-ernmost arch of the Tower, with its carved Angels, and to the Rood, which it frames; to the Screen, with its delicate open work, only veiling the beyond, with a very transparent veil, to the dark oak, or other wood, of the Choir Stalls with their fretted canopies; and so to the bright Sanctuary with, perhaps rays of light from a southern-like sun, lighting, but half veiling with light, the Reredos, with its sculpted Saints and the Christ in glory, blessing, above all. . . .

The pavement of the interior should be of American marbles— simpler in the Nave and Aisles, richer in the Choir, and especially rich in the Sanctuary.

The work is a great one. Its importance, from every point of view, is great. It is a grand opportunity. We shall be glad to do what we can to expedite the work, and hope it may be taken in hand soon.

Lastly, our desire and our hope is to raise your great Cathedral that it may inspire hearts with a joyful devotion, and unite them in the carrying out of a great monumental, National and religious work in your Capital of Washington.

Faithfully yours,

H. Vaughan G.F. Bodley, R.A., F.S.A.
Pemberton Building, Boston, 7, Gray's Inn Square,
America London

Note

We have not designed a Chapter House, understanding that it is con-templated to build a large Hall for Church meetings and gatherings, etc. Such a Hall could serve as a Chapter House, or there could be one attached to it of the dimensions required for Chapter purposes. The desirable offices could be built in connection with this large Hall.

This Building should follow on the completion of the Cathedral, which is of first import. The Hall and other buildings should be designed to be in harmony with the Cathedral, though they should have a more Domestic character of Gothic architecture. They should not be too high, so as not to interfere with the views of the Cathedral itself. But it will be an artistic advantage to have well-designed buildings near it. We should be glad to design such erections. There would be ample and good space on the site for them. We think they would be best on the ground to the southwest of the Cathedral, approached from the avenue, and not far from it. There could be rooms for a caretaker and other offices.

————

Anson Phelps Stokes on *Art and the Color Line*

Anson Phelps Stokes (1874–1958) was a Cathedral canon from 1924 to 1939. The former Secretary of Yale University was active in promoting improved racial relations in Washington and increased American ties with Africa, causes he advanced in his extensive writings and through the Phelps Stokes Fund, the New York family's philanthropic arm. *Art and The Color Line*, excerpted below, is a May 1939 appeal he made to The Daughters of the American Revolution's officers, requesting them to change their rules on the use of Constitution Hall to allow distinguished negro artists, such as the singer Marian Anderson (1897–1993), to appear. The D.A.R.'s refusal to allow Anderson to perform there became a cause célèbre. The President's wife, Eleanor Roosevelt, resigned her D.A.R. membership, and Miss Anderson was invited to deliver her recital to a large audience at the Lincoln Memorial on Easter Day, April 9, 1939. Stokes's manner was never confrontational, but was that of a careful teacher who found a variety of ways to raise challenging moral and ethical questions. He was a gradualist on racial integration, believing that public opinion was becoming more enlightened and the courts would be the main arena to bring about racial integration.

Although *Art and the Color Line* is one of Stokes's best-known publications, he was not originally a member of the Marian Anderson Citizens' Committee, but was asked to lead it in the D.A.R. meeting when the chairman, Professor Charles H. Houston, Vice-Dean of Howard University Law School, was out of town. The seven other members of the committee included several members of the Howard University Law School, the National Association for the Advancement of Colored People, and Mrs. Gifford Pinochet, wife of the former Governor of Pennsylvania, and a civic activist with whom the American contralto stayed during her Washington visit. In January 1943 the D.A.R. invited Marian Anderson to sing at Constitution Hall in a concert to raise funds for war relief. She appeared in another concert there a decade later, and launched her final world tour in 1964 with a concert in Constitution Hall, saying she had no place for bitterness in her heart, and that Constitution Hall was a beautiful concert venue.

Art and the Color Line

Madame President: I greatly appreciate the opportunity you have given us for a quiet, constructive conference with you on the issues connected with the recent refusal of the D.A.R. to permit the use of Constitution Hall for a concert by Miss Marian Anderson. We are here because of your kind letter of May 20th to Mr. Charles H. Houston, the Chairman of the Marian Anderson Citizens' Committee, in reply to his letter of April 19th. It seems advisable to begin with a brief historical survey of the events leading up to this meeting.

I. Résumé of Marian Anderson Incident, Washington, 1939

The first request for the use of Constitution Hall for a concert by Miss Anderson was made by Howard University School of Music in early January. The request was repeated in a more formal letter on January 18th just prior to the meeting of the National Board of Management, as you doubtless know. . . . This second application was refused because of the rule of the Society to the effect that white artists alone may be presented at concerts of this character. It is unnecessary at this time to enter into the details of these and other efforts to secure the Hall or to explain various circumstances which may have complicated the issue.

Arrangements were made with the Department of the Interior by which the concert was held in the open air in front of the Lincoln Memorial before about 50,000 people, both white and colored, including a distinguished group of Senators and other public men from the North and South. The concert was a brilliant success and there was perfect order throughout. Incidentally, Miss Anderson's brief address in response to the ovation which greeted her was a model of courtesy and consideration. She lived up to her reputation, not only as a distinguished artist, but as a woman of rare culture and dignity.

Under the above circumstances the Marian Anderson Citizens' Committee under date of April 13th renewed its request for use of the Hall for next year, and it is with the major issues involved in this request that a sub-committee is meeting with you today.

In our presentation to you we have specially in mind that The Daughters of the American Revolution is an organization incorporated by the Congress of the United States "for patriotic, historical, and educational purposes," and that among its special objectives, as stated in the Act of Incorporation, are *"to cherish, maintain and extend the institutions of American freedom; to foster true patriotism and love of country, and to aid in securing for mankind all the blessings of liberty."* Because of these patriotic objectives with which, as thus stated, we are in complete sympathy, and because of the unusual national character of the organization, we feel that we are justified as citizens of the District of Columbia in respectfully asking consideration for certain views which we consider have their definite bearing upon your policy in its relations to the public. Were the D.A.R. merely a social club or a purely private association without recognized public responsibilities we would hesitate to approach you on the subject. We fully recognize that you represent a great national patriotic association and that Constitution Hall, built through the generous interest of your members, has been of great service to this community and to the Nation. You may well take pride in "the contribution to the cultural life of Washington," made by this beautiful hall, referred to in your recent report to the 49th Continental Congress. This contribution has been made largely through the concerts and public meetings which you have allowed in the Hall on payment of the required fees by responsible organizations. . . .

III. Objections Raised and Answered

Let us now consider seriatim the major objections that have been raised:

(1) *That the granting of the request,* according to the report of the President General made before the Thirty-Eighth Continental Congress of the D.A.R. in April 1939, *would "under the conditions existing in the District of Columbia," be inadvisable, as it would be "contrary to accepted custom."*

We believe that the President General could not have been fully cognizant of the present situation in the District in making these statements, for there have been some marked improvements in local public opinion in recent years as far as granting recognition to our colored citizens in matters of both cultural opportunity and public recognition. For instance, contrary to the usual custom in the South the busses, trolleys and taxicabs are now open to the public irrespective of race. The same is true of the waiting room and dining room in the railroad station. It is also true of the public libraries of the District, including the Congressional. Colored people are permitted to attend all lectures, meetings and concerts in Government halls, including the concerts in the Library of Congress. There is also no segregation in the Courts and it is notable that there has been for many years a Negro Judge on the Municipal Court, before whom cases have frequently been tried by representative white lawyers of Southern birth. Indeed, the Bar Association of the District, whose members are mostly Southern, recently petitioned the President for the continuance of Judge Cobb, an honored Negro jurist. . . .

A few specific examples of interracial audiences and of Negro participants in cultural events may be worth citing:

Miss Anderson has appeared in the past in concerts with interracial audiences both at the Armstrong High School and at the Rialto Theater. As is well known, she has appeared at the White House.

Paul Robeson and Roland Haynes, two of the best known Negro singers, have both appeared before interracial audiences in the large Washington Auditorium, which having been taken over for government offices, is no longer available.

A few years ago the Interracial Committee, of which I was then Chairman, arranged without difficulty, for an Exhibition of Negro Art at the National Museum. The artists were all colored sculptors or painters, but those who attended were divided almost equally between both groups of citizens.

The services at Washington Cathedral are always open to and considerably patronized by colored people. This is true particularly of sacred concerts. At the recent Confirmation Service held by Bishop Freeman, about one third of those confirmed in the Cathedral and of those in the audience were colored.

In closing may I say that I speak, I am sure, for every member of the committee in stating that you may put your professional requirements for artists to appear in Constitution Hall as high as you like and we shall gladly respect them. Only we ask you to remember that art should recognize no color line, and we are dealing in this case with musical art in one of its highest forms. The papers have been full recently of the anniversary of Henry Burleigh, the great soloist of St. George's Episcopal Church of New York City. Although a colored man he has sung in this distinguished church in the metropolis for over a generation. His voice and his bearing have been an inspiration to tens of thousands of people, as have been those of other Negro singers such as Roland Hayes, Paul Robeson, and Miss Anderson herself.

We see no adequate reason why the color line should be drawn in the case of a really great singer such as Marian Anderson. We repeat this is a matter of art. We ask in this American democracy—especially at a critical time in our history when foreign social and political ideologies inconsistent with our national traditions are clamoring for acceptance, for fair play for American genius—for an opportunity for white and colored persons interested to hear world famous artists, when they come to Washington, in Constitution Hall—the only really suitable hall in view of the regrettable absence of a municipal auditorium. We ask you not to discourage a group representing one-tenth of our citizens who have made amazing progress since emancipation and who are specially qualified through the genius of some of their singers to make a contribution to the culture and inspiration of the Nation's Capital.

Phelps Stokes Fund Office
101 Park Avenue, New York City
August 16, 1939

Bishop John T. Walker Combines the Offices of Bishop and Dean

John Thomas Walker (1925–1989) was Bishop of Washington from 1977 until his death on September 29, 1989. The first African American Bishop of Washington, Walker had originally come to Washington as a Cathedral missioner in 1966, under Dean Francis B. Sayre, He was elected as suffragan bishop of Washington in 1971, and bishop coadjutor in 1976. He succeeded Bishop William

F. Creighton as diocesan bishop in 1977. The switch in roles from working for the Dean to having the Dean work for him highlighted an obvious tension about the two roles—who ran the cathedral: dean or bishop? Essentially, the dean publicly challenged the bishop and threatened to resign if the Bishop assumed management of the cathedral, which Walker did. Sayre retired, and maintained only minimal contact with the institution that had been central to his life for over twenty-seven years. Walker explained his actions in a paper on "Mission and Ministry of Diocese and Cathedral."

Mission and Ministry of Diocese and Cathedral, A Statement by The Right Reverend John T. Walker September 13, 1977

At the outset of my episcopacy I would like to address a most important policy consideration—the relationship of the mission and ministry of the Diocese and the role of the Bishop in the life of each.

Bishop and Diocese

Fundamentally, I see the role of the Bishop in the life of the Diocese in the same way as my predecessor. The Bishop, together with his staff, carries out his pastoral office by using the authority and resources of his office to support and guide the parish churches in carrying on their ministries. He provides stimulus, consultation and fiscal support as needed, all with the purpose of assisting the visibility of his parish churches.

The Bishop is also a boundary person standing between the church and society. As a witness of God's judgment on both, he is required to remind the church of its calling to work diligently for a just society and to remind society that without justice it will perish. The prophetic office is made flesh by program as well as pronouncement. Hence, we minister directly to the aged and children in need through diocesan programs and institutions.

In saying these things I am intending to continue the same perspective as Bishop Creighton although there may be differences in emphasis and style. I expect to maintain the same strong position that the parish is the front line of our corporate authority. By contrast, I see my role in the life of the Cathedral somewhat differently.

Cathedral Commission Report

The Cathedral Chapter, through a special Commission of which I was a member, began a review of the Cathedral mission and organization in the Spring of 1976 which culminated in the Commission report to Chapter in April, 1977. The Commission made several statements about the relation of Cathedral and Diocese and Bishop;

1. The Cathedral as "Chief Mission Church of the Diocese of Washington" is in mission and ministry intrinsically tied to the Diocese and is a natural extension of the mission and ministry of the Bishop and Diocese of Washington.
2. The Cathedral has a most important national mission due primarily to its unique location in the nation's capital. This is dependent upon a substantive mission and ministry to the people who live in the greater Washington area and this Diocese.
3. The Cathedral has a rich relationship with the city and the nation. It has been a leader in the ecumenical movement and in the development of closer ties with other faiths as well. Thus it is a valued resource to the church at large.
4. The Charter and By-Laws of the Cathedral place the Bishop of Washington at the center of its life as President of the Cathedral Foundation and its chief pastor.
5. Harnessing the resources of Mount Saint Alban is a common task under a single leader, the Bishop of Washington offers opportunities for service to the church and community envisioned by the founders of the Cathedral.

Organizational Implications

I agree wholeheartedly with the Cathedral Commission both as to its recommendation for a coordinated and complementary ministry of Diocese and Cathedral and its view of the Bishop as the central leader of both. Further, it remains my hope that we will complete the Cathedral in the near future. It is timely to reshape the mission and to emphasize the mission and to emphasize the larger ministry of the Cathedral with the office of the Bishop. Their combined resources under a unified leadership can greatly enrich both the church and society which they serve.

There are obvious organizational implications of such a position. The Bishop, rather than a Dean, will be the chief executive of the Cathedral. In the Bishop and through his authority can the Cathedral and its institutions be brought into a common ministry with the Diocese. Accordingly, when Dean Sayre's resignation becomes effective, January 17, 1978, I will not nominate a successor. This is a return to the organizational structure which existed for much of the Cathedral's history. I intend to operate as the Dean of the Cathedral for at least five years to give the plan a good solid test. As Bishop and Dean, I will function as chief liturgist and spokesman of the Cathedral and am already scheduled to participate in every season of the church year and at all major festivals.

Obviously, the Bishop cannot be the daily operating head of the Cathedral and do justice to all his responsibilities. A second step will be to appoint a Provost of the Cathedral who will function as my "executive vice president" for the Cathedral Foundation. Merely to change the position title and description is not enough to insure that the central aim will be carried out: bringing the Cathedral and Diocese together under the leadership of the Bishop. Therefore, I will on January 18, 1978, appoint Canon Charles A. Perry, Executive Officer of the Diocese to be Provost of the Cathedral Foundation as well. He and I will allocate our time between the two institutions and he will be my principal manager in both. Appropriate changes will occur in responsibilities of both Cathedral and Diocesan staff to support this change without loss of present program and resources.

Where We Go Next

I am making known my intensions four months in advance of Dean Sayre's departure so that the two policy making bodies, the Cathedral Chapter and Diocesan Council, will know my mind and can join with me in the months ahead as we move to implement these decisions. Also, I believe to be fair to the Cathedral and Church House staffs they must know both the general direction in which I wish to move and the firm decisions that have been made.

The Diocesan Council in June approved my request for extra-budgetary funding to insure an orderly transition in Episcopal leadership. I intend to meet with all elements of the Diocese during the Fall and Winter to listen to their priorities and to talk with them in more detail about my hopes. The effort begun by the Cathedral Commission which I cited earlier will be continued by Chapter members and Chapter staff. I intend to use the Fall and Winter for further exploration and discussion of the directions I have described with all the elements of Cathedral life.

I have not gone beyond the basic steps I have outlined. The details will be worked out in the months ahead. Ultimately, they will be decided by the appropriate policy making bodies, Cathedral Chapter and Diocesan Council. I anticipate that the common mission will yield a number of Cathedral and Diocesan structural simplifications and shared functions and some cost savings. I trust that it will strengthen our ability to carry forward our joint mission within our limited resources. I intend to move slowly, to hear from all of you, to retain the best of the past and to eventually bring all of our resources together into a cooperative and shared mission and ministry.

Rowan LeCompte, Master Stained Glass Artist, Lectures on His Life's Work

Rowan LeCompte was only sixteen when his first stained glass window was accepted for a chapel in Washington National Cathedral, where he produced more than forty-five windows, including the great West End Rose Window, and six mosaic murals. The somewhat shy, diminutive artist spent over seven decades at the Cathedral, and designed works for fifty other churches as well, including the chapels at Princeton University and Trinity College, Hartford, Connecticut, and the New York State Capitol at Albany. Born in Baltimore in 1925, LeCompte who died in February 2014, was the son of a biscuit baker and his wife. The youth always had strong artistic and architectural interests, and was largely self-taught. A family visit to Washington National Cathedral in 1939, when he was still in high school, was a revelatory experience, as was meeting the Cathedral's architect, Phillip Hubert Frohman, who bought one of LeCompte's first works for a Cathedral chapel, and became a lifelong mentor and friend.[1]

The American artist Norman Rockwell featured LeCompte, working on a stained glass window of the Resurrection, on the cover of *The Saturday Evening Post* on April 16, 1960. Although his work was widely known and in many institutions, LeCompte is best known for his West End Rose Window at Washington National Cathedral. It is one of 231 cathedral windows made over 83 years by twenty artists. Over 25 feet in diameter, it contains 10,500 pieces of colored glass and took almost four years to complete and install. LeCompte was assisted by the Cathedral's German-born master craftsman, Dieter Goldkuhle as fabricator and installer. The window was completed by Easter Day 1976 and dedicated the following year in the presence of Queen Elizabeth II and President Jimmy Carter.

LeCompte, designer of all 16 clerestory windows overlooking the Cathedral's long nave, made his last major window at age 84, working out of his small studio room near Charlottesville, Virginia. On March 24, 2001, he gave a cathedral lecture on his life's work, from which the remarks below are excerpted.[2]

★ ★ ★ ★ ★

I don't want to be overly egocentric at all, but I must give you a little bit of background to describe properly my relation to this building. I was born in Baltimore in 1925. Four years later came the Depression and my family always had food on the table, but money was very scarce. Nevertheless, it was a family that cared very much for music. My mother was a constant, quiet gardener, a very loving and gentle person. My father was temperamentally a fireball, but immensely energetic. I had actually the good fortune to be the second of only two children. Because my parents had a son in 1913 who was nearly twelve years older than I. Consequently, I grew up in a household

1 Elody R. Crimi and Diane Nye. *Jewels of Light, The Stained Glass of Washington National Cathedral,* Washington National Cathedral Guidebooks (Washington, DC: Washington National Cathedral, 2004): 22–26, 33–36. A 97-minute film on the Cathedral work of Rowan LeCompte and master stained glass artisan Dieter Goldkuhle was made over six years by Peter Swanson, a documentary film maker, in 1212. Peter Swanson, *Let there be Light* (Leicester, MA: Global Visions & Associates, 2012).

2 The lecture is contained on the Washington National Cathedral website, Lecture Transcript, Rowan LeCompte's Lecture, March 24, 2001. (http://www. nationalcathedral.org/learn/lectureTexts/MED–4565U–TT0011_shtml)

with a loving mother and a harried and often impatient, but certainly loving, father. But a heavenly, younger father, younger than
my real father, my brother. His name was Stewart LeCompte, and
to my delight, his children and grandchildren are here today. . . .
It happened that one of my mother's sisters visiting from Canada
proposed a trip to Washington during a visit of hers during the
summer of 1939. She offered to bring me over, and we would see all
of Washington we could see. Since it was semi-unknown to me, that
was going to be a great excursion. And over we came on the train,
on a crisp morning, the first of July in 1939, an African American
taxi driver at Union Station offered to show us all the sights. So we
got into his taxi and the fee was going to be $5.00 for the entire
morning.

And in the blinding morning sunlight we went up to the white
gleaming steps of the Lincoln Memorial, which was only seventeen
years old, and it didn't look like the melting sugar cube it begins to
resemble now because the air was cleaner then and the sky was bluer.
But in one of our turns through Northwest Washington we chanced
to turn a bend, and I don't know where this could have been, but
it was perhaps down Massachusetts Avenue. And I saw something
from the cab window that was not on our schedule, but that I had
recognized instantly as resembling a marvelous photograph in a 1922
copy of the *National Geographic* that I had looked at during long days
in sick bed as a child. It was a white building covered with spires.
I'd never seen a cathedral in my life, but I thought this must be the
Washington Cathedral. And I remember Margaret turning to me and
saying, "Would you like to see that, dear?" And I definitely did want
to see it, so we came.

In those days one entered on the South Transept steps which
were made of concrete, and you walked up to a great piece of unbuilt
structure which was covered with tar paper and came to a big tin
door in a tin wall which was covered with scaffolding. The door
opened, and we came into a space that from the outside seemed to be
black, but once in the door I could see we were in a magic twilight,
a heavenly place. I had never seen such a thing! A great, soaring,
mysterious space and it was filled, to my delight, with music. The
organ, which had just been installed, was being used for practice.
And the awe of the interior, the dim light, the magic of the North
Rose shining there in the gloom. It wasn't gloom; it was mystery.

It was anything but gloom. It was a magic place. And filled with a degree of awesomeness and beauty and spirit. How else can I say it, that I had never seen in my life before, or experienced. And I was simply struck, if not dumb, I was certainly bowled over.

Well, the next day back in Baltimore, I was at the Enoch Pratt Library reading what there might be on stained glass. And of course there was a lot. And over the weeks I read as much as I could. And in late October 1939, actually presumed to make a little watercolor study for a stained glass window. It's of course a laughable little trifle, but I can't help being touched when I see it because it suggested that I was already enchanted. That really is true.

I tried to teach myself the craft. And of course there were many things I did not learn by myself, but I nevertheless, was able to start assembling little panels, usually less than a square foot for my own satisfaction and instruction. And then these things began to be commissioned by high school teachers or family friends. For five dollars you could get a neat little panel about 5" square with a head derived from one of the thirteenth century windows at Chartres. In due course as the years passed, I finally built up experience of some forty of these little stained glass window sections, many of them with figural subjects . . . I wrote to the most famous stained glass artist of that time in this country, who was Charles J. Connick, who lived in Boston and whose studio was there. He was imminent, both as a stained glass artist and as a writer, and a friend of writers. He had done, among other things, the great Rose Window in the West End of St. John the Divine in New York. Anyway, I wrote Mr. Connick to ask if I could be his apprentice. And he wrote back immediately that this would be an interesting proposition, but he would need to see a piece of my work. So I made a little panel, about a foot tall, and eight inches wide, with a figure of St. Paul in it. Now I had only the scraps from this transom shop to work with, and there was one kind of red, and one particularly poisonous green, but there were two different blues, all of this was cheap commercial rolled glass called mistakenly "cathedral glass"—it's what you would never put in a cathedral. In any case, I completed this thing and sent it off to Mr. Connick, and he returned it with a letter of the most stinging criticism. He could not have given me a greater gift— because it wasn't crushing. But he told me what he had thought, and what he thought of the drawing was not unprintable, but almost. And he also criticized my glass selection, but in that I felt perhaps a little justified by the fact that I didn't have any other source of supply. In any case, I decided to work very much on drawing and did that,

> [LeCompte then discussed visiting the Baltimore Pro-Cathedral of the Incarnation, where he was introduced to its architect, Philip Hubert Frohman, also architect of Washington National Cathedral, who said "you are welcome to visit me at any time in my office, I'd be glad to talk with you about stained glass."]

Upon my arriving there, we just sat and spent the afternoon talking. I had a thousand questions for him. And he was so generous in giving me his time and sharing his feelings about windows and his experiences of various artists that I was in great awe of. [Eventually Frohman asked the high school senior to try his hand at making a proposed window for the yet-to-be-built St. Dunstan's Chapel. LeCompte's proposal was accepted by the Building Committee, he would have to donate the window and install it, but a committee member offered him $100 to cover expenses.] In due course, the window was installed by me and my friend Philip Henry Lebovitz, a school chum now at last deceased, on a cold Saturday, Saturday March 28, 1942. Towards the evening it began to sleet and then it turned to snow. Mr. Frohman took us frozen kids down to Union Station and bought us a bowl of oyster stew and then put us on the train to go home. I came back. It snowed that night eleven inches! In any case, that was an epoch in my life, and I needn't say any more about it. That summer Mr. Frohman offered me a job as a draftsman in his office, and I'm sure I produced nothing of any use to him, but it was an education and a delight to be near him many days. . . . I hope that the future will love it as we have loved it. I hope that a greater sense of mystery can be achieved as the science of lighting is perfected so that we see not the lighting fixture, but only the architecture that is illuminated.

I hope the place will be filled with music, as some French churches are all the time, even when there's no one there because they have some marvelous sound system playing Gregorian or other music constantly. Because music in a building like this transforms it. It becomes transfigured. Especially Bach, of course, because it's just Gothic architecture turned into sound. But it has a structural quality that is sublime.

Washington National Cathedral Chronology

1891:   December 8: Meeting at home of Charles C. Glover to discuss building of a cathedral

1893:   January 6: Congress grants a charter for the Cathedral Foundation

1895:   Diocese of Washington is established separate from Diocese of Maryland
December 4: Washington Diocese first convention, Henry Yates Satterlee elected on eleventh ballot

1896:   March 25: Henry Yates Satterlee is consecrated first bishop of Washington in Calvary Church, New York City

1898:   September 7: Part of Mount Saint Alban land bought for $245,000
October 23: Peace Cross is installed on cathedral grounds to commemorate end of Spanish-American War, President William McKinley speaks
May 17: King Hall ministerial school for negro students is closed for lack of funds and students

1900:   October 1: Cathedral School for Girls opens

1905:   June 1: Cornerstone is laid for what becomes St. Alban's School for Boys

1906:   Cathedral land is free of debt, chapter votes in favor of Gothic architecture for new building, architects George F. Bodley and Henry Vaughan are hired

1907:   June 7: Original drawings for English gothic cathedral arrive in Washington

September 29: Foundation Stone of cathedral is laid, President Theodore Roosevelt speaks, as does the bishop of London

1908:   February 22: Death of Bishop Satterlee

1909:   January 25: Consecration of Alfred Harding, former rector of St. Paul's, as second bishop of Washington

1910:   Edgar "Daddy" Priest, an English musician, is named organist and choirmaster of cathedral, d. 1935

1912:   May 1: First services are held in recently completed Bethlehem Chapel

1916:   Formation of All Hallows Guild to plan cathedral close gardening; installation of G.C.F. Bratenahl, former rector of St. Alban's parish, as first resident cathedral dean

1921:   Philip Hubert Frohman begins tenure at cathedral architect

1922:   April 17: Work is resumed on Great Choir foundations

1923:   April 30: Bishop Harding dies; James Edward Freeman, former railroad executive and rector of Epiphany Church, is elected third bishop of Washington

1924:   February 6: Burial in cathedral of Woodrow Wilson, 26th President of the United States

Anson Phelps Stokes becomes a cathedral Canon, retires in 1939

1925:   Easter: First copy of quarterly magazine, *The Cathedral Age,* is published

1926:   Summer: The Bishop's Garden opens

Cathedral Christmas cards are published, a valuable source of revenue

1927:   Completion of crypt chapels of St. Joseph of Aramathea, Chapel of the Resurrection

1928:   Construction of north aisle of choir begins, laying of corner-
        stone at the College of Preachers

1930:   Good Friday: CBS broadcasts three-hour service nationwide,
        first such broadcast from cathedral

1932:   May 5: First service in Great Choir and sanctuary

1932–   Anson Phelps Stokes makes a lengthy study visit to Africa,
1933:   lectures on "Race Relations in the U.S." in numerous African
        universities

1935:   September: Robert Barrow, St. Alban's School and Yale
        University graduate, becomes organist–choirmaster, resigns
        in 1939
        December 8: Radio talk by Archbishop William Temple of
        York

1937:   May 6: Installation of Noble C. Powell as second cathedral
        dean

1938:   November 10: Great organ is dedicated, 8,354 pipes, later
        increased to 189 ranks, 10,647 pipes

1939:   Paul Callaway becomes organist–choirmaster, retires in
        1977
        April 9: Access denied to the D.A.R. Constitutional Hall;
        Marian Anderson sings before nearly 70,000 persons at
        the Lincoln Memorial; Canon Anson Phelps Stokes helped
        arrange the concert, wrote an influential pamphlet, *Art and
        the Color Line*

1940:   October, Episcopal Church's General Convention meets in
        Washington, National Cathedral is designated as seat of the
        presiding bishop

1942:   May 10: Cathedral dean ZeBarney Phillips dies of wrongly
        filled prescription
        May 13: Debut of Cathedral Choral Society (150 voices) with
        Verdi's *Requiem*

1943:   June 6: Death of Bishop Freeman

Theodore O. Wedel comes to Washington as warden of College of Preachers, with wife, Cynthia Clark Wedel; retires in 1960

1944:   April 19: Angus Dun is consecrated as fourth bishop of Washington

1945:   May 10: $5,000,000 campaign is launched; fiftieth anniversary of Diocese of Washington

1947:   January 14: Installation of Henry Knox Sherrill as presiding bishop

1949:   November: Weekly radio series *Cathedral Prayer* begins

1950:   September: John W. Suter, custodian of the Book of Common Prayer, resigns as dean to resume parish ministry and St. Paul's School chaplaincy

December 24: First Christmas Eve telecast of candlelight service

1951:   May 6: Installation of Francis B. Sayre as fifth dean of Washington National Cathedral

July 4: Presentation to cathedral of silver cross and candlesticks by King George VI of England

John M. Burgess, head of Episcopal Church activities at Howard University, becomes the first black canon at National Cathedral, later is elected bishop of Massachusetts

1952:   February 15: Memorial service for late King George VI attended by President and Mrs. Harry S. Truman and diplomatic corps

1954:   March 15: First meeting of American cathedral deans, sponsored by Dean Sayre

May: Visit of Haile Selassie, Emperor of Ethiopia

Summer: Building in the nave resumes, launching of fiftieth anniversary fund drive

1955:   April 1: Joseph Ratti, master stone carver, falls from scaffolding to his death

1956:   November 11: Dedication of the Woodrow Wilson Bay
        October 20: War Memorial Chapel is dedicated in presence
        of President and Mrs. Eisenhower, Queen Elizabeth II, and
        Prince Philip

1958:   June 15: Dedication of bay for Mabel Thorpe Broadman,
        founder of the American Red Cross

1959:   January 14: Installation of Arthur Carl Lichtenberger as pre-
        siding bishop
        May 27: Funeral service for John Foster Dulles, former secre-
        tary of state

1960:   January: Construction is resumed on south transept

1961:   June 16: Dedication of north cloister and administration
        building

1962:   January 1: Beginning of work on central tower
        September 15:   College of Church Musicians opens with Leo
        Sowerby as director, closes in 1968 with Sowerby's death,
        and for lack of funds
        November 1: Installation of William F. Creighton as fifth
        bishop of Washington in presence of archbishop of Canterbury
        Michael Ramsey

1963:   September 22: Dedication of cathedral carillon of matched,
        tuned bells

1964:   May 7: Dedication of Gloria in Excelsis Tower with five
        musical services throughout day

1965:   January 27: Installation of John E. Hines as presiding
        bishop
        January 28: Memorial service for Sir Winston Churchill

1966:   John T. Walker joins cathedral staff as canon missioner

1969:   Cynthia Clark Wedel serves as president of the National
        Council of Churches (1969–1972) and World Council of
        Churches (1975–1983)

1968:   March 31: Dr. Martin Luther King, Jr., preaches his last Sunday sermon at National Cathedral, four days before his assassination

1970:   March 28: Funeral of President Dwight David Eisenhower

1971:   John T. Walker is elected suffragan bishop of Washington

1973:   Cynthia Clark Wedel publishes *Women Priests in the Catholic Church?*

1974:   April 21: Dedication of the Space Window, designed by Rodney Winfield, on the fifth anniversary of the Apollo moon landing; window contains a small rock chip from the moon

1976:   June: Creation Rose Window by Rowan LeCompte is completed

1977:   January 8: Women included in cathedral ordination service held by Bishop Creighton, with Bishop Walker as preacher
July 18: Cathedral construction halted for lack of funds; accumulated debt is over $12 million, with $800,000 annual interest payments
September 15: Bishop Walker issues statement on "Mission and Ministry of Diocese and Cathedral," announcing intention to combine roles of bishop and dean in one person
September 24: John T. Walker succeeds William F. Creighton as diocesan bishop

1978:   January 17: Retirement of Francis B. Sayre as cathedral dean on his sixty-third birthday; Bishop Walker becomes dean, names Charles B. Perry as provost

1981:   October 7: Memorial service for Anwar Sadat

1982:   May 1: Pilgrim Observation Gallery open to public
November 10–12: Reading of the names of Vietnam War dead

1983:   April 5: First stone in the west towers is set in place, marking final major construction phase

1984: Cathedral construction resumes as Capital Campaign eradicates debt
December 23: Archbishop Desmond Tutu preaches at cathedral

1986: Ronald H. Haines elected suffragan bishop of Washington

1989: September 29: Death of Bishop John T. Walker; his death was announced at service marking installation of last stone in cathedral tower, completing eighty-three years of construction work

1990: June 30: Bishop Ronald H. Haines, suffragan, is elected diocesan bishop, retires a decade later

1991: November: Nathan D. Baxter is elected cathedral dean, resigns in 2003

1993: August 31: Michael P. Hamilton, senior canon, retires; Hamilton organized numerous conferences and forums and edited books on environmental, medical, racial, gender, political, and social issues over three decades at National Cathedral

1997: June 14: Service marking the merger of three Lutheran denominations into Evangelical Lutheran Church in America

2001: January 1: With Bishop Haines's retirement, Jane Holmes Dixon becomes pro tempore bishop, retires in 2002; second woman bishop in the United States, third in the Anglican Communion

2002: June 1: John Bryson Chane is consecrated as eighth bishop of Washington

2003: June 30: Nathan D. Baxter, dean since 1992, resigns, is elected bishop of the Diocese of Central Pennsylvania in 2006
Summer: Michael McCarthy, founder and director of the London Oratory, is named cathedral music director

2005: April 23: Samuel T. Lloyd, III, installed as dean of Washington National Cathedral

2009:   September: Former White House executive Jan Naylor Cope is appointed cathedral vicar

2011:   Samuel T. Lloyd resigns as dean, to return to Trinity Church, Copley Square, Boston, as priest-in-charge

August 23 (1:53 pm): A 5.8-magnitude earthquake shakes the cathedral, knocks off four tower pinnacle stones, leaves a gash in the roof, topples gargoyles and masonry, causing approximately $21 million in damages

November 12: Marian Edgar Budde, formerly rector of St. John's Church, Minneapolis, is consecrated as ninth bishop of Washington

2012:   July 31: Gary R. Hall, former dean and president of Seabury-Western Theological Seminary, Evanston, Illinois, is announced as tenth dean of Washington National Cathedral

2013:   January 22: National Prayer Service at cathedral for the inauguration of Barack Obama's second presidential term

Bibliography

Ahlstrom, Sydney E. *A Religious History of the American People*. New Haven, CT: Yale University Press, 1972.

Anderson, Eric and Alfred A. Moss, Jr. *Dangerous Donations: Northern Philanthropy and Southern Black Education, 1902–1930*. Columbia, MO: University of Missouri Press, 1999.

Bacon, Mardges. *Ernest Flagg: Beaux-Arts Architect and Urban Reformer*. New York, Cambridge, MA: MIT Press, 1986.

Berg, A. Scott. *Wilson*. New York: G. P. Putnam's Sons, 2013.

Brent, Charles H. *A Master Builder: Being the Life and Letters of Henry Yates Satterlee, First Bishop of Washington*. New York: Longmans, Green and Co., 1916.

Companion on the Way: The Collected Letters of Catherine (Kitty) Dun, Wife of Angus Dun, Bishop of the Episcopal Diocese of Washington, 1944–1962. Washington: Washington National Cathedral, 2006.

Crimi, Elody R. and Diane Ney. *Jewels of Light: The Stained Glass of Washington National Cathedral*. Washington: Washington National Cathedral, 2004.

Federal Writers' Project, Works Progress Administration, American Guides Series. *Washington, City and Capital*. Washington: Government Printing Office, 1937.

Feller, Richard T. and Eileen M. Yago. *Symbolism and Iconography, Cathedral Church of St. Peter and St. Paul*. Washington: 1990.

Feller, Richard and Marshall W. Fishwick. *For Thy Great Glory*. Culpeper, VA: Community Press, 1965.

Harrison, Robert. *John Walker. A Man for the 21st Century*. Cincinnati: Forward Movement, 2004.

Hein, David. *Noble Powell and the Episcopal Establishment in the Twentieth Century*. Urbana: University of Illinois Press, 2001.

Hempstone, Smith, ed. *An Illustrated History of St. Alban's School*. Washington: Glastonbery Press, 1981.

Hewlett, Richard Greening. *The Foundation Stone, Henry Yates Satterlee and the Creation of Washington National Cathedral*. Rockville, MD: Montrose Press, 2007.

Inventory of Diocese of Washington Archives. Vol. I. Washington: Historical Records Survey, 1940.

Inventory of Washington Cathedral Archives, Volume II. Washington: Historical Records Survey, 1940.

Johnson, Howard A., ed. *This Church of Ours, The Episcopal Church: What It Is and What it Teaches About Living.* Greenwich, CT: The Seabury Press, 1958.

Keiler, Allen. *Marian Anderson, A Singer's Journey.* New York: Scribners, 2000.

Kevin, Robert and Cynthia Wedel. *The Ordination of Women.* Cincinnati: Forward Movement, 1975.

Lea, William S. *Theodore Otto Wedel, An Anthology.* Cincinnati: Forward Movement Miniature Book, 1972.

Living Stones, Washington National Cathedral at 100. Washington: Washington National Cathedral, 2007.

Marty, Martin E. *Protestantism in the United States: Righteous Empire.* 2nd ed. New York: Charles Scribners' Sons, 1982.

Meyer, Donald B. *The Protestant Search for Political Realism, 1919–1941.* Westport, CT: Greenwood Press, 1973.

Morgan, William. *The Almighty Wall, The Architecture of Henry Morgan.* Cambridge, MA: MIT Press, 1983.

Paret, William. *Reminiscences.* Philadelphia: George W. Jacobs, 1911.

Pike, James A., ed. *Modern Canterbury Pilgrims and Why They Chose the Episcopal Church.* New York: Morehouse-Gorham, 1956.

Row, Christopher D. "A World Without End: Philip Hubert Frohman and the Washington National Cathedral." Ph.D. diss., Harvard University, 1999.

The Peace Cross Book, Cathedral of SS. Peter and Paul, Washington. New York: R.H. Russell, 1899.

Truman, Margaret. *Murder at the National Cathedral.* New York: Ballantine Books, 1990.

Tulloch, G. Janet. *Happy Issue, My Handicap and the Church.* Greenwich, CT: The Seabury Press, 1962.

Saint, Lawrence. *The Romance of Stained Glass.* Huntington Valley, PA: publisher unknown, 1959.

Satterlee, Henry Yates. *The Building of a Cathedral.* New York: E.S. Gorham, 1901.

———. *The Calling of the Christian and Christ's Sacrament of Fellowship.* Washington: Church Militant, 1902.

———. *A Creedless Gospel and The Gospel Creed.* New York: Charles Scribners' Sons, 1895.

———. *To the Clergy and Laity of the Diocese of Washington.* Washington: publisher unknown, 1902.

———. *The Fundamental Principles of Christian Unity: Lectures Delivered in Lent, 1902 Under the Auspices of the Churchman's League of the District of Columbia.* Washington: Church Militant, 1902.

———. *Life Lessons from the Prayer Book: a Manual of Instruction for Bible Classes.* New York: James Pott, 1889.

———. *New Testament Churchmanship and the Principals Upon Which it was Founded.* New York: Longmans, Green and Co., 1899.

Schuyler, Hamilton. *A Fisher of Men: Churchill Satterlee, Priest and Missionary—An Interpretation of His Life and Labors.* New York: E.S. Gorham, 1905.

Shepherd, Massey Hamilton, ed. *The Liturgical Renewal of the Church: Addresses by Theodore Otto Wedel.* New York: Oxford University Press, 1960.

Stokes, Anson Phelps. *Reminiscences of Anson Phelps Stokes, 1874–1954, For His Children and Grandchildren and Stories and Some Comments and Reflections.* Lenox, MA: 1956.

———. *What Jesus Christ Thought of Himself: An Outline Study of His Self-Revelation in the Gospels.* New York: The Macmillan Co., 1916.

Van der Meer, Haye. *Women Priests in the Catholic Church? A Theological-Historical Investigation.* Translated by Arlene and Leonard Swidler. Philadelphia: Temple University Press, 1973.

Wedel, Cynthia Clark. *Celebrating Thanksgiving.* New York: The National Council of the Protestant Episcopal Church, 1941.

———. "The Church and Social Action," *The Christian Century,* 87 (August 12, 1970): 959–962.

———. *Citizenship—Our Christian Concern.* New York: National Council of the Churches of Christ in the U.S.A., n.d.

———. *Ecumenical Rivalry and Cooperation.* Cincinnati: Forward Movement Publications, ND.

———. *Employed Women and the Church.* New York: National Council of the Churches of Christ in the U.S.A., 1959.

———. *Faith or Fear and Future Shock.* New York: Friendship Press, 1974.

———. *Reflections on Ministry, Implications of Personhood, Gender and Vocation.* Cincinnati: Forward Movement Publications, ND.

———. *The Vine and the Branches, An Introduction to the Ecumenical Movement.* Cincinnati: Forward Movement Publications, ND.

Wedel, Mrs. Theodore O. *Health and Welfare Needs of the Nation and the Place of Church Agency.* New York: Department of Christian Social Relations, Diocese of New York, 1954.

Wedel, Theodore Otto. *The Christianity of Main Street.* New York: Macmillan, 1950.

———. *The Coming Great Church.* New York: Macmillan, 1945.

———. *Episcopal—Presbyterian Unity, A Comment on "A Basis of Union."* Poughkeepsie, NY: Chronicle Press, 1946.

———. *The Gospel in a Strange, New World.* Philadelphia: Westminster Press, 1963.

———. "The Group Dynamics Movement and the Church," *Theology Today,* 10 (January 1954): 511–524.

———. *The Medieval Attitude Toward Astrology, Particularly in England.* New Haven, CT: Yale University Press, 1920.

———. *The Pulpit Rediscovers Theology.* Greenwich, CT: The Seabury Press, 1956.

Wharton, Edith. *The Age of Innocence.* New York: Modern Library, 1998.

Index